SHORT **BREAKS**
from and within the UAE

there's more to life...
ask**explorer**.com

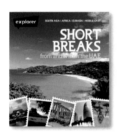

Short Breaks From And Within The UAE 2013/1st Edition
ISBN 978-9948-20-156-4

Front Cover Photograph – main image – Gerard Larose – Seychelles Tourism Board.
Bottom left to right: Taj Hotels Resorts & Palaces; Sri Lanka Promotion Bureau;
Medium Rare Advertising & Marketing on behalf of the Turkish Cultural
& Tourism Office, Dubai; Atlantis Holidays; Explorer.
Printed and bound by Emirates Printing Press, Dubai, United Arab Emirates.

Explorer Publishing & Distribution
PO Box 34275, Dubai, United Arab Emirates
Phone   +971 (0)4 340 8805
Fax   +971 (0)4 340 8806
Email   info@askexplorer.com
Web   askexplorer.com

Welcome...

One of the biggest advantages of living in the UAE is the opportunity to see more of the world. Exotic locations that can take a full day of travel from places like the UK, US, Australia and Canada, can be reached in as little as a couple of hours from Dubai or Abu Dhabi – and with the added bonus of no jetlag.

Whatever you're into – nature, culture, fashion, art, adventure, snow, sun, water – you'll find it in South Asia, Africa, Eurasia and the Middle East. And the best thing is that these destinations are less than five hours away from or within the UAE, so a trip can be slotted easily into a weekend or midweek break.

Drawing on the knowledge, passion and miles travelled by the Explorer team, we bring you the best places to visit and the ultimate things to do in just three or four days. From classic to iconic, gritty to glitzy, unusual to unexpected – here are 20 destinations to capture your imagination.

Your short break starts here...

 Since 1996, Explorer has been the UAE's Number 1 source for all the information you need about living life under the Gulf sun to the fullest. And for even more insider tips and inspiration, including details of the latest happenings in Dubai, Abu Dhabi and beyond, askexplorer.com has all the answers.

 **99** Things To Do in
AMMAN

For more information about things you can do in Amman, visit www.VisitJordan.com/99things

Hop on the tour through Sharjah NOW!

Sharjah Aquarium and Maritime Museum

Al Qasba

AL QASBA

Etisalat - Eye of the Emirates Observatory Wheel

Kids Area

Restaurants

Maraya Art Centre

Sharjah Fountain Shows

Splash Park

Mini Golf

Resturants

Iconic
Waterfront

Architected with family entertainment in focus, Al Majaz Waterfront is conveniently located to provide a unique one-stop-shop for families and individuals. The splendid Sharjah Fountain dances in front of its semi-circular courtyard making an amazing scene for breakfast, lunch or dinner. Choose the time, the cuisine and companions; Al Majaz Waterfront with its selective dining brands and various entertainment options offers you an unforgettable experience.

@AlMajazWF   AlMajazWF   AlMajazWaterfront
AlMajazWaterfront   almajaz.ae

Beaches

Al Majaz Waterfront

Central Souq

Al Noor Mosque

Family-Oriented Destination

With a landmark on the horizon, the Etisalat - Eye of the Emirates wheel stands a witness to the new fun filled water canal, Al Qasba. Catering to individual tastes yet providing collective activities, Al Qasba is meant to be the joy of your loved ones. Take wonderful pictures of sunset; enjoy the traditional yet modern ambience bringing your family and friends together in a safe, charming and elegant atmosphere. Retreat onto spacious outdoor seating areas and choose from a selection of cuisines. The global assortment of dining options is mouthwatering. Let your young explorers find their way to the Kids Fun Zone, it is designed with the best safety measures to put your minds at ease.

@AlQasba   AlQasbaShj   AlQasbaShj   AlQasba   alqasba.ae

Heritage Area

Museums

Souqs

A Treasured
Heritage

Presently, the Heart of Sharjah boasts some of the UAE's finest museums and collection of masterfully restored traditional homes. Although far from complete, the art galleries, traditional souqs, exceptional architecture and ongoing events have firmly established the Heart of Sharjah as a leading cultural and tourism destination not only in Sharjah, but also in the UAE.

@heartofshj   heartofshj   Tel. +971 6 544 8847
heartofsharjah.ae

Fish Market

Heart of Sharjah

Sharjah Museum of Islamic Civilization

City Sightseeing® Sharjah
Hop On - Hop Off

جولة سياحية في الشارقة
اصعد - انزل

Al Mahatah

العربية   English   Deutsch   РУССКИЙ

١٢٤ Languages   17 Bus stops   OFFICIAL TOUR

Al Noor Mosque

The Best Way to Discover **Sharjah**

Sharjah is a lively and exciting city, with interesting artefacts and monuments located at every corner. The City Sightseeing Sharjah tour buses provide tourists and visitors a novel way to discover all its charms and its rich cultural heritage.

A day on this 'Hop-on-Hop-off' double decker bus tour allows visitors to take in the most enjoyable and memorable experiences in Sharjah, as it plies across all the emirate's famous landmarks.

CitySS_Sharjah   CitySightSeeingSharjah
CitySightSeeing.ae

For operational inquiries   للمعلومات عن العمليات
+971 6 525 5200   Sharjah Contact Center   مركز الشارقة للإتصال
www.citysightseeing.ae   80080000

Spirit of Seychelles

explorer

there's more to life...

THERE'S MORE TO LIFE THAN BRUNCH

UAE & OMAN
ULTIMATE EXPLORER
OFF-ROADING, DIVING, CAMPING, HIKING, WEEKEND BREAKS AND MUCH MORE

ask**explorer**.com/shop

   ask**explorer**

FEEL THE THRILL

Do they scream for their mums here?

Or here?

Live the ultimate water adventure
Book tickets online today at yaswaterworld.com or call +971 2 414 2000

Yas Waterworld
ABU DHABI

askexplorer.com

LET
US
STAY
WITH
YOU.®

Let us offer you Arabian hospitality at its finest.

Let us teach you about our rich Qatari heritage.

Let us wrap you in luxury and comfort.

Let us keep a place in your heart.

Rate is per room/per night, based on single or double occupancy, exclusive of taxes, gratuities, fees and other charges; does not apply to groups; cannot be combined with any other offer and is not applicable for Rewards redemption. Advanced reservations are required. No refund or credit for unused portion. Void where prohibited. Offer is subject to availability. Daily breakfast is available in select hotel restaurants and not valid for in-room dining. Destination Experience is per stay and varies by hotel. Credit is applied per night, has no cash value, and is not valid on room rate, alcohol, or third party services. Valid through December 31, 2013.

SHARQ
VILLAGE & SPA

Contents

Lake Nemrut, Turkey

Introduction

Mount Nemrut National Park, Turkey

Before you leave

From relaxing beach breaks to weekend shopping trips, underwater adventures to wildlife safaris, you'll be surprised at how much you can see and do in just three or four days.

Whether you want to watch the sunrise over the majestic African plains, sun yourself on the world's best beaches, traverse the tea plantations of exotic Asia, or simply lose yourself in a bustling European bar scene, it's all within easy reach of the UAE. Time is precious – so the idea of travelling less than five hours to enjoy the sights and sounds of another country in three to four days is certainly appealing. What's more, psychologists believe that people who use their holiday allowance for a series of short breaks instead of longer ones are happier, as excitement levels get a regular injection.

A weekend or midweek break isn't a long time to explore a place, but there are ways to make the most of your time – and not return more exhausted than when you left.

If possible, book your flights for the Thursday evening so that you don't have to take a day off work. While it's a good idea to book hotels, guided tours and drivers before you leave, some things are best kept unplanned. Instead of making dinner reservations, try asking some of the locals or be guided by your tastebuds when you're actually there.

The hardest decision is where to go. Start by checking the world map (p.xxix) and destination finder (p.xxviii). Then, visit flightcentre.ae for the lowest airfares from Dubai, and accommodation sites such as booking.com to get the best hotel deals. Whether it's a last-minute getaway or a pre-planned escape, there's a short break just waiting to be booked.

When to go

There are two major public holidays in the UAE that are popular for travel: Eid Al Fitr (which marks the end of Ramadan) and Eid Al Adha (which marks the end of the pilgrimage to Mecca). Each holiday lasts from one to three days and often coincides with discounted flights from Emirates, Etihad, flydubai and other operators. Summer (June to August) is a popular time for travel to escape the heat, but coincides with the school holidays. If you're travelling with friends or as a couple without kids, you might want to avoid family-friendly holiday resorts. Of course, with 20 destinations to choose from, all just a few hours away, there's always a right time to go.

Where to stay

Within each chapter you'll find a range of suggestions, from five-star luxury to budget-friendly beach huts. Explorer has selected some personal favourites, which we've featured as handpicked hotels. These stays can often be experiences in themselves and, with so little time, offer all you need to feel completely looked after. Don't forget to check the transfer time between the airport and your hotel – you don't want to be spending half your break in a taxi!

Budget breaks

Going on holiday doesn't have to mean breaking the bank; a relatively modest budget is all you need for a great escape, whether you want to soak up some culture, explore the outdoors or simply sunbathe. Goa is a great budget break option for beach lovers, while Azerbaijan and Georgia both offer stunning scenery and challenging terrain to reward explorers willing to go off the beaten track. The archaeological wonders of wallet-friendly Cyprus are just a few hours' flight away, although if it's history you're after, there is plenty to be found in the Middle East.

Lap of luxury

Of course, if you are planning to go all out, there are destinations where splashing your cash will earn you a ticket to a true paradise. For the best short break that money can buy, look to the five-star resorts of idyllic archipelagos such as the Seychelles and the Maldives. Both destinations boast pristine beaches, turquoise oceans, and luxurious villas where your every holiday wish is granted, from gourmet restaurants to luxury spas. You may blow the budget, but it's sure to be an unforgettable break.

Family fun

When it comes to family holidays, the perfect destination will be one that has enough activities to keep kids of all ages entertained as well as attractions that the whole family can enjoy together. Cyprus and the Maldives are both good choices, with many resorts boasting dedicated kids' and teens' clubs to keep younger holidaymakers happy while their parents enjoy a romantic meal or trip to the spa. Plus, these also offer lots of family-friendly activities, from watersports to day trips. Closer to home, the UAE has a fantastic choice of family attractions, from gargantuan theme parks like Ferrari World and Yas Waterworld to the endless entertainment options at The Dubai Mall.

Weird & wonderful

We have also highlighted our quirkiest finds, from Kenya's Giraffe Manor, where the long-necked creatures might interrupt your breakfast, to Kerala's wacky houseboats compete with Jacuzzi, and Sri Lanka's converted tea factory where colonial meets chic at the country's highest point.

The Leela Palace, Udaipur

How to book

Be sure to shop around for accommodation, and check booking websites such as agoda.com and booking.com for the best deals. To save time and hassle, you can often book a package that includes flights and accommodation as well as car hire and guided tours. And, if you're staying in the UAE, don't forget to check askexplorer.com for hotel reviews and activity ideas, and many more inspiring travel features.

Mare Anglaise, Seychelles

Checklist

It's much easier to plan a last-minute adventure when you're not travelling too far or for too long, which is a big advantage of taking a short break. The downside, however, is that it's easy to forget the essentials when you're packing up at short notice. With that in mind, here's a handy checklist to make sure things run smoothly.

☐ Car hire – Do your research and find out ahead of time whether you need to rent a car or if it would be easier and more convenient to simply hire a driver or use taxis during your stay.

☐ Luggage – Check your allowance. You might do well to save both money and time at the airport by travelling light

☐ Passport – Make sure that your passport is not going to expire any time soon; many countries require a minimum of six months' validity from your date of travel.

☐ Travel insurance – Your travel insurance should provide comprehensive cover for whatever activities you might be planning, as well as the basics such as lost luggage, missed flights or illness.

☐ Vaccinations – Each chapter includes a list of the recommended vaccinations, but visit cdc.gov for the latest medical advice.

☐ Visas – Be sure to check the recommended government websites to find out whether you need a visa for the country that you're planning to visit.

Essentials

Short Breaks includes destination-specific information at the beginning of each chapter, from climate to currency, time zones to language. This is intended as a guide, so be sure to check with your embassy on the latest travel advice, especially for Egypt, Lebanon and Turkey.

We have indicated the best time of year to visit each country based mainly on climate, but this doesn't mean you can't go at other times. In fact, these destinations can be much cheaper and quieter off-season. Just check that your activities are available before you book – you don't want to plan a beach holiday during the monsoon season. See the directory on p.352 for useful numbers and websites.

Selected by Explorer

The following chapters are not your usual round-up of checklists and travel tips: each one has been written by Explorers using first-hand travel experience. We've trekked the trails of Nepal; sipped tea straight from the plantations of Sri Lanka; snorkelled the crystal seas of the Seychelles; and sought out Beirut's best bars and clubs.

Take your pick

With the world at you fingertips, the hardest thing is deciding what you want to get out of your short break, who you want to travel with, and where in the world you want to go. To help you get inspired, we've highlighted the best activities for each destination, as well as the best time to go and the average flight time. See the chart and the map overleaf.

Outdoor adventures
There's no shortage to the amount of outdoor adventures that can be pursued in and around the UAE; the only limit is your own ambition. If you're planning a day trip or overnight stay close to home, consider Oman, or the northern emirates of Fujairah and Ras Al Khaimah, for outdoor pursuits like dune bashing, mountain biking, hiking and diving. However, for a once-in-a-lifetime break, there's no beating a trip to Kenya and the unforgettable Masai Mara National Reserve, where you can go on safari, spot the Big Five and admire the African plains from a hot air balloon.

Culture & heritage
It's amazing how far back in time you can travel during a short break. There are plenty of short haul destinations to keep history buffs entertained, whether you're interested in ancient cities, Roman ruins or religious artefacts. Walk amongst archaeological sites and ruins dating back thousands of years in Cyprus. In Jordan you'll find the 5,000-year-old Nabataean city of Petra, while in Turkey you can wander the legendary city of Troy, explore the temples of Ephesus or simply marvel at the 4th century Hagia Sophia in Istanbul.

Surf & sand
Here in the UAE, we are blessed with some fabulous seaside spots, from the buzzing city beaches of Dubai and Abu Dhabi, to the deserted stretches of rugged coast in Fujairah. But within a five-hour radius are some of the world's most beautiful beaches. It's not far to the bohemian beach scenes of Goa and Kerala, where you can party and meditate in equal measure with your toes firmly in the sand. Or there's Sri Lanka's booming surf scene, which comes alive once tourist numbers have died down at the end of the peak season.

City sights & late nights
Shopping, sightseeing, stellar nightlife... Whatever you want from a city break, there's a huge variety within easy reach. Magnificent Muscat, with its pretty architecture and bustling souks is just a short hop away, and slightly further afield are the bars of the Middle East's ultimate party destination, Beirut. And for a true taste of culture, walk the streets of Baku or Amman to find restaurants, cafes and street stalls serving the most authentic local cuisine.

Nature & wildlife
From the heights of the Nepalese Himalayas, home to the tallest mountains in the world, to the other-worldly volcanic landscape of Ethiopia's Danakil Depression, the hottest place on earth, we've included some of the world's most extreme natural wonders. In between these you'll find the greenest, serenest rolling hills, tropical jungles, vast lakes and untouched coastlines. From whale-watching to sunrise safaris, see some incredible wildlife; from elephants and lions to tigers, dolphins and bears.

Everest Skydive

Baku Flame Towers, Azerbaijan

South Asia

Destination	Page	Beach	City	Culture & heritage	Nature	Outdoor adventure	Wildlife	Flight time (hrs)	January	February	March	April	May	June	July	August	September	October	November	December
Goa	p.3	●		●	●		●	4	●	●	●	●	●				●	●	●	●
North India	p.19		●	●	●		●	3.5	●	●	●							●	●	●
Kerala	p.33	●		●			●	4	●	●	●						●	●	●	●
Maldives	p.47	●			●	●	●	5	●	●	●	●	●							●
Nepal	p.63		●	●	●	●	●	4.5	●	●	●	●						●	●	●
Sri Lanka	p.77	●	●	●	●		●	4.5	●	●	●	●	●				●	●	●	●

Africa

Destination	Page	Beach	City	Culture & heritage	Nature	Outdoor adventure	Wildlife	Flight time (hrs)	January	February	March	April	May	June	July	August	September	October	November	December
Egypt	p.95	●	●	●		●	●	4	●	●	●	●	●	●	●	●	●	●	●	●
Ethiopia	p.109			●	●		●	4	●	●	●							●	●	●
Kenya	p.125	●			●	●	●	5	●	●	●				●	●	●	●		●
Seychelles	p.141	●			●		●	4.5				●	●	●	●	●	●			

Eurasia

Destination	Page	Beach	City	Culture & heritage	Nature	Outdoor adventure	Wildlife	Flight time (hrs)	January	February	March	April	May	June	July	August	September	October	November	December
Azerbaijan	p.159		●	●	●			3			●	●	●	●	●	●	●	●		
Cyprus	p.179	●		●	●			4			●	●	●	●	●	●	●	●	●	
Georgia	p.197		●	●	●			3.5				●	●	●	●	●	●	●		
Turkey	p.211	●	●	●	●			4.5			●	●	●	●	●	●	●	●		

Middle East

Destination	Page	Beach	City	Culture & heritage	Nature	Outdoor adventure	Wildlife	Flight time (hrs)	January	February	March	April	May	June	July	August	September	October	November	December
Bahrain	p.233		●	●		●		1	●	●	●	●							●	●
Jordan	p.249	●	●	●	●			3			●	●	●	●	●	●	●	●	●	●
Lebanon	p.265	●	●	●				4	●	●	●	●	●	●	●	●	●	●	●	●
Oman	p.279	●	●	●	●	●	●	1-2	●	●	●	●						●	●	●
Qatar	p.295		●	●		●		1	●	●	●							●	●	●
UAE	p.311	●	●	●	●	●	●	0	●	●	●	●						●	●	●

● Recommended by Explorer

South Asia

South Asia

Goa

Snooze in hammocks on the beach, see the countryside by motorbike, and eat some of the best seafood in the world in India's palm-fringed state.

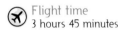
Flight time
3 hours 45 minutes

Door to door
45 minutes by car from the airport to popular north Goan resorts; up to 2 hours to reach south Goa

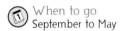
When to go
September to May

Famed for white sandy beaches and hedonistic partying, and just under four hours' flight from the UAE, Goa remains a firm favourite as a short haul destination for UAE residents looking to let their hair down.

The northern part of Goa is the place to head when lazy sunny days and long revelrous nights are what you're after. It's the epicentre for hippies lost in time, commercialised beaches and wild nights out. In southern Goa the atmosphere is far more laidback and visitors can enjoy authentic Goan cuisine, empty beaches, excellent hotels and wonderfully cheap beach huts complete with hammocks and the obligatory background music courtesy of Bob Marley. Unless you've chosen one of the luxurious hotels near the airport, it's wise to base yourself in the south and take mini

excursions to the north, allowing you the chance to visit interesting sites and cultural attractions. Should you fancy a little of the hedonism only found in parts of Calangute and Baga, it's easy enough to travel there.

Goa stretches for over 100km of coastline and its inland areas include the lower-ranging Western Ghats mountain range, palm forests and paddy fields. While its attractions are spread out across the state, most can be reached within an hour or two and travelling between destinations gives visitors a good chance to enjoy the scenic landscape of lush green palm jungles, broken by houses and villas painted in fluorescent colours and dazzlingly white churches. Your hotel concierge can arrange tours; alternatively, grab a map and hire a taxi to travel around the sights.

Pocket-sized appeal

Located on the western coast, Goa is India's smallest state by a substantial margin, but its pocket-sized appeal exerts a powerful charm. You'll feel the difference immediately on arrival in Goa's tiny but charming little airport – the familiar sub-continental bustle and jostling that you might be accustomed to in other parts of India give way to a measured dreaminess akin to island life. With a population of 1.5 million, this is where the swarming cityscapes of urban India give way to coconut groves, meandering cows and blue skies, with the occasional blare of a scooter or tuk-tuk horn.

Goa
Essentials

Goa's let-it-all-hang-out reputation has attracted Indian and foreign tourists since the early 1970s.

Getting there
Fly direct from Dubai to Dabolim Airport with Air Arabia, or via Mumbai with Jet Airways, or via Doha with Qatar Airways.

Visas
Most visitors must obtain a single or multiple entry visa (valid for between 15 days to six months) prior to arrival in India. Apply online at blsindiavisa-uae.com or visit the visa office in Dubai located in the Khaleej Centre, Bur Dubai.

Time
One hour 30 minutes ahead of the UAE.

Climate
Goa has a tropical climate with daytime temperatures of 25°C-30°C and heavy monsoon rains from June to September.

Language
Konkani; English is widely spoken in most urban areas.

Currency
Indian Rupee (INR). 100 INR = Dhs.6.5.

Vaccinations
Hepatitis A, Hepatitis B, Polio and Typhoid. Malaria tablets are recommended.

Best for... shoestring budgets
India is one of the world's cheapest destinations and it's possible to travel on Dhs.180 a day or less if you plan and haggle well. Food and drink is also cheap and a bottle of Goa's finest ale costs Dhs.3. Accommodation-wise, beach towns are dominated by seafront bungalows, which rent for as little as Dhs.20 per night.

The Leela Goa

A short break to Goa is more than enough time to explore this exotic Catholic-Hindu enclave of India.

North Goa

North Goa is best known for its package holidays and party-friendly resorts along the Calangute and Baga beaches (p.16-17). As well as experiencing the grungy, hedonistic party scene, there's culture, history and nature to enjoy in the capital city Panaji, the village of Anjuna, and beyond.

Sahakari Spice Farm

Old Goa

Once the magnificent Portuguese capital of Goa, these days all that remains of Old Goa in Panaji is a handful of imposing churches, cathedrals and ruins. Se Cathedral is worth a look, while one of the most interesting in the area is the Basilica of Bom Jesus, considered one of the best examples of baroque architecture in India. This UNESCO World Heritage Site contains the preserved remains of the body of Saint Frances Xavier in a glass casket.

Yoga retreats

India was where yoga was born, and Goa is the most Western-friendly place to study the discipline. Yoga Magic near Anjuna is a popular retreat that offers daily yoga classes, accommodation in Rajasthani-style hunting tents and delicious vegetarian meals. yogamagic.net

Spice farms

Goa's tropical climate and dense forests make it an ideal place to grow spices and many of the spice farms are open to visitors. Try Sahakari Spice Farm, where, for only 400 rupees, you'll get a crash course in the history, medicinal and culinary uses of spices such as nutmeg, curry leaves, turmeric and cardamom, and finish with a traditional lunch. There's also the option to purchase a range of spices and teas to take home. For an additional cost, you can ride elephants around the compound or get wet in an elephant bath. sahakarifarms.com

Se Cathedral, Old Goa

Anjuna Flea Market

This classic market has been around since the 1970s and covers most of the area behind the south side of Anjuna beach. What began as hippies selling off their possessions to afford a ticket back home, has now become a commercial spectacle on a grand scale. Every Wednesday, vendors sell a massive collection of artefacts and collectibles, creating an irresistible one-stop shopping experience.

Ayurvedic treatments

Shamana Spa at the Grand Hyatt Goa offers a wide range of treatments and massage techniques, but an Ayurvedic massage will give you the authentic local experience. This traditional Indian massage philosophy involves lots of heavenly oil that is applied with long and slow strokes to warm the muscles and relax the body. Guests stepping into this haven of serenity can make use of the spa's impressive wellness facilities, including a Roman bath-style Jacuzzi, large indoor swimming pool, and separate male and female saunas and steam rooms.
goa.grand.hyatt.com

Mangeshi Temple

One of the largest and most popular Hindu shrines in Goa is located roughly 8km southeast of Old Goa and is dedicated to Mangueshi – an incarnation of Lord Shiva. Before entering, purchase an offering of colourful flowers from one of ladies sitting outside the Temple walls and pass this onto the priest inside – a ritual known as Puja. The priest will take your offering and, in return, give you his blessing.

Drink-Joy

The typical drink of Goa is feni or fenny, a rather exclusive alcoholic drink that is not sold in any other part of India. This Indian liquor is of two types – cashew feni and coconut feni; it has a strong shelf life and drinking styles vary. It is usually drunk with cola, soda, and lemon juice, or as a base for a cocktail.

Mandovi River

A boat cruise on the Mandovi is a must-do; head west to watch the sunset or east to sail past Panaji and the green island of Chorao. Santa Monica runs day, evening and full moon cruises, with Goan dancing and traditional buffet adding to the charm.
goaindiatourism.org

Fort Aguada

Walk along the high sides of this fort for great views out to the Indian Ocean. Built in 1612 to protect the northern shores of the Mandovi estuary from Dutch raiders, the fort has a four-storey Portuguese lighthouse.

Souza Lobo

Souza Lobo is a Goa institution with spicy coastal food to satiate both a local and traveller's desire for authenticity. Locals have been coming here for generations not simply for the view but the prime location too. Be prepared to scoff down sublime prawn curry, sausages and fried fish.

 Canoe or take a boat trip through the mangroves along Cumbarjua Canal in search of crocodiles. It's the only place in Goa where they can be found.

South Goa

The unique charms of India's coastline state are arguably best showcased in South Goa. It's bigger, less developed, boasts more colonial architecture and by far the best beaches. It's 15 miles of unspoilt, uninterrupted stretches of white sand and the perfect hideaway for a short break.

Silent raves

Goa's iconic headphone party known as Silent Noise is held at Neptune's Point in South Goa – a stunning peninsula where happy clubbers navigate the winding path across a bridge, up a jagged rock face before arriving at this noise-less dance party. Everyone is connected to the music with wireless headphones and DJs play simultaneously, competing to get the crowd to tune into their set. Add in lasers, visuals and thousands of revellers, and you've got a mini-rave every week. silentnoise.in

Dolphin tours

Hire a local boatman at the north end of Palolem Beach to ferry you up to Butterfly Beach and back, relishing the views of untouched coastline along the way. If you sail off in the mornings, you're also likely to spot a pod of dolphins following your trail.

Deep-sea fishing

Bring home a fresh catch on a deep-sea fishing trip. With your expert local guide, board a large, covered canoe on a beach in Goa and spend three hours fishing and relaxing. Anything you catch, you can take back to shore and cook. viator.com

Salcete Wildlife Sanctuary

If you've got a hankering to seek out wild animals, this wildlife sanctuary is for you. Close to the Karnataka border in Salcete, it's home to deer, sloth bears, leopard cats, and many other animals in their natural habitat.

Palolem Beach

Dudhsagar Waterfall

As India's fifth largest waterfall, Dudhsagar is a fantastic place to visit, especially during monsoon season. The name comes from the milky appearance of the waterfall; Dudhsagar meaning 'ocean of milk'. The tiered waterfalls are surrounded by the thriving green forests of the Western Ghats and fall from an astounding height of 2,000 feet. Swimming is allowed here too.

Martin's Corner

Word has it that any visit to Goa is not complete until you go to Martin's Corner and, after sampling the tiger prawns coated in creamy garlic butter, it's not hard to see why. The seafood is particularly outstanding and the restaurant prides itself on serving authentic Goan dishes. The atmosphere inside this modest wooden restaurant is consistently lively with Indian revellers taking to the stage for a spot of karaoke while diners gorge on crab xacuti. martinscornergoa.com

Curry mornings

If you want to know more about the secrets of Indian cooking, On The Menu, a cooking school overlooking the river holds weekly sessions where visitors learn about the wonderful, hidden flavours of India. holidayonthemenu.com

Seafood by candlelight

At night, the popular stretches of beach in the south are lit up by candlelight with each of the shoreline venues setting up tables and chairs in preparation for nightly seafood barbecues. While the choice is plentiful, try to pick one where the seafood is chilling on ice, just for peace of mind. The proud chef at Camp San Francisco is more than happy to explain what's on offer and how best to serve each hearty dish. You won't be disappointed with the giant, meaty kingfish coated in authentic Goan spices. It's phenomenal. campsanfrancisco.com

Sunburn Festival

Sunburn Festival launched six years ago as South Asia's first electronic music festival, and featured heavyweights like Carl Cox and John 00 Fleming. The festival practically founded Goa Trance, a type of pulsing, transcendental electro music that's enjoyed by thousands of revellers annually in December.

Goa
Places to stay

The Leela Goa

North Goa

Amarya Shamiyana

Sleeping under canvas may not be everyone's cup of tea but even the most hardened hotel-lover will be a camping convert after a night here. At the start of the season, four bleached-white shamiyanas (Urdu for tent) are pitched within a private grove of coconut trees that border the shores of Ashvem Beach. But these are no ordinary tents; in fact, they are more like mini-marquees complete with a master bedroom, private veranda and an ensuite bathroom with walk-in rain shower.
amaryagroup.com

Grand Hyatt Goa

Designed to resemble a grand, 17th century Indo-Portuguese palace, the Grand Hyatt is the ultimate five-star hotel in Goa where luxury is standard. A lush 28-acre resort with over 300 rooms and suites, seven restaurants and bars, an indoor/outdoor spa, and an enormous outdoor pool; at the Grand Hyatt Goa, your every whim is catered for.
goa.grand.hyatt.com

The Leela Goa

For over-the-top luxury, you'll have difficulty finding better than this 75-acre resort that includes a secluded beach and a magnificent view of cliffs and coves where the two-storey, salmon-coloured villas are arranged along a winding artificial lagoon. Go for upmarket Goan cuisine at its signature Jamavar restaurant, or alfresco at Riverside.
theleela.com

Pousada Tauma

While Pousada Tauma is not your run-of-the-mill five-star tourist hotel, this one stands out for its distinctive local character. Fashioned entirely out of Goan laterite stone and set around a beautiful pool with cascading water, each suite is uniquely styled and themed with eccentric Goan antiques.
pousada-tauma.com

For a budget-friendly hotel alternative, try browsing through the listings on airbnb.com. There's a variety of accommodation types, from beach huts to tree houses, that are available for short-stay rentals. Owners often let out a room in their own homes too.

Holidays in Goa should carry a health warning – they're highly addictive

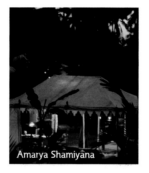
Amarya Shamiyana

Grand Hyatt Goa

The Leela Goa

South Goa

Dwarka

If you're after complete seclusion, Dwarka should fit the bill. To get there, you drive through villages and down a dirt road. Ten huts are set around a lagoon and overlook the ocean, which is blissfully free of hawkers as it's inaccessible by road. At Dwarka, it's all about being at one with nature, and you can go for jungle walks during the day before lounging around a bonfire at night. dwarkagoa.com

Neptune Point

If you're travelling to Goa on a shoe-string and want to experience true travelling life, try Neptune Point in Palolem. While these beach huts are certainly minimal in terms of furnishings and décor, not to mention particularly flimsy walls, it is one of the liveliest sets of beach huts in the area. Reserve a sea-facing beach hut and you'll wake up to one of the most beautiful views in the world. neptunepoint.com

Romance Beach Huts

A firm favourite on Agonda Beach, these sea-facing huts are painted in bright colours

Taj Exotica

and stand on two-metre high stilts, a stone's throw away from the water. The huts are a bit more expensive than most on Agonda Beach, but they're also more spacious and better decorated, and come with a hammock. romancebeachhuts.com

Taj Exotica

Located on the southwest coast of Goa, this Mediterranean-style resort has a way of slowing down time to a tranquil tempo. Set in 56 acres of lush gardens, Taj Exotica is a favourite spot for high-end travellers. The tropical-inspired design creates a lush and relaxing paradise. tajhotels.com

Dwarka

Taj Exotica

Handpicked hotel
Relax & unwind

Goa Marriott Resort & Spa
goamarriottresort.com

Distance from airport
50 minutes

With stellar views out towards the Mandovi River and a beautiful infinity pool, this luxury retreat is an oasis of calm.

Just 30 minutes away from the bustling beaches of Baga and Calangute, Goa Marriott Resort & Spa offers the perfect respite from the chaotic roads beyond its gates. In fact, as soon as you pass security and enter the lobby, receive your shell necklace and replenish your thirst with a delightful purple lemonade concoction, you will feel so far away from the hustle and bustle that the laidback surroundings will hypnotise you into full-on holiday-mode.

An idler's idyll

The Goa Marriott Resort & Spa offers a truly idyllic setting, rising up from the riverside, where guests take pleasure in relaxing on hammocks or performing sun salutations along the narrow beach. There is one stunning infinity swimming pool where afternoon cocktails and snacks can be enjoyed at the relaxed pool bar, while the narrow stretch of coast allows for a lovely evening stroll.

Marriotts in general are the no-nonsense go-to hotel for those looking for a sure-bet, and this property is no exception, with its attentive staff, sleek, modern fittings and occasional wafts of a warm sea breeze. Even entry-level accommodation is plenty roomy, with an easy-on-the-eye palette of muted tones and subtle Indian touches in the selection of art and sculptures.

The hotel's all day dining restaurant, Waterfront Terrace & Bar, serves up a delicious selection of breakfast treats from typical Indian cuisine to omelettes cooked to order and a sprawling array of mezze options. No task is too small for this dedicated team and the pastry chef comes round every morning to serve fresh

cakes and biscuits to guests. For that special romantic evening, Simply Grills is one of the area's most popular outdoor restaurants and is located alongside the infinity pool with views out across the bay. Fill your bellies with delicious barbecue meats and seafood before enjoying a night cap at the A.Z.U.R bar.

And, if by chance, there's an ounce of stress left in you, then you can always take a trip to the delightful Quan Spa which features a range of traditional and Ayurvedic treatments to soothe weary bodies and dissolve stress completely.

Location, location

While Goa Marriott Resort & Spa is the epitome of resort-holidaying, where all that you desire is available for your indulgence, the location of the hotel is still a perfect base for seeing the sights. Old Goa, the hedonistic party beaches of the north, the luscious spice plantations and dizzying hippie markets are all within driving distance and the concierges are more than willing to help organise a travel itinerary.

But if, like most, you'd rather hide away in the luxurious confines of the hotel, with a cocktail in hand and delicious food at your beck and call, there's absolutely no shame in that either. After all, it's your holiday.

Limo pick-up
Dabolim Airport is notoriously packed with touts trying to make a quick buck from tired tourists. Save the hassle and pre-arrange a hotel limo to pick you up.

Sunshine & sunsets

Enjoying beach life

North vs South
Head north to party on the commercialised beaches of Baga and Anjuna, then travel to the quieter and pristine shores of the south.

Goa's charm lies chiefly in the wealth of beautiful beaches lining the shores, each with its own distinct appeal.

Agonda Beach
This very quiet yet beautiful stretch of coastline is about a 20-minute motorbike ride from Palolem and attracts the more laidback travellers looking for complete peace and quiet. While there may not be much to do except hang around in a hammock with an ice-cold Kingfisher beer (for Dhs.3), Agonda is one of the most mesmerising spots to watch the sun set. It's no wonder why so many people end up staying far longer than they intended.

Anjuna Beach
While it has changed dramatically since its original days, Anjuna still retains a touch of the unconventional. A trip to the dream beaches of the 1960s hippie trail is worthy of a visit if only to witness the hoard of travelling hippies that have somehow got lost in time here. It's still very much a party town; head to Curlie's, a very popular place for an evening drink, an alternative crowd and the odd impromptu party. Also, try to get here on a Wednesday to see the legendary flea market (see p.7).

Arambol Beach

Once a sleepy fishing village called Harmal, Arambol Beach has become the newest hippie haven of Goa. Each season, the locals are joined by hundreds of backpackers, who are also attracted to the laidback environment and live music scene there. The popularity of Arambol as a beach destination is growing every year but, so far, it still retains an uncommercialised feel. Local pressure has ensured there are no resorts built here to privatise the land; basic guesthouses, particularly huts on the beach, are the only type of accommodation on offer, and, quite frankly, who would want it any other way?

Baga Beach

Bordered by Calangute Beach to the south, and Anjuna Beach to the north, Baga Beach may be the most tourist-heavy beach in the country. But, for those who like action, it's one of the most happening beaches on the coast. You'll find everything from watersports to fine dining restaurants there, along with a pulsating nightlife that carries on into the early hours.

Morjim Beach

Situated in northern Goa, Morjim is home to the endangered Olive Ridley sea turtle. Kitesurfers also frequent the beach as the shallow waters and wide spaces create the perfect surfing location.

Palolem Beach

Picturesque Palolem Beach is a semi-circle shaped beach with shady palm trees and soft sand. Since it was discovered, it's become a backpacker haven. It may not be as deserted as it once was but Palolem is still the ultimate beach destination in south Goa. The little coastal town has shops and restaurants but still manages to retain its unspoilt charm. The beaches are relatively empty except for a few local fishermen with their boats, not to mention the ubiquitous cows laying about and enjoying the sun.

Arambol Beach

Palolem Beach

Cover story

While Goa's reputation as one of the most liberal Indian states means that sunbathing in a bikini is entirely acceptable, it is important to remember that topless sunbathing is illegal and wearing flimsy shorts or a bikini anywhere other than the beach is disrespectful.

Anjuna Beach

Jaswant Thada, Jodhpur

North India

In a nation known for its colour and opulence, Rajasthan and Delhi outshine their neighbours with a dazzling landscape of palaces, monuments, forts and bazaars.

 Flight time
3 hours 20 minutes

 Door to door
40 minutes by car from Delhi airport to New Delhi; 30 minutes by car from Jaipur airport to Jaipur; four hours' drive or 30 minutes' flight from Delhi to Jaipur

 When to go
October to March

From the Pink City of Jaipur and the red sandstone of Rajasthan's forts, to the gleaming white marble of the Taj Mahal and the 'Blue City' of Jodhpur, northern India is a vibrant, colourful land. There are the parched ochre dunes of the Thar Desert sands, the silver streets of Chandni Chowk and the array of reds and oranges of a classic New Delhi sunset across the city's rooftops. The neighbouring regions of Rajasthan, Delhi and Uttar Pradesh are fascinating, diverse, historically rich, romantic and, above all, make up one of the most beautiful places on earth.

If ever there was a time to step out of your comfort zone, it is in Rajasthan – where maharajah-gilded palaces, exuberant festivals and sprawling tiger reserves are set amongst a contrasting landscape of haunting desert, serene lakes and green hills.

The capital of this massive state is Jaipur, a fairytale and exotic land of breathtaking palaces, local handicrafts and historic monuments. Neighbouring Delhi, home to India's capital city New Delhi, embodies everything there is to love and hate about India's frenzied urbanity. It's a city with a wealth of cultural, spiritual, artistic and culinary delights – and where sacred cows wander crowded streets, hawkers sell brightly coloured tapestries, rich silks and exotic fabrics, and pedestrians are narrowly avoided by the cars and rickshaws that fight their way along narrow streets.

The Golden Triangle

This well travelled route hosts three of North India's greatest cultural gems, including Delhi, Agra and Jaipur. Popular with first timers to India or those on a shorter timeframe, most tourists fly to Delhi, travel southwards to the site of the famous Taj Mahal at Agra, then west to the ethereal Pink City of Jaipur. The circuit is about 1,000km by road, and each leg is about five hours' drive; the faster and very scenic way to travel the Golden Triangle, however, is by speedy Shatabdi train. This is your chance to see the ancient Qutab Minar and witness the enthralling chaos of New Delhi, stand at one of the world's most iconic landmarks, and ride an elephant to the Amber Fort amongst the desert landscapes of Rajasthan. And all in just three or four days.

North India
Essentials

This map is not an authority on international boundaries

In a nation that bursts with smiling faces and infectious, jingoistic pride, you won't be out of your comfort zone for long.

Getting there
Fly from Sharjah, Dubai or Abu Dhabi to Delhi with Air Arabia, Emirates, Etihad and Jet Airways. Fly from Dubai or Sharjah to Jaipur with Air Arabia and Air India Express. Flights from Dhs.900 return.

Visas
Most foreign nationals need to obtain a visa before entering India. BLS (blsindiavisa-uae. com) visa service delivers your passport and visa back to you, usually within four days.

Time
One hour 30 minutes ahead of the UAE.

Climate
Broadly speaking, it has a subtropical climate with a monsoon season from July to September. Temperatures average 26°C-45°C in summer and 8°C-22°C in winter.

Language
Hindi, but English is widely spoken.

Currency
Indian Rupee (INR). 100 INR = Dhs.6.5.

Vaccinations
Hepatitis A and B, Polio and Typhoid. Malaria tablets are recommended.

Best for... train journeys
Perhaps the quintessential Indian experience, trains are a great way to meet the locals and absorb the melting pot of India on the move. Travelling on overnight services allows you to cover vast distances while saving time. Services run surprisingly regularly, fares are extremely cheap and you can book tickets online at makemytrip.com.

Jaipur

Amber Fort

It's easy to fall head over heels in love with this country – from cosmopolitan, frenetic Delhi to the magnificent forts and palaces of Jaipur.

Jaipur

The architectural opulence of Rajasthan's lively capital, a city truly built for a king, is a sight to behold.

City Palace

Housing the Maharaja Sawai Man Singh II Museum, this stunning palace was built by the Rajputs in the 18th century, and the royal family still reside in the complex. The Peacock Gate alone is worth seeing for its exquisite detailing, and the museum is a fascinating insight into Rajput regal life.

Palace of the Winds

Towering above the old town's main thoroughfare, this ornate facade was built for the royal ladies in purdah. The thin walls are covered with stone lattice work which allowed them to watch the activity of the town, but prevented people from seeing in.

Amber Fort

Bazaars & markets

The labyrinthine central market of Jaipur is a riot of colour, with brightly dressed locals selling all handicrafts and edible treats. For the finest Indian sweets a stop at the LMB store in Jauhari Bazaar is a must. The adjoining restaurant serves up delicious chaat (snacks) and Rajasthani thali in kitsch surrounds.

Raj Mandir Cinema

This stunning art deco building has a lobby decorated in icing sugar pinks and blues with glittering mirrors and chandeliers. It's like stepping into a fairytale palace.

Amber Fort & Palace

Well worth the short journey from the Pink City, this is one of Rajasthan's most spectacular royal forts and reminiscent of China's Great Wall. The incredibly grand interior bears intricate mosaics, mirrors and frescoes, while a sound and light show transforms the imposing exterior each evening. Elephants are on hand to carry visitors to the fort in true royal style.

Sariska National Park

Conveniently located between the area's biggest transport hubs of Jaipur and Delhi, Sariska is home to the Royal Bengal tiger, and is popular with visitors eager to get a glimpse of one. As well as an abundance of wildlife, the area has a wealth of history, with Kankwari Fort and ancient Shiva Temples, that go back as far as the sixth century, both fascinating sites to visit.

Jodhpur

Rajasthan

Journeying through this Indian state is every bit as magical as you'd imagine, with a glittering landscape of lakes, forests and desert, and majestic architecture.

Jaisalmer
Right in the heart of the Thar Desert is Jaisalmer. While it's fun to whiz around the city in a tuk-tuk, stopping to admire Jaisalmer Fort, the real spectacles are the breathtaking sand dunes and water tanks.

Jodhpur
At the centre of the 'Land of Kings' is this bustling city famed for its majestic monuments and temples, such as Jaswant Thada, and vivid blue houses. Batman fans may recognise buildings from *The Dark Knight Rises*, most notably Mehrangarh Fort. Perhaps the most impressive of Rajasthan's forts, this was described by Rudyard Kipling as 'the work of angels, fairies and giants'.

Udaipur
Romantic and picturesque, Udaipur gives a perfectly proportioned slice of Indian life. It's built around Lake Pichola, an awe-inspiring artificial lake encircled by temples, lush greenery, bathing ghats and palaces. Enjoy views of the city from the water aboard a traditional shikara boat or hire a guide for a day-long excursion to City Palace. This architectural spectacle neighbours a bustling bazaar, and further afield is the magnificent Kumbhalgarh Fort.

Tiger trail
After a brief hiatus when the government closed India's tiger reserves, tiger tourism is back in a big way and Ranthambore National Park is one of the best places in India to spot these elusive creatures. It's also home to other wildlife, including leopards, crocodiles and chameleons.

Mehrangarh Fort

 To enjoy the tranquility and wildlife of the Thar Desert stay overnight in a tented camp. From riding a camel across the Sam sand dunes to cooking flatbread on an open fire and sleeping under the stars – it's an unforgettable experience.

Humayun's Tomb

On the buses

The best and fastest way to see the city sights is to jump onboard the Hop On Hop Off bus tour (hohodelhi.com), which visits the top 20 attractions across Delhi, with the added bonus of witty anecdotes from English and Hindi speaking guides.

Delhi

For a city break with a difference, explore the maze-like lanes and alleys of Old Delhi and the tree-lined avenues and colonial buildings of the capital, New Delhi.

Delhi belly

From shawarma to fresh fruit beer, momos (dumplings) to banta, a delicious lemon-based drink that's an ideal refreshment for hot Delhi weather, there's plenty to sample on a fulfilling food tour of Delhi. urbanadventures.com

New Delhi

First impressions of a country count – and if this is your first stop-off in India, it won't disappoint. It's a sprawling metropolis with a heady cocktail of spice, incense and petrol in the air. Catch the metro to visit architectural wonders such as Humayun's Tomb, with its domes, decorative pillars and water features, and Qutab Minar, an early Indo-Islamic feat of engineering. A visit to Gandhi Smriti will show you the exact spot where Mahatma Gandhi, the Father of the Nation, was assassinated on January 30, 1948. The towering archway of India Gate is a striking war memorial best viewed at sunset.

Old Delhi

The best way to soak up the melee of smells and sights of the old city is by spending some time walking along its streets. Cars, rickshaws, hand-pulled carts, and animals all compete for space in this frenetic city, but a pair of comfy shoes and map will get you off on the right foot. Old Delhi's most famous monument, the Red Fort, stands as a powerful reminder of the Mughal emperors who ruled India; there's nothing better to imagine the ancient era than the sound and light show at the fort each evening. A shocking contrast to the wide, orderly streets of New Delhi is the network of narrow, winding bazaars in the 300-year-old Chandni Chowk – India's ultimate shopping destination. Other treasures include the incredible Jama Masjid, India's largest mosque.

India Gate

When to visit

The Taj Mahal is open from dawn to dusk, and is closed on Fridays. Adult entrance costs around Dhs.50 for non-Indian nationals. Upon reaching the Taj Mahal, an onslaught of 'guides' will jostle for your attention – and your money. These are not licensed guides and should be avoided – they will basically harass you until you pay them to go away.

Agra

The enduring pull of the 350-year-old Taj Mahal is reason enough to make the pilgrimage to Agra.

Taj Mahal

One of the world's most cherished and iconic landmarks, the Taj Mahal is on every self-respecting traveller's bucket list. Built by the Mughal emperor Shah Jahan as an expression of devotion to his late wife, India's most famous tomb is a must for anyone visiting North India. With more than three million visitors every year, you won't be alone, but when you're soaking up the exquisite architecture and intricately detailed craftsmanship, all else will fade to the periphery. The best time to visit is early morning, in time to watch the dawn light bathe the monument in an ethereal glow.

Agra can be reached on a day trip from Delhi, but the city does have some other impressive sights, including Agra Fort, that make an overnight stay worth the stop.

Fatehpur Sikri

For an interesting day trip, Fatehpur Sikri is 40km west of Agra. This fascinating ghost town was built during the 16th century by Mughal emperor Akbar as a new capital. Geographically speaking, it wasn't his best idea and due to a lack of groundwater reserves the city was abandoned after he died. A wander round the beautifully preserved red sandstone palaces and Islamic monuments serves as a wonderful insight into the Mughals and their civilisation.

From Delhi, Agra is just three hours, and companies such as onthegotours.com offer private guided tours. Delhi Tourism and Transportation Development Corporation (delhitourism.nic.in) runs a cheaper bus tour, three times a week. It's a 14-hour day trip with an early 5am start, but there's plenty of time to snooze en route.

Taj Mahal

Taj Lake Palace

Rajasthan

Manvar Resort & Camp

Aman-i-Khas

Experience Ranthambore National Park, one of India's best for spotting tigers, from this luxurious tented base close to a natural watering hole. Excursions into the park in open-top vehicles can be arranged if you can drag yourself away from the comfort of the camp and its spa facilities.
amanresorts.com

The Blue House

This budget-friendly option in Jodhpur is a family-run place with great views of Mehrangarh Fort, which is lit at night to give it an even greater sense of majesty. Rooms are simple but with fun décor, and home-cooked meals can be enjoyed on the rooftop.

Manvar Resort & Camp

The latest trend for exploring Rajasthan is from a luxury camp, and this desert camp in the Thar Desert is one example. Comfortable en suite safari tents are plushly furnished. Evenings are an experience, with traditional music and dance around the campfire. Your toes may be in the sand but this is some seriously upmarket glamping. manvar.com

The Oberoi Udaivilas

This sumptuous resort in Udaipur is built in the style of a traditional Indian palace with fountains, courtyards and gardens. Accessed by boat ride across Lake Pichola, all the rooms have terraces and a pool. Yoga and meditation sessions are available at the resort spa, a haven of serenity overlooking the lake. oberoihotels.com

Taj Lake Palace

Rising like a mirage from the shimmering waters of Lake Pichola, this ridiculously grand hotel will make you feel like a maharajah. Its romantic setting in the middle of the lake ensures unbeatable views, while attentive staff, dressed in traditional regalia, will pander to your every whim. tajhotels.com

Luxury camps are the hippest way of experiencing the land of the kings

Taj Lake Palace

Aman-i-Khas

Although Judi Dench, Bill Nighy and co. were rather disappointed to wash up at the *Best Exotic Marigold Hotel*, the actual location for the film is a rather charming heritage hotel, Ravla Khempur, which is set amongst some beautiful scenery in a remote and peaceful part of Rajasthan. (ravlakhempur.com)

Jaipur

Alsisar Haveli

A taste of regal Rajasthani life doesn't have to break the bank, and Jaipur's heritage hotels have been lovingly restored to provide an evocative base from which to explore the city's history. Rooms at Alsisar Haveli, located in the heart of the Pink City, are richly furnished with antique furniture. alsisarhaveli.com

Barwara Kothi

Owned and run by Jaipur nobility, Barwara Kothi gets great reviews from travellers for its reasonable rates, homely atmosphere, spotless rooms and friendly hosts. It is conveniently close to the city centre in a bright colonial villa. barwarakothi.com

lebua Lodge at Amer

Just outside Jaipur, away from the chaos of the city, is this quirky and serene 'camp', with futuristic cubic tents, each with TV, AC, wi-fi and marble bathrooms. Unique five-star chic without the sterility. lebua.com

Tree House Resort

Be at one with nature in a 'nest' at this quirky-yet-luxurious tree dwelling camp. Tree houses come in different sizes, from one room to an enormous five-room tree-mansion. Facilities are top-notch, so you'll be rather surprised to see that there are branches poking through the ceiling. treehouseresort.in

lebua Lodge at Amer

The Oberoi Amarvilas

Delhi

LaLiT New Delhi

For a more chic experience of India's chaotic capital, the LaLiT is a haven of calm. An antithesis to the flamboyance of the city's architecture, the clean decor of this trendy hotel retains a level of plush sophistication without overdoing it. Rooms are spacious, and the spa offers Ayurvedic therapies to wash away the furore of the city. thelalit.com

Taj Mahal Hotel

Luxurious surroundings and impeccable service are pretty much guaranteed from Indian hotel giant Taj Group, and this New Delhi institution is no exception. A social hub for the city's in-crowd who are attracted to its prime address, award-winning bars and restaurants and glamorous setting, the Taj Mahal Hotel is a safe bet for those looking for the Delhi high life. tajhotels.com

Agra

The Oberoi Amarvilas

With arguably one of the best views in the world, this luxurious resort facing the Taj Mahal is almost as lavish as the monument it reverently overlooks. While this prime position doesn't come cheap, a front row seat as the sun rises atmospherically over the Taj Mahal is surely a priceless experience. oberoihotels.com

The Oberoi Amarvilas

In the footsteps of maharajahs

Sightseeing by train

Few destinations can excite the imagination quite like India, and exploring this diverse and fascinating destination by train is a travel fantasy for many. The Maharajas' Express Treasures of India tour allows you to do just that, taking in some of its brightest gems over just three nights and four days, including Agra, Ranthambore, Jaipur and Delhi.

Day one

The Maharajas' Express departs from where most journeys around India begin: New Delhi, leaving the capital city first thing in the morning. After a traditional welcome, the whistle blows and it's full steam ahead. A lavish brunch is served as the crowded urban landscape of New Delhi transforms into green countryside sprinkled with dusty rural villages. Pulling into Agra in the afternoon, it is time for a tour of UNESCO World Heritage Site, Agra Fort. This impressive monument dates back to the Mughal Emperors of the 16th century. The train is then stationed in Agra for the night, so it's time to relax, have some dinner, and hit the bar for a champagne-fuelled evening.

All aboard
The Maharajas' Express three-night Treasures of India tour departs once a month, from October 2013 to April 2014. (the-maharajas.com)

If you're craving an adventure coloured by centuries' old history, then the Maharajas' Express should be your next stop.

Amber Fort

Taj Mahal

Maharajas' Express tour involves a visit to the 16th century Amber Fort and Palace, regarded as one of Rajasthan's most magnificent forts. After lunch you can visit the City Palace or Jantar Mantar, an 18th century astronomical observation site. There's time to shop for jewellery in the chaotic markets, unwind at a spa or on the golf course, or take the unique opportunity to witness an elephant polo match – as bizarre as it sounds and yet oddly compelling.

Heading home
Finally, there's one last night to spend on the train for the journey back to Delhi. On day four, you'll wake up in the capital city, refreshed and exhilarated, having tasted the past lives of royalty. It's time to depart the train after a quick breakfast, but there's plenty to absorb in the country's charismatic capital if you need one last afternoon of culture before catching the flight home.

Home comforts
You might not expect much luxury when travelling by train, but the Maharajas' Express really does feel like a home away from home. All the passenger cabins have an LCD TV, DVD player, phone and internet access, and individual temperature controls.

Day two
The second day begins with a visit to India's most instantly recognisable icon: the Taj Mahal. After enough time to admire (and photograph) this centuries-old homage to love in the early dawn light, it's time to board the train for lunch, and a journey to a far wilder attraction: Ranthambore National Park. A game drive at the reserve takes you on a quest to find the elusive Royal Bengal tiger amongst the foliage of the wilderness, before getting back onboard for dinner as the train whisks you rhythmically towards Jaipur.

Day three
Arriving in Jaipur is truly unforgettable, and at its heart is the old town, the walled Pink City. The colour, which is similar to that of the red stone used in Delhi's central monuments, doesn't come from the stones; in fact, the buildings were painted. This dates back to a visit from the Prince of Wales in the late 1800s, when the town was turned pink to honour his arrival. Since Jaipur was once the seat of Indian royalty, it's time to take in some regal relics and awesome architecture. The final full day of the

Ranthambore National Park

South Asia

Kerala

Beautiful beaches, meandering backwaters, tea plantations and tiger reserves – Kerala's mesmerising backdrops are havens of calm and encompass the best of India's natural wonders.

Flight time
4 hours

Door to door
1 hour by car from Kochi airport to Alappuzha; 6 hours' drive from Kochi to Poovar; 1 hour by car from Trivandrum airport to Poovar

When to go
September to March

Kerala is a land blessed with nature's best: sprawling backwaters, fields upon fields of tea, bountiful beaches and historical cities with colourful stories to tell. Stretching down the Malabar coast between the Arabian Sea and the Western Ghats, Kerala's scenery is stirring and hugely varied.

The capital of Thiruvananthapuram and historic harbour city of Kochi are both rich in palaces, churches, spice markets and early colonial architecture. A winding network of serene rivers and lakes is the state's star attraction, so fly to Kochi and head to Alappuzha to explore the backwaters by houseboat. Or, to experience beach life, fly to Trivandrum and catch a water taxi to the unspoilt Poovar Island Resort. To really get under the skin of Kerala, head out to the lush green landscapes and the tourist-free hill stations of the Western Ghats.

It's the people of Kerala that make it such an enchanting place to explore. Keralites welcome visitors with an infectious sense of the joys of life – and you're probably more likely to spot an Indian tiger than an unhappy local. And, wherever you travel, an incessant beeping of car horns along the frenetic streets, brightly coloured shops displaying even brighter fashions, and food stalls exuding a pot-pourri of aromas, all provide a splendid assault on the senses.

Kerala may be a paradox of chaos and calm, but it is an irresistible mix – so sit back, chill out and enjoy Keralife.

God's own country

For a short break in Kerala, it would be easy to simply pitch up on one of its many sublime, white sand beaches with a coconut cocktail in hand, and not leave until final boarding. But there are many other ways to relax – cruising through the backwaters of Kerala on a houseboat, or visiting the numerous Ayurveda spas and wellness retreats for traditional Indian massage therapies. Feeling more adventurous? Then take the short trip to one of several national parks that offer the chance to spot a tiger, as well as elephants, leopards and a host of wildlife. Alternatively, you can head up to the cooler, cardamom-infused air of the Western Ghats' hill stations, which are a wonderful base from which to explore tea plantations, streams and waterfalls.

Kerala
Essentials

The Western Ghats shelter the state from the hot northern winds, keeping summer temperatures relatively cool.

Getting there
Fly from Dubai, Abu Dhabi and Sharjah to Kochi (Cochin) and Thiruvananthapuram (Trivandrum) airports with Emirates, Etihad and Air Arabia. Air-India Express also runs a direct flight from the UAE. Flights from Dhs.1,200. Emirates also flies to Kozhikode (Calicut) from around Dhs.1,600.

Visas
Most visitors must obtain a single or multiple entry visa (valid for between 15 days and six months) prior to arrival in India. Apply online with BLS visa service (blsindiavisa-uae.com).

Time
One hour 30 minutes ahead of the UAE.

Climate
Tropical Kerala is pleasant to visit for most of the year. The hottest months are March to May, when temperatures can reach 37°C. The monsoon season brings torrential rain from June to August.

Language
Malayalam; English is widely spoken.

Currency
Indian rupee (INR).
100 INR = Dhs.6.5

Vaccinations
Hepatitis A, Hepatitis B, Typhoid, Polio. Malaria tablets are recommended.

Great for... self discovery
Kerala shies away from the loud and brash cities that India is famous for, and shows you serene mountains and quiet waters instead. A haven of peace and tranquility, it is a popular destination for yoga and Ayurvedic retreats. You can unwind, de-stress, or lose weight with ancient healing and wellness practices for all budgets.

An enticing combination of beaches, backwaters and hills – all packaged in an enchantingly beautiful state.

Kochi

Forget what you've heard about India's cities – Kochi is a whole different kettle of fishing nets, with a noticeably different pace. But, if its laidback atmosphere doesn't draw you in, then the lush green scenery, fresh seafood and picturesque buildings surely will.

Fort Cochin

Hire bikes to explore the compact heritage quarter of the city, visit the fish market to get a sniff of the catch of the day, and stock up on spices from the colourful market. History lovers will appreciate St. Francis Church, the oldest European church in India. End the day with a sunset cruise around the harbour to admire the handcrafted Chinese fishing nets common to the Kerala coast.

Alappuzha

Museums & monuments

Treasures from the past make for an interesting afternoon stroll around the city. The 16th century Mattancherry Palace is home to colourful displays of royal costumes and rich murals that illustrate scenes from epic Sanskrit narratives. The Maritime Museum showcases the origin, history and evolution of the Indian Navy, and the intriguing Jewish synagogue and Jew Town is a must-see for any visitor. While you're on the historical trail, make a beeline for Hill Palace Museum to learn about the glory of the Rajas and the history of Kerala.

Food, glorious food

While seafood is the pride and joy of Kochi, there are many other local delights to try, from the 57 varieties of crispy dosa (a rice batter pancake filled with black lentils) served at Pai Brothers to the toddy (a mildly alcoholic beverage made from the sap of palm trees) at Nettoor Shap near Le Meridien Hotel. Just leave room to try the catch of the day at the Casino Hotel – think prawns cooked with spices in a banana leaf. Waiter!

Alappuzha

One hour south of Kochi is Alappuzha, a slow-paced town that's popular for catching a houseboat (see p.44). The town also hosts the Nehru Trophy, a snake boat race held in August when hundreds of people compete in huge rowing boats, and even more enjoy the spectacle.

Western Ghats

When you tire of walking the streets of Kochi or lounging on soft, surf-lashed sand, you can venture up into the cooler climes of the Western Ghats mountain range, where tranquil is brewed to a 'tea'.

Hill stations

Far away from the skylines and smog of the UAE is the fresh mountain air, the mist clad hills and the panoramic views of the little-explored peaks of the Western Ghats. Head for one of many hill stations to enjoy hiking trails through gorgeous tea plantations. A few hours east of Kochi is Munnar, Kerala's highest and most popular hill station, surrounded by acres upon acres of greenery dotted with tea pickers. Alternatively, head to Thekkady through miles of rubber, coffee and tea plantations.

Periyar Tiger Reserve

There is probably no better place in India to watch Asiatic elephants at play than the Periyar Tiger Reserve. While sightings of any tigers are quite rare, a hike through this lush green forest is breathtaking, with monkeys swinging through the overhead vines and exotic birds flying by. It's a three to four-hour trip from Kochi, so break up the journey and rest your head at one of the many secluded lodges surrounding the reserve. periyartigerreserve.org

Worth a look

Kerala's capital city, Thiruvananthapuram, is often bypassed in favour of the state's more enticing destinations, but the Sree Padmanabhaswamy Temple is worth a look for its gothic-like facade, and the many fabric shops may well entice you to buy a sari.

Smile!

As your fascination with life in Kerala blossoms, it's important to remember that the intrigue goes both ways; be prepared to be stared at, especially if you're fair-skinned, but your best bet is to make like the locals and smile.

Wellness retreats

If you're looking for a quiet corner of the world to relax and rejuvenate, plan a trip to the home of Ayurveda and yoga. People from all walks of life are drawn to Kerala to find the light, find themselves, or simply find a few days' peace. Kerala's retreats range from the humblest Ashram to the most luxurious of resorts.

Ayurvedic resorts

Many budget and luxury resorts across Kerala offer Ayurvedic packages, where you will experience the deeply cleansing, reviving power of Ayurveda, eat food prepared to the Ayurvedic tradition and enjoy daily Ayurvedic massages. As the home of this 5,000-year-old holistic healing tradition, based on the idea that everyone has a unique constitution related to the elements, Kerala has retreats for all budgets.

Holistic hideaways

The Woodhouse Beach Resort in Varkala (woodhousebeachresort.com) offers one to five-day treatments that include a consultation with a doctor, while staying in ocean-facing villas. The lakeside Sarovaram Ayurvedic Resort near Kollam (sarovaramkollam.com) runs tailormade packages for a minimum of three days. Once checked in, you'll have the opportunity to see something of India should you choose.

Yoga retreats

India's gift to the suppleness of the world, yoga has a devoted following that flocks to Kerala's famous yogis to further master the practice. Yoga newcomers and those not so advanced also come to learn the basics and get a taste of the zen life – which, considering the sheer beauty of the landscapes and the serenity of daily life in Kerala, isn't hard to find. Retreats usually involve a daily regime of yoga, meditation and vegetarian meals. Sivananda Yoga Vedanta Dhanwantari Ashram (sivananda. org) in the foothills of the Western Ghats runs rejuvenating yoga vacations for a minimal donation.

Poovar

One of the biggest draws of Poovar, a tranquil coastal village, is its pristine beaches. The diverse and beautiful landscape boasts backwaters, mangroves and estuaries to explore as well as endless stretches of golden sand. Check into the Poovar Island Resort (see p41).

Beaches

Some of India's most beautiful beaches are in Kerala, and accommodating lazy, sun-drenched days are what Keralites do best.

Kovalam

South of Thiruvananthapuram is Kerala's busiest beach village. Several bays heave with activities, watersports (surfing is increasingly popular) and five-star hotels.

Varkala

Far enough north of the capital and set below some gorgeously rugged, palm-topped cliffs (so not one for those afraid of steps), Varkala is a more rustic, laid-back beach experience than Kovalam, with some authentic eateries perched on the clifftop.

Cherai

North of Kochi on Vypeen Island, Cherai is a unique stretch of beach lined with coconut groves and sandwiched between the backwaters and the sea – enjoy an exquisitely serene sunrise over the former and a typically stunning Kerala sunset over the latter. Swimming is safe and dolphins can be spotted from the shore.

Marari

This deserted stretch of beach a short drive from Alappuzha is glorious for those looking for quiet solitude and relaxation. Watch local fishermen haul in their boats, witness village life and eat tasty local thali – the ubiquitous Indian lunch, and every traveller's dream tray of curries. Accommodation varies from rustic homestays to the luxury of Marari Beach Resort (p41).

The Leela Kovalam

Vivanta by Taj – Malabar, Kochi

Beach & backwaters

Bright Water Luxury Houseboats, Alappuzha

A wonderfully relaxing way to enjoy the serene backwaters around Alappuzha, these houseboats vary in size, some with upper decks and even plunge pools, and can accommodate groups or couples. The gentle breeze, rhythmic chug of the boat's engine and morning chipper of the birds are the perfect soundtrack to accompany coconut cocktails from the on-deck armchairs.
brightwatercruise.com

The Leela Kovalam

A five-star haven nestled on a rocky outcrop between Kerala's most famous beaches, the Leela is a destination in itself. A divine infinity pool overlooks the Arabian Sea, as does an open meditation room at its Ayurvedic spa, allowing for some holistic relaxation of mind and body. theleela.com

Les 3 Elephants, Cherai

A boutique eco-resort situated between the backwaters and the beach in Cherai, this gets the thumbs up for its environmentally-friendly luxury. Cute, comfortable thatched bungalows overlook the backwaters and the fishing nets that are typical to the area.
3elephants.in

Poovar Island Resort

This quirky coastal cocoon is close to Trivandrum airport. While 'deluxe' in Kerala might not be a literal translation of the UAE's five-star luxury, personality is a major attraction, and Poovar has bags of it. The resort attracts a mix of yoga types on a strict cleansing diet, honeymooning couples enjoying Ayurvedic pampering, and travellers collecting memories. Opt for one of the floating cottages and spend a blissful few days soaking up the slow pace.
poovarislandresorts.com

Spice Village

Wherever you stay in Kerala, you're never too far from lush greenery, glassy waters or sweet sandy beaches

Take it easy

Unwind completely at Marari Beach (cghearth.com/marari-beach) without even trying. There's no TV, or beach parties or surfing, just the opportunity to lie back on a near-empty beach and watch the waves.

The Leela Kovalam

Soul & Surf

Brunton Boatyard

The Leela Kovalam

The Raviz, Kollam

Jutting out on a lush peninsula in the Kollam backwaters, The Raviz is a modern luxury Indian experience. Daily activities include the usual yoga and meditation, as well as village walks, bamboo rafting, fishing and much more. It all makes for some great exploration of the waterways and local area.
theraviz.com

Soul & Surf, Varkala

The perfect Indian beach blend – ride the waves with the help of qualified instructors and free your mind and body with clifftop yoga sessions. Or just laze on the sand from dawn to dusk – it's your prerogative. Stay in simple but comfy accommodation with lush gardens gazing over the Arabian Sea; and it's just a few steps down to the beach. A stylish 'surf camp' for the free spirited.
soulandsurf.com

A gorgeously atmospheric eco-resort high up in the wilderness of the Western Ghats, Spice Village (cghearth. com) is a great base for exploring Periyar Tiger Reserve. It's also good for enjoying the surrounds and the authentic food – some produce is grown onsite, while cooking demos let you into the secrets of Kerala's coveted cuisine.

Kochi

Brunton Boatyard

This is wonderfully colonial thanks to its former life as a Victorian shipyard, and perfectly positioned on the bank of the harbour. With its fantastic outdoor pool and excellent eateries, what's not to love?
cghearth.com

Fort House Hotel

A quaint and reasonably priced family-run hotel, right by the water in the Fort Cochin area. This is one of the oldest European settlements in India and still retains its colonial feel with medieval Dutch, Portuguese and British architecture.
hotelforthouse.com

Le Meridien Kochi

Experience both the backwaters and the city from this serene base, which has rooms overlooking the waterways. A boat runs between its two locations on opposite sides of the channel, and it's still close enough to the centre of Kochi for easy exploring.
starwoodhotels.com

Vivanta by Taj, Kochi

Tucked away on Willingdon Island, in the heart of Kochi's impressive harbour, this branch of Taj Vivanta is a good base for exploring the city, with views of the green shores of the harbour. The spa offers an 'Ayurveda Journey' – a three-day package of holistic treatments. vivantabytaj.com

Vivanta by Taj – Malabar, Kochi

Venice of the East

Relax **on Kerala's backwaters**

Glide through a labyrinth of canals, lakes, coconut groves and water birds on a backwater houseboat.

A popular way to seriously slow down the pace and be utterly pampered is to see Kerala's beautiful backwaters with a languorous few days spent on a private houseboat. It's not a particularly eventful journey, but it is a blissful chance to switch off, and take in the serenity of Indian life.

Finding a floating home

There is a wide range of comfortable houseboats, and these quirky wicker-crafted vessels come in all sizes and statures to accommodate groups or couples, and can even come with a Jacuzzi or splash pool. It is best to book online before your trip, and there are many companies running tours out of Alappuzha. Prices range from the more basic accommodation to the luxurious, and depending on the number of bedrooms and

Carry on cruising
One and two-night round trip cruises from Alappuzha (also known as Alleppey) can be booked at alappuzha-tourism.com

storeys, and increase during the high season from October to March. Prices are lowest from April to September when monsoon rains can whip up choppier waters, although the weather usually only lasts for short bursts. Two nights lazing around on a houseboat is long enough to have surrendered to the quietude of life on the backwaters. If you have the time, however, an extra day could really have you in the grip of Keralife.

In good company

The right crew can make for a wonderfully fun trip. Not only will they treat you like royalty with welcome drinks, garlands and gracious service, they will be as companionable or unobtrusive as you want them to be. If you're game, it is a chance to get to know some locals and learn about life in Kerala, and you could be saying goodbye at the end of your cruise with genuine sadness. The crew will usually include a captain, a deckhand and a chef to cook up some aromatic local cuisine, and maybe even some fresh catch. Be sure to check your crew are licensed and read some testimonials on tripadvisor.com before booking.

On the water

Setting off from Alappuzha can feel like Grand Central Station in terms of hustle and bustle, but with kitted out longboats in place of buses and trains. Once away on your own floating home, solitude is soon found across Vembanad Lake (the longest in India). Entering the glassy-calm waterways takes you meandering past palm-fringed paddy fields and villages devoid of modern amenities, where clothes and people are washed in the backwaters and children splash merrily on their way home from school.

During your trip you can usually stop at a couple of remote fishing villages and find deserted beaches, rice farms and Catholic churches, and inhabitants that, aside from a few children asking for school pens, will be as bemused by you, as you are intrigued by them. It is a unique opportunity to witness first-hand the humble simplicity of life here.

Friends & couples

A cruise can make for a super-relaxing, romantic break for a couple, or a (slightly) more lively occasion for groups of friends, with up to eight bunks per boat. Expect to pay from 3,500 rupees for two people for a 24 hour trip.

Get stuck in

As time seems to stand still and inactivity becomes the pursuit of the day, your chef will be whipping up a wonderful range of local dishes for breakfast, lunch and dinner, in huge quantities. Whether he is diving for mussels buried in the backwater's bed and frying them in an assortment of spices, or nipping off to find some home-brewed coconut concoction to accompany a night of cards and story swapping, there is nothing for it but to get stuck in.

South Asia

Maldives

It's the go-to place in the Indian Ocean for relaxation. And with its tropically terrific beaches and heart-stoppingly perfect resorts, the Maldives is a desert island paradise.

Flight time
5 hours 5 minutes

Door to door
Resort transfers from Male by boat or seaplane vary from 30 to 90 minutes; 10 minutes by boat from the airport into Male

When to go
December to April

Anyone who picks the Maldives for a short break not only has the joy of experiencing the sunny side of life, but also has every right to be smug as they walk into the office on a Sunday. This picture-perfect island nation in the Indian Ocean is made up of 26 atolls containing almost 2,000 coral islands, of which around 200 are populated. Of the populated islands, approximately half are resort islands offering a wide variety of options for holiday-makers, from the obscenely-priced to the more affordable.

You would be forgiven for thinking that videos and photos of the Maldives found in glossy magazines have been digitally remastered – because surely the ocean can't be that blue and the sand that golden? However, when your seaplane touches down

on your resort island you will quickly realise that this *is* paradise. As one of the world's best destinations, if not the best, for diving and snorkelling, there are few places on earth where you can walk from a stunning beach straight into the ocean and see a lively coral reef a few feet below you. Time seems to slow down in the Maldives and spending a few days in awe of the ocean, relaxing in a hammock over impossibly pristine beaches, or sipping cocktails and dining on all-inclusive seafood buffets can certainly make for a dream holiday.

The Maldives is a place to get away from the rat race and discover a whole new world beneath the sea. While it comes with a price, it is one worth paying for a slice of heaven on earth.

Dive in & explore
As the lowest country in the world, the Maldives is very much about the ocean on which its dream desert islands sit. With one of the richest marine biodiversities on the planet, the biggest draw is the diving and snorkelling. The view above sea level is pretty much blue skies, green trees and impossibly white sand (not that you'd complain) while the ocean reveals a whole new world of marine life in technicolour glory, from reef sharks to turtles, stingrays to a plethora of tropical fish. Whether you're PADI certified, want to be, or just fancy a spot of snorkelling, the Maldives offers one of the best options for underwater exploration.

Maldives
Essentials

Whether you are a party of two looking for an amorous adventure or a family of five, this awesome archipelago fits the bill.

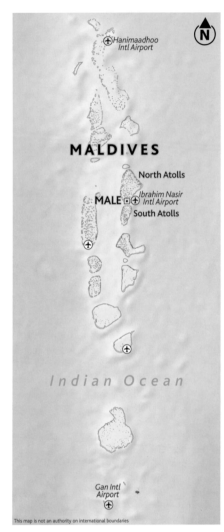

Hanimaadhoo Intl Airport

MALDIVES

North Atolls

Ibrahim Nasir Intl Airport
MALE
South Atolls

Indian Ocean

Gan Intl Airport

This map is not an authority on international boundaries

Getting there
Fly from Dubai or Abu Dhabi to Male airport with Emirates, Etihad or flydubai from Dhs.1,400 return. Resorts will arrange for seaplane or speedboat transfers from Male, adding the (often hefty) charge to your check-out bill.

Visas
Visitors to the Maldives will be granted a 30-day tourist visa on arrival.

Time
One hour ahead of the UAE.

Climate
The Maldives has a tropical climate with average temperatures hovering around 30°C. Between January and March it is dry, although monsoons from the northeast can still bring rain. The chance of rain increases between May and November and humidity is higher too. However, this is also when resort prices are lower. March to October is the best time to visit for surfers, as this is when the swells are at their biggest.

Language
Dhivehi; English is widely spoken.

Currency
Maldivian Rufiyaa (MVR).
100 MVR = Dhs.24

Vaccinations
Hepatitis A, Hepatitis B and Typhoid.

Great for... total escapism
Although the Maldives is only a few hours' flight from the UAE, you'll feel a million miles from anywhere, with the sophisticated skyscrapers and cosmopolitan chaos of home a distant memory. You can go to do nothing but lie by the pool or beach and perhaps visit the spa, or you can get active in the ocean with a pick 'n' mix of watersports.

Forget about island hopping. Aside from the occasional excursion, select a resort, dig your toes into the sand and relax.

Island life

Islands vary in size, from the very small uninhabited islands which can disappear when a reef's current changes, to the bigger islands such as Male at 1.7 square kilometres. In the end, deciding which island to pick really depends upon your budget. If you want exclusivity, opt for one of the 100 or so resort islands; however, if you're working on a tighter budget then there are guesthouses on Male and some of the inhabited islands. Take into consideration, however, that while you may be able to bag a bargain on your flights and accommodation, you still need to set a fairly high budget for your food and drink. It isn't easy to travel between the islands, so choose carefully when picking your home away from home.

Male

All international flights land in Hulhule, the airport island that is part of Male, the capital; visitors then take a connecting seaplane flight or speedboat from here to their chosen resort. In a country of around 275,000 people, the capital is home to two-thirds of the population, and the busy streets of Male are a world away from the serenity of the other islands. While Male is the largest of the islands, there is not much to see or do, although there are several hotels available if you land at night (seaplanes only fly during daylight hours). From the airport island, you can take a 10-minute boat ride to get to the main island of Male. If you do have a few hours spare, there is a traditional market on the northern side of the island selling local produce and souvenirs, and the Friday mosque is an interesting example of coral architecture.

The Atolls

From Male you head north or south to one of the 26 atolls that make up the Maldives. Each individual atoll comprises a coral reef that surrounds a lagoon and is divided by deep channels. Within the atoll sphere resides a series of islands, each with its own animated coral reef where all manner of marine life have made their home. Each resort is a world in itself with activities and restaurants to keep you entertained. Depending on where you are staying, you may be able to enjoy excursions to some of the inhabited islands for cultural tours.

Catch of the day

The Maldives offers bountiful fishing opportunities. Most resorts offer fishing trips and often you'll be able to barbecue your catch of the day on one of the uninhabited islands.

Watersports

As 99% of the Maldives is made up of ocean it's not surprising that a large amount of time is spent in the water. In addition to the obvious snorkelling and diving, many resorts offer stand up paddleboarding, windsurfing, and waterskiing. All resorts have professional diving schools, with the option of house reef dives – so close to the shore that they can be explored by beginners as well as experts – or boat dives, which go into deeper waters for wreck dives. The Maldives' stunning coral reefs in shallow waters are just as fun to explore by snorkel though. Other trips include night dives, and snorkelling safaris with underwater cameras.

Well-being

Thanks to its serene natural surroundings, the Maldives is the perfect location for total relaxation. You will notice that most resorts have "& Spa" attached to their title and with good reason; taking time out to enjoy a relaxing treatment is a must, even when you're already in paradise.

 Need a refreshing beach or pool-side drink? Try coconut water, straight from the sliced-open fruit.

Kuramathi Island Resort

Male

If you are staying in the capital for a night or two, there are a few luxury options and budget hotels that can be reached by car from the airport at Hulhule or by boat if on the island of Male. There are also several breathtaking resorts scattered across the North and South Male Atolls – just a short taxi (or speedboat) ride from the airport.

Sheraton Maldives Full Moon Resort & Spa

This slice of luxury on a private island in the North Male Atoll is the perfect holiday spot for ocean lovers, hosting a range of watersports in its lagoon and boasting 40 dive sites nearby. It's also a great choice for a family holiday: kids will love the playground and daily activities at the Sheraton Adventure Club, while grown-ups enjoy some well-deserved chill-out time at the luxury Shine Spa for Sheraton. starwoodhotels.com.

Taj Exotica Resort & Spa

Thanks to its handy location on the South Male Atoll, the Taj Exotica Resort & Spa is an excellent choice of hotel for those short on time, as it's just a 15-minute speedboat ride from the airport. This stunning island resort is surrounded by one of the largest lagoons in the Maldives, and whether you're looking for a romantic break or a family getaway, you're sure to enjoy the luxurious over-water villas, sparkling private plunge pools and infinite ocean views. tajhotels.com

Traders Hotel

Located in Male, the Traders Hotel is a great stopover option and offers a chance to experience another side of island life. The rooftop pool bar is the perfect spot from which to watch the comings and goings of the city. You can dine on French and Japanese nibbles and sip fruity mocktails while taking in the view. shangri-la.com/traders

Taj Exotica Resort & Spa

Taj Exotica Resort & Spa

Sheraton Maldives Full Moon Resort & Spa

Remember that in the Maldives each island is home to just one resort – so choose yours carefully. Do your homework and think about what you want: a romantic short break or a memorable family getaway? Consider the size of your chosen destination: a bigger resort will feel livelier, but fewer villas will make for a more exclusive experience.

Family-friendly

On first impression, you may assume that the Maldives is a destination reserved for honeymooners and other couples in search of luxury and romance. However, there is a wide range of resorts offering fun for all the family, making it the perfect place to spend some quality time with the kids.

Constance Halaveli

While parents unwind, kids can search for hermit crabs and send balloon wishes high into the sky. Children aged 10 and over can also do a PADI scuba diving course, and children as young as five can have a diving experience of their own with SASY (Supplied Air Snorkelling for Youth).
halaveli.constancehotels.com

Kuramathi Island Resort

One & Only Reethi Rah

Kuramathi Island Resort

Tots & teens

More resorts in the Maldives are recognising the importance of catering for mini-holidaymakers, too. Some offer such features as spa treatments for kids and teens, while others such as the Niyama resort offer a 'kids eat and sleep for free' promotion during selected dates.

Kuramathi Island Resort

At the Bageecha Kids Club, there's a whole host of activities on offer for children, from nature walks to treasure hunts and marine life lessons. The latter is a great option before taking a family snorkelling trip. Best of all, you can opt for an all-inclusive package, and leave your worries (and wallet) behind during your stay. kuramathi.com

One & Only Maldives at Reethi Rah

Who says a family holiday has to sacrifice luxury? This resort is a good choice for families wanting a luxury hideaway and VIP treatment. This luxury resort in the North Male Atoll caters well for families of all ages, with its signature KidsOnly programmes for children aged four to 11 and teens aged 12 to 17. Supervised by fully-qualified counsellors, younger guests get to enjoy their own section of the resort with their own clubhouse and swimming pool.
reethirah.oneandonlyresorts.com

Viceroy Maldives

The Viceroy's Generation V programme is available for kids aged four to 12 and focuses on educating children about the local culture and environment through fun activities including shell painting, kite making and snorkelling. The hotel also offers babysitting services, and the option of 24-hour in-villa dining to enjoy once the kids are asleep in bed. The deluxe beach villas come with a twin-sharing bedroom in addition to a master suite.
viceroyhotelsandresorts.com

One & Only Reethi Rah

Couples only

From newlyweds on their honeymoon to a husband and wife renewing their vows, or simply a couple in search of the ultimate romantic break, you cannot fail to be touched by the magic of the Maldives.

Anantara Kihavah

Whether you want to get married on the beach or on a yacht, in an underwater restaurant or diving in the ocean, the wedding packages here are out-of-this-world. For couples looking for extreme romance this resort offers private dining, couples' spa treatments and private pools.
kihavah-maldives.anantara.com

Conrad Maldives Rangali Island

A unique experience at this six-star resort is the mini submarine perfect for couples to take a romantic 30-minute underwater cruise. Plus, you can renew your love in a ceremony on the beach or even underwater. A fantasy resort where everything you know is left far behind once you get off that seaplane. conradmaldives.com

Huvafen Fushi

This astoundingly beautiful resort has all manner of memorable romantic experiences on offer, from underwater weddings and sunset cruises to low-key ceremonies on the powder-white beach. Be sure to take some time to unwind with a couples' treatment in the legendary LIME spa, home to the world's first underwater treatment rooms.
huvafenfushi.peraquum.com

Soneva Fushi

This intimate resort is just perfect for love birds – it even touts its own Romantic Experience which includes private beach dinners, dolphin cruises, spa treatments, wine and chocolate tasting and night snorkelling for two. soneva.com

Huvafen Fushi

On a budget

The Maldives have always been well known as a notoriously pricey holiday destination (albeit one that's worth every single dirham). However, it is possible to enjoy a Maldives short break without breaking the bank – you just need to budget carefully and choose the right resort.

Asseyri Tourist Inn

Located on the inhabited island of Hanimaadhoo, this hotel offers a range of room types from singles to a private cottage perfect for families. While the resort is alcohol-free, the restaurants are still very good and the ocean of course remains just as mesmerising as any of the luxury resorts. The reef within a vast sand bank here is a great place to learn kitesurfing too.
asseyri.travel

 Keep costs down with an all-inclusive food and drink package. Make sure you try a few local delicacies. Seafood features heavily and the cuisine is strongly influenced by south Indian cooking, particularly Kerala; meals are typically hot, spicy, flavoured with coconut, and traditionally served with rice.

Fun Island Resort & Spa

A 45-minute speedboat ride from Male, this resort has 50 beach bungalows with private terraces and access to the beach itself. Dining is a little limited with just two restaurants, but there are plenty of activities to keep you busy throughout the day, including windsurfing, canoeing, snorkelling and island hopping. There's even a PADI accredited diving centre on site that organises lessons and excursions.
funislandmaldives.com

Kuredu Resort

There are two resorts and four categories of rooms at this destination providing a lot of choice for guests, from the more affordable garden villas to the Jacuzzi beach villas as well as luxury pool villas and water villas. The stunning hotel boasts plenty of dining options and you can even boost your holiday budget by selecting one of the all-inclusive packages. kuredu.com

Makunudu Island Resort

Just under an hour by speedboat from Male in the North Male Atoll, this resort has just 36 beach bungalows, offering a truly secluded desert island experience. This is a great choice for a few days away from it all, when your to-do list consists of nothing but sunbathing, getting pampered in the spa, or some leisurely snorkelling. And you don't need deep pockets to enjoy it either.
makunuduisland.com

Guesthouses

For a really low budget, staying in a guesthouse on one of the inhabited islands instead of a luxury resort on a resort island should also do the trick. However, keep in mind that most of the hotels and guesthouses on inhabited islands don't serve alcohol. Elsewhere, Thulusdhoo is a popular island for budget surfing breaks, with guesthouses such as Surfers World Guest House being just a 30-minute speed boat ride away from Male. All rooms, though basic, have en suite bathrooms and there's the option of full board, breakfast only or bed only. Located near some excellent surfing spots – including Chickens, a tropical goofy footers dream – this is ideal for surfers and backpackers.

Low season breaks

If you're set on staying at a luxury resort, such as the Kuramathi Island Resort or Niyama, visit during the off-peak seasons. The Maldives enjoys warmth all-year round, but during the low season (May to November) there is a higher chance of rain. However, the temperatures remain in the upper 30s and the significantly lower hotel rates (which sometimes drop to at least half of the peak season price) make it a great time to escape the UAE summer. If you're very clever and book in advance, the best time to go is on the cusp of high season. That way you can still enjoy a drier holiday but pay half of what the guests who stayed there just a couple of weeks before paid!

Surf's up

If your idea of a beach break involves catching the perfect wave, then you're in luck. Not only is March to October a cheap time to visit, it's also when the swells are at their best.

Niyama

Kuramathi Island Resort

W Retreat & Spa Maldives

Sundowners

Of course, not everyone heads for the Maldives in search of a family holiday or romantic break. For some, the idyllic archipelago is a place to unwind and let their hair down in luxury restaurants and bars, against a backdrop of unreal beauty.

Club Med Kanifinolhu

Club Med's private Maldives resort is the perfect holiday destination for those looking to enhance (and show off) their beach bodies, with an array of athletic activities on offer including aquagym, beach golf, soccer, kayaking, and more. Afterwards, take a trip to the luxury spa for a well-earned pampering session, then fill your evenings with tropical fruit-inspired cocktails and live music. clubmed.co.uk

Niyama

Niyama

Home to the world's first underwater nightclub Subsix, this unique resort in the Maldives is a party paradise. With international DJs, a rooftop bar offering laidback grooves, and the must-visit restaurant Edge – an overwater eatery accessible only by boat – as well as campfire dining, this is the ultimate in hedonistic holidaying. Recharge with the pampering NIYAMA Recovery treatment at the excellent LIME Spa. niyama.peraquum.com

Velassaru Maldives

Cocktails and Cuban tunes in Fen Bar's Havana night set the scene for this opulent island resort of indulgence, with its beach and water bungalows and villas as well as the 270msq Velassaru Water Suite. Don't forget to visit overwater eatery Teppanyaki for some of the freshest sushi you'll ever eat, or beachside restaurant Sand for alfresco dining with panoramic views of the Indian Ocean. velassaru.com

W Retreat & Spa Maldives

With its WET beach parties and DJ nights, this resort is perfect for party people looking to combine a luxury paradise island stay with great activities and energetic evening entertainment, including 15BELOW, the Maldives' only underground nightclub. The team of resident mixologists will make sure that you have an exotic creation in your hand for sundowners and beyond. wretreatmaldives.com

W Retreat & Spa Maldives

Love is in the air

Reignite the romance

Ticket to paradise
Travelling to the resort involves seaplanes, speedboats and buggies, but your reward is a private paradise for two.

Couples wanting a secluded break with a romantic backdrop can stay in a stilted water villa at the Shangri-La.

What is it that makes the Maldives so synonymous with romance? For decades, this enchanting archipelago in the Indian Ocean has been shorthand for idyllic islands, unreal beauty and honeymoon bliss. You don't even need to be planning your honeymoon in order to make the most of this destination; the manageable flight time from the UAE means that it's just as good for a short romantic break as a once-in-a-lifetime trip.

There's nothing quite as romantic as feeling like you and your beloved are the only two people in the world – a sense of intimacy and seclusion that can easily be achieved if you know which Maldivian island to choose.

For a truly hidden gem, there are few places as romantic as Shangri-La's Villingili Resort & Spa (shangri-la.com/maldives). The journey to its intimate location on Gan Island in Addu Atoll involves an hour-long flight crossing shimmering aquamarine water and a scattering of islands, plus a 15-minute speedboat trip and, quite possibly, a buggy ride into the jungle to your hidden villa. But the travel time is more than worth it to arrive at your own personal paradise.

Two's company

It wouldn't be a trip to the Maldives without exploring the world beneath the waves. The archipelago has some of the globe's best diving and snorkelling sites, and there are few outdoor activities quite as romantic as drifting blissfully on the surface of the ocean alongside your loved one. The resort has its own house reef, for just such an occasion.

 The stunning CHI spa, tucked away between the jungle and the sea, offers some wonderfully relaxing couples' treatments, including a cowrie shell massage that uses the large, smooth shells to soothe tired muscles and melt your cares away.

Table for two

Shangri-La offers spectacular restaurant dining: gourmet cuisine plus gorgeous ocean views. Perhaps the most romantic option, however, is organising a private meal. You can have your dinner served in one of the tranquil spa pavilions, within your villa or on the beach under a palm tree.

Island getaway

Bright turquoise waves lap gently at powder-soft sand as palm trees sway languidly in the ocean breeze. The beauty is spellbinding, and that's before you even get to your jaw-dropping luxury villa. You can opt for the Swiss Robinson Family-esque tree house hideaway, or a beach villa with private access to your own stretch of sand and sea. The archetypal Maldivian over-water villas on stilts are also available. Each romantic haven has its own unique luxurious touches, from private infinity pools to open air showers.

Privacy is key to the appeal of the Shangri-La resort. The island's uniquely dense vegetation has been incorporated into the hotel design to add to the romantic seclusion by screening you from the outside world. It feels as though you could spend your entire short break seeing no one but each other. However, if and when you do decide to drag yourself away from your villa, or indeed from the resort, there are plenty of things to see and do. Why not take a cycle tour of the island on the resort's 'his and hers' bikes? You'll discover your own secret coves and strolls that you won't find on any tourist map.

Nepal

With its jaw-dropping mountain scenery, helter-skelter of a capital city, and unbeatable trekking trails, Nepal remains one of the world's greatest adventures.

Flight time
4 hours 15 minutes

Door to door
From 45 minutes to 2 hours by car, depending on traffic, from the airport to Kathmandu Valley

When to go
September to May

It's famed as a trekker's paradise, and there's an undeniable urge to head off into the mountains once you land in Nepal. For many an adventurer, now could be the time to tick the Himalayas off your bucket list. After all, since the 1960s people from the west have been making personal pilgrimages to Nepal to experience the awe of the world's tallest collection of mountains as well as the simple, spiritual way of life.

Landlocked between Tibet and India, Nepal spans the terrain from the subtropical jungle to the icy Himalayas, and contains eight of the world's 10 highest mountains. Its cultural landscape is every bit as diverse, with Buddhism and Hinduism coexisting harmoniously. A short break in Nepal can combine sightseeing, nature and adventure.

From the lakes and leisurely trekking trails of Pokhara to the hustle and bustle and cultural sights of Kathmandu; from the wildlife adventures of the Chitwan National Park to the lush green hillstations of Nagakot – there is much to experience on Everest's doorstep. More than 80 per cent of the population live directly off the land; whether you trek, hike, bike or drive through Nepal's communities, engulfing yourself in their humble way of life is perhaps the best experience of all.

Of course, Nepal is not without its problems; roads are poorly maintained and the city smog creates a blanket of pollution. But this certainly shouldn't put you off. Instead, wander away from commercialised routes. The beaten track is remarkably thin and easy to escape.

Adventurous long weekends

Explorers and intrepid climbers brave the dramatic landscape of Nepal for months at a time, but that doesn't mean that you have to. On the contrary, you can quite easily connect with the cultural soul of this enchanting country and see the Himalayas – without having to walk the entire six-month long trek itself – during the course of a long weekend. Whether you stay in Pokhara, Chitwan or Nagakot, there's far more than just trekking in Nepal (p.72-75). It's a country full of cultural treasures, of extreme sports and unique landscapes all waiting to be explored.

Nepal
Essentials

A land of snow peaks and Sherpas, yaks and yetis, monasteries and mantras are all waiting to be seen in Nepal.

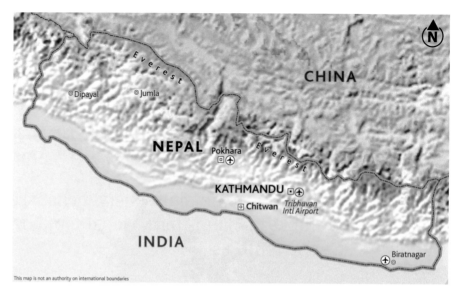

This map is not an authority on international boundaries

Getting there
Fly from Dubai, Abu Dhabi or Sharjah to Tribhuvan International Airport with flydubai, Etihad and Air Arabia, from Dhs.1,500 return. Internal flights to Pokhara are available with Buddha Air.

Visas
All foreign nationals, except Indian nationals, need a visa, costing from US$ 25 for 15 days. For most nationalities this can be obtained on arrival at the airport. Visit immi.gov.np.

Time
One hour 45 minutes ahead of the UAE.

Climate
Summer (June-August) can get very hot, with temperatures reaching 40°C. Winter temperatures drop to 0 to -10°C. Trekking season is from September to May and the rainy season is from June to September.

Language
Nepali. English is spoken in tourist areas.

Currency
Nepalese Rupee (NPR). 100 NPR = Dhs.4

Vaccinations
Hepatitis A and B, Malaria tablets and Typhoid.

Best for... trekking
While the thrill of high-altitude trekking in Nepal was once available only to a gung-ho few, recently, the journey has become more accessible. Most treks follow established routes where you can eat and sleep in simple inns for cheap. Trails are steep, but you walk at your own pace, and no standard trek goes above 5,500m.

Nyatapola Temple, Bhaktapur

Everest region

Nepal is a playground for the adventure enthusiast with a huge variety of outdoor pursuits to choose from.

Ultimate adventures

Are you ready for a high-altitude adventure within a truly soul-warming environment? Then pack your rucksack and get ready to experience the best that Nepal has to offer.

Short treks
Although a short break does not give you enough time to trek to Everest Base Camp, you can still experience the beauty of the mountains in four to five days. Walk through the Kathmandu Valley to Balthali, or fly to Pokhara and explore the Annapurna region. It's the ideal way to soak up the Sherpa culture, walking past colourful prayer wheels, monasteries and museums, and across adrenaline-pumping swing bridges. Evenings are rewarded with hot food and conversation around a campfire at one of the many tea lodges en route. himalayan-trails.com

A round of golf
You know a course is going to be tough when it is designed and constructed by an ex-British Army Gurkha officer. The visually stunning Himalayan Golf Course outside Pokhara is surrounded by beautiful snow-capped mountains and set in a huge canyon with a fast-flowing river that runs through the course. Since its opening in 1998, it has generated worldwide praise for its difficulty and beauty. himalayangolfcourse.com

Bungee jumping
It may be called the Last Resort, but it certainly won't be the last time you'll want to do Nepal's highest leap off of the country's longest suspension bridge. The 160-metre plunge towards one of Nepal's wildest rapids might also give you time to enjoy an incredible (and upside down) view of the Bhote Kosi River. The camp is a thrill-seeker's heaven, with canyoning, rafting and other extreme sports on offer, just three hours from Kathmandu. thelastresort.com.np

Paragliding over Pokhara
Pokhara is the starting point for many treks to the Annapurna Himalayas as well as other adventures including paragliding. Ride in a truck up the side of the mountain and along several hairpin turns, then get ready to strap into the harness, run off the side of a cliff, and float your way back down to earth while soaking up the gorgeous views of the valley and mountain ranges.
nepal-paragliding.com

On safari

Try a two-day escorted elephant-back safari in the Chitwan National Park, keeping an eye out for monkeys, exotic birds and, if you're lucky, tigers and rhinos. Scout for wildlife in jeeps or canoes, or go jungle-walking. Group tours are organised by intrepidtravel.com

Everest skydive

Pokhara region

Everest skydive

You could spend months preparing for, and eventually climbing, the world's highest mountain or you could fly above it on a plane and skydive past it. The self-proclaimed 'world's most elite skydiving adventure' allows you to jump from a whopping altitude of 8,848 metres in front of the Everest summit. everest-skydive.com

Mountain biking

Looking for hardcore adventure? You'll need two wheels and iron lungs for the Yak Attack, the highest mountain bike race in the world, set amongst the splendid Himalayan peaks of Nepal's Annapurna region. This 400km race at an altitude of over 5,400m, is one of the toughest races on earth where mud, landslides, rickety suspension bridges and freezing temperatures are your worst enemies. yak-attack.co.uk

Kayaking & canyoning

Royal Beach Camp offers kayak clinics from its camp on the Trisuli River. Add-ons include canyoning and rafting trips. Head to the office just north of the Kathmandu Guest House. royalbeachnepal.com

...and relax

Indulge in the best irony possible by getting a massage from an 'untouchable'. Relegated by society, Nepal's below-caste members get a helping hand from Himalayan Healers, an organisation that trains them to heal others through various kinds of massage, while empowering them to heal themselves of low self esteem, and rescuing them from generations of the worst kind of drudgery. It's a truly uplifting experience. himalayanhealers.org

 Do as the locals do and drink raksi, a potent drink made from rice that's very strong on the nose... and liver.

Nepal
Places to stay

The Dwarika's Resort, Dhulikhel

Kathmandu

Ambassador Garden Hotel

This 18-room building is one of the oldest of the small hotels in Thamel, and was opened to commemorate the owners great grandfather who was the Ambassador to China in the 19th century. The gentle and family-friendly nature of the service, combined with comfortable and delightfully quaint rooms, create a home away from home experience that you just won't want to leave. aghhotel.com

The Dwarika's Hotel

Located just a stone's throw from the famous Pashupatinath Temple and the Buddhist stupa at Bouddhanath – and yet just a few minutes away from the airport – this hotel is an ideal base from which to explore Nepal's capital, housing many interesting artefacts from the 13th century. Its new sister property, The Dwarika's Resort in Dhulikhel, is an holistic lifestyle retreat with an incredible view. dwarikas.com

Kantipur Temple House

The eco-friendly Kantipur Temple House offers a quiet oasis amidst Kathmandu's historical (but often frenzied) treasures. It features a lovely rooftop garden overlooking the ancient Swayambhunath Temple. All the rooms feature exposed red brick walls and handmade wooden furniture. Each room has a seating area and private bathroom. It's the perfect place to relax on the way to or from a trek.

kantipurtemplehouse.com

Royal Penguin Hotel

Another fine option is this quirky little hotel situated down a quiet side street of Thamel – one of the most popular tourist areas of Kathmandu. There are plenty of bars, restaurants and shops nearby and the rooms make for a very comfortable stay with excellent service from staff.

royalpenguinhotel.com

Kantipur Temple House

Waterfront Resort

For something quite unique, book the Hotel Shanker – a former Rana palace

The Dwarika's Hotel

Samsara Resort

This three-star guesthouse has been designed as a peaceful haven in Thamel, the main tourist district, which has a wealth of dining and shopping options. There's also a lovely garden where you can relax, enjoy a drink or meet new friends. The rooftop restaurant – the highest in Kathmandu – offers magnificent views of the Langtang Himal to the north. samsararesort.com

Cheap digs

Accommodation rates are generally very cheap in Kathmandu with basic rooms charging as little as Dhs.30 per night. Five-star hotels in the region start at Dhs480 per night.

The Dwarika's Resort

Chitwan

River Bank Inn
Located in the serene location on a bend of the river Rapti, this 12-roomed guesthouse gazes out onto the grassland of Chitwan National Park. From here you can organise different excursions into the park before lounging around in the beautiful terraced restaurant. riverbankinn.com.np

Unique Wild Resort
A basic but comfortable collection of chalets guarded by trees, this lovely resort also offers a complete safari experience. You can track the animals inside the national park from the top of an elephant or ride in a jeep with one of their skilled nature guides.
uniquewildresort.com

River Bank Inn

Pokhara

Hotel The Kantipur
Despite having over 50 rooms, there's a cosy feel to this impressive looking guesthouse. While it is relatively basic in terms of amenities, the absolutely stellar views of the Annapurna and Machpuchhare mountains from almost every room more than makes up for it. hotelkantipur.com

Shangri-La Hotel
If you're after a little luxury, the Shangri-La is arguably the most elegant of the lot. Located at the foot of the Annapurna peaks, this resort stays true to traditional design with impressive restaurants and a relaxing and authentic environment. hotelshangrila.com

Trek-O-Tel
This smart and modern hotel is located in Lakeside East. The interior is tastefully decorated and understated. The rooms are housed in octagonal stone blocks that are surrounded by a pretty garden.
acehotelsnepal.com

Waterfront Resort
Pokhara's Waterfront Resort is only a 10-minute drive from Pokhara airport and lies on the tranquil rural northern shore of the beautiful Phewa Lake. Rooms are comfortable, air-conditioned and each with a lake-view balcony; it's a great place to relax and unwind. ktmgh.com

Annapurna Range, Pokhara

Gateway to the Himalayas

Sightseeing in the capital

Krishna Temple, Patan

Nepal's capital has a rich history spanning nearly 2,000 years, with many of the sights clustered in the old part of the city. Navigate Kathmandu's narrow streets and enjoy the city before heading to base camp.

A trip to Kathmandu can leave the traveller enchanted, but the Nepalese capital's highs and lows can also overwhelm. A city of over a million people, Kathmandu is a place of constant noise and traffic, and the occasional boisterous protest. In town for the weekend? Here's how to spend it memorably.

Thursday

Thamel is the party capital of Kathmandu and rooftop bars and clubs pump music out into the streets while Everest beer flows – just what you'll be after, upon landing. Head to any one of the hotel's rooftops for a view of the throbbing neon lit Thamel and the sprawling city of Kathmandu. If you're feeling adventurous, venture through the twisting streets and mingle with the flip-flop and baggy pant-clad backpackers. Local merchants whisper in your ears to gauge your interest in their array of produce (from tiger balm to other miracles of Mother Nature). Head over to the oasis known as Garden of Dreams, a hidden oasis in Kathmandu's urban jungle which was created by a Marshall to depict Nepal's six seasons. Protected by a high wall, and a 160 NPR entrance charge, the gardens have been refurbished and are beautifully maintained – so much so that you could be walking through London's Kew Gardens rather than being a stone's throw from the craziness of Kathmandu.

Friday

Hop in a taxi for a round of hardcore sightseeing. The city is one part mesmerising, one part magical and two parts mayhem. The broken streets are charismatically chaotic – dilapidated cars sound their horns, motorbikes cough plumes of smoke and pedestrians precariously dart in and out of the traffic. Dive into the foray and weave your way to the Monkey Temple, called thus

Deal or no deal

Nepal is very cheap but haggling is expected. Whether you're picking up a yak wool hat or replica prayer wheel, you'll still find yourself negotiating over a hundred rupees (Dhs.5).

for the hundreds of sacred monkeys living in its grounds, around 5km from Thamel. The site overlooks Kathmandu and on a clear day gives you an uninterrupted view with the mountains in the distance. Visitors bring offerings to the Gods and pray for good fortune and health. They chant the common mantra 'Om Mani Padme Hum' whilst turning the multitude of prayer wheels that you will find at every spiritual site in Nepal.

Saturday

Stroll through Baktapur City (City of Devotees) which dates back to the 12th century and is home to Dattatreya Square. In Lalitpur (City of Beauty and Fine Arts) you can join the crowds at Patan Durbar Square where a multitude of shrines act like park benches for locals who sit for a while, surrounded by the different Gods of Buddhism. In the afternoon, take a taxi to Baber Mahal Revisited, an upscale entertainment complex housed in the beautifully renovated stables of a palace.

Swayambhunath, The Monkey Temple

All the best kept secrets

Discover **the world from the top**

From hilltop expectations to heart-stopping encounters in Nepal's lesser known locations.

Kathmandu is a fascinating city and the poverty, pollution and ever-growing population are all part and parcel of the experience. However, after a couple of days there, you might be craving the serenity of the mountains.

Chitwan National Park

For the ultimate nature trail, take a small 16-seater plane, courtesy of Buddha Air, from Kathmandu to Chitwan. After 30 minutes flying over those elusive mountains, you'll arrive in Bharatpur where you can arrange a tour into Chitwan National Park. Book yourself into any one of the humble lodgings here and use them as your base for a couple of nights while you explore the park, which is home to various species of wildlife, including wild tigers, rhinos, and elephants. When planning a visit to Chitwan, try to give yourself enough time for several safaris. The wildlife is unpredictable and you can't rely on sightings every time. Make sure to save at least one day to paddle in a wooden canoe down the river in search of crocodiles. You'll also want to make time to board an elephant for a trip through the jungle.

Nagakot

A two-hour drive up and you'll reach Nagakot – a hill station that stands at 2,100m above sea level (Kathmandu is 1,600m). People often head here for the incredible view of the mountains and to simply get away from it all. You can enjoy a dinner in darkness before staying at the humble Niva Niwa Lodge (nivaniwa.com) and awaken at sunrise to see the glorious mountain range coming slowly into sunlight. On a clear day, you can see Everest in the east and Annapurna in the west.

Package deal

Many people visit Chitwan on package tours arranged through travel agents in Kathmandu, Pokhara or overseas. This is by far the easiest approach if you plan to stay at one of the upmarket lodges inside the park.

Pokhara

Drive 160km to Pokhara for a hiking adventure towards Sarangkot, a viewpoint at 1,600m above sea level (Pokhara at base level is around 800m). Nepal's second city, at least in tourist terms, Pokhara is the end point for the famous Annapurna Circuit trek and the starting point for a dozen more treks through the mountains of the Annapurna Range. There are several quality tour guides in the area such as Earthbound Expeditions (enepaltrekking.com) whose guides make hiking up natural or man-made steps look like a walk in the park.

Pokhara represents a last chance to stock up on creature comforts before hitting the mountain trails. For others, it's a place to enjoy a steak dinner and cold beer after days of basic meals in the hills. Even if you aren't a dedicated trekker, there's plenty here to keep you busy. Pokhara has numerous museums and there are some fascinating caves, waterfalls and Tibetan villages in the surrounding hills. For the adventurous, travel agents offer a slew of activities, from trekking and microlight flights to river rafting and jungle safaris. Paragliding from Sarangkot viewpoint has to be one of the most thrilling experiences around.

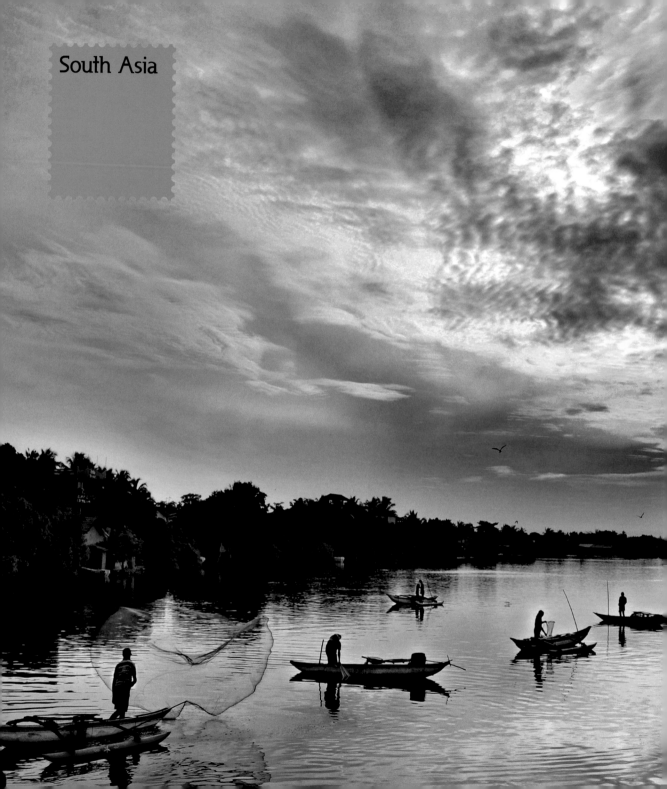

Sri Lanka

The teardrop-shaped island of Sri Lanka gives a bite-sized version of India, with an exotic mix of palm-fringed beaches, hill plantations and cultural sights.

Flight time
4 hours 40 minutes

Door to door
4 hours by car from Colombo airport to Galle; 4.5 hours to Dambulla; 4 hours to Kandy; 2.5 hours from Mattala airport to Nuwara Eliya

When to go
September to April

Rainforest, unspoilt beaches, well-populated game parks, great surf, gorgeous hotels offering exceptional rates. Have we got your attention yet? Add into the mix a charming blend of Buddhist, Hindu, Muslim, Christian and indigenous cultures, along with spicy, traditional curries, rotis and egg hoppers – and you have the ideal Sri Lankan holiday.

For such a compact island, there's an astonishing number of heritage sites here – from colossal ancient monuments and rock carvings to sprawling ruined cities and a 5AD king's palace in the clouds. That said, the beaches are pretty special too. From the airport all the way down to the south, there are sandy shores aplenty where you can sip from fresh coconuts in the shade of wind whispering palms. And for a refreshingly cool climate and 'head in the clouds' moment, head to the Hill Country, which is dotted with tea plantations, colonial villages and winding roads.

With flights now to the south of the island, as well as to Colombo on the west coast, it's never been easier or quicker to touch down in this land of plenty. Yes, the roads are still somewhat basic, bumpy and rather winding – and it will take you three or four times longer to reach your destination than you think – but treat the journey as part of the holiday rather than a means to an end. Buy freshly picked cashew nuts and baked rotis from street sellers, dodge roaming goats and cows, play I Spy for cotton trees, and simply admire the natural beauty as you pass by.

The perfect blend

An interesting blend of ancient heritage, rich culture and diverse landscapes makes Sri Lanka an ideal destination for a short break. If you fancy a culture hit then you can head to the Cultural Triangle or Kandy; if it's a cool climate and peace and quiet you are seeking then a few days in the Hill Country will be ideal; and if it's relaxation and romance you want then you can lounge in hammocks on the white sandy beaches of the south. And for those who want it all, and are game for a road trip, you can see the ruins of a spectacular rock fortress, an ancient Buddhist cave temple, the tea-growing hills, whales and dolphins, and of course elephants – all in just four days.

Sri Lanka
Essentials

This gem of an island has some of the most varied landscapes on the globe, so there is something for everyone.

INDIA

Bay Of Bengal

Trincomalee ◎

Sigiriya □
Dambulla □

SRI LANKA

Colombo Intl ⊕ □ Kandy
Airport
□ Nuwara Eliya
□ **COLOMBO**

Mattala Rajapaksa
Intl Airport
⊕
Hikkaduwa □
Mirissa
Galle □ □ ◎ Hambantota

Indian Ocean

This map is not an authority on international boundaries

Getting there
Fly from Dubai and Abu Dhabi to Colombo Airport with Emirates, flydubai, Mihin Lanka and Sri Lankan Airlines, from Dhs.980 return. Fly from Dubai to Mattala airport on the south coast with flydubai, from Dhs.1,000 return.

Visas
All visitors to Sri Lanka must have Electronic Travel Authorisation (ETA) before entering the country. Apply online at eta.gov.lk/slvisa. A tourist visa costs Dhs.110.

Time
One hour 30 minutes ahead of the UAE.

Climate
Sri Lanka is at its warmest from April to August and coldest in January. Temperatures range from around 27°C in the lowlands and along the coast, to a cooler 16°C in the hill country. The south-west monsoon is from May to July and the north-east monsoon is December to January.

Language
Sinhala, Tamil and English.

Currency
Sri Lankan Rupee (LKR).
100 LKR = Dhs3.

Vaccinations
Hepatitis A, Hepatitis B, Malaria, Polio, Rabies, Tetanus and Typhoid.

Great for... family breaks
There are plenty of attractions to occupy young minds: from meeting 'Nellie' at Pinnawala Elephant Orphanage to running wild around the ruins at Polonnaruwa. Prams are not ideal for Sri Lanka's bumpy paths so bring a backpack carrier, as well as kids' sunscreen and mosquito repellent. An iPad is a life-saver for the long car journeys.

Sigiriya Rock

Sri Lanka
Highlights

Dambulla Cave Temples

Polonnaruwa

Sri Lanka is as much about relaxation as it is about wildlife and history — from hot sandy beaches to cool hillside villages.

Cultural Triangle

If you fancy a culture hit, then head straight to the heart of the country from the airport. Lay down roots in Dambulla or Kandy, and explore the remains of various cities, temples and monuments dating back over 2,000 years.

Pinnawala
The perfect stop-off on your journey from the airport to Dambulla or Kandy is this elephant orphanage where stray and injured wild elephants roam freely on a 25-acre coconut plantation. Arrive at 10am or 2pm to see newborns and elderly matriarchs parade through the town to the Ma Oya river for a leisurely bath. Watching the bottle-feeding is beyond cute.

Pinnawala Elephant Orphanage

Polonnaruwa
The island's medieval capital, where the showstopper is the remains of the Royal Palace, once a magnificent seven-storey, thousand-room structure with frescoes. Because the grounds are so extensive, it's impossible to see everything, so you'll be making just a few stops at the key pieces of architecture and decoration.

Dambulla Cave Temples
The largest and most well-preserved complex of caves towers 160 metres over the surrounding plains. The major attractions are spread over five caves, which contain statues and paintings related to Lord Buddha. It's best to visit them in reverse order, starting at Cave 5, to see the caves in increasing degrees of magnificence. At the bottom of the steps up to the caves there's the rather bizarre Golden Temple — topped by a 30-metre seated golden Buddha.

Sigiriya Rock
Worthy of being called the 'eighth wonder of the world', Sigiriya is Sri Lanka's answer to the Taj Mahal. This ancient castle was built in 5AD, and today you can admire the remains of the upper palace at the flat top of the rock. The Lion staircase, a gigantic figure that leads to the palace garden on the summit, is nothing short of breathtaking. It's a pretty steep climb to the top, so best to head over there early morning or late afternoon; the walk takes about 45 minutes and starts off nice and slow.

Sigiriya Rock

Spices, arts & crafts

There are several places to stretch your legs on the journey from Dambulla to Kandy, one being Matale Spice Garden. Learn about the various spices grown across the island, stroll around the fragrant greenery in the shade of huge tropical trees, taste a herbal brew or enjoy an Ayurvedic massage. There's also plenty of wood carving and silk workshops en route – expect a short guided tour and then a hard sell (and, if you're lucky, a cup of tea!).

Kandy

The stunning 17th-century Temple of the Tooth Relic is believed to house the left upper canine tooth of the Lord Buddha himself. While it's a daily draw for white-clad pilgrims bearing lotus blossoms and frangipani, it is also one of the most visited attractions of this attractive city. The tooth is removed from the shrine in late July for Esala Perahera, a 10-day torchlight parade of dancers, drummers and ornately decorated elephants. If you have time, take a stroll around Peradeniya's Royal Botanical Gardens. Or, stop for lunch at one of the many hill-side restaurants for scenic views over Kandy Lake, at the heart of the city.

Slowly does it...

Sri Lanka's roads are either busy and slow due to the volume of traffic, or empty and slow due to the numerous twists and turns. The golden rule is to hire a driver and go with the flow! Expect to pay around Dhs.160 a day, including all fuel and driver accommodation. Hasantha is tourist board-approved and highly recommended; email nilupul7h@yahoo.com.

Temple of the Tooth Relic

You're more than likely to want to drive straight past Colombo to the beach, or just avoid it altogether. But, if you do have time pre-flight, the capital is worth some exploration. Hop on board an open double-decker bus for a city tour to witness the charm of Colombo, including the National Museum and its ancient royal regalia; the restaurants, spa or handicraft store at the oldest building in the area, The Courtyard; and the small, captivating Seema Malakaya on Beira Lake.

Hill Country

Head to the central highlands, take a deep breath and enjoy the cool fresh air while hiking hills and exploring emerald tea plantations. There are some heady mountain roads to climb to get there from Colombo or Kandy, but plenty of distractions en route.

Tea plantations

The Hill Country is filled with rows of tea plants and dotted with workers picking the leaves. For a sip of Sri Lanka, Rothschild's living and working museum is an enlightening experience – and the tea tasting at the end refreshing in so many ways.

Nuwara Eliya

The highest town in Sri Lanka is known for its typically colonial hotels, strawberries and golf course. Nuwara Eliya really comes alive during Buddhist New Year with horse racing and parties. Boating, hiking, golfing, horse riding and visits to tea plantations are a must do when visiting this scenic hill station. It even has very frequent – and very British – showers of rain!

Adam's Peak

It's a tough trek to Adam's Peak, and an early start of 3am to enjoy the breathtaking sunrise. But, the views are worth every knee-buckling step to the top. A good place to stay, or simply enjoy afternoon tea, is the Agar Tea Estate at the foot of the mountain.

In the wild

Udawalawe National Park most resembles an African game park, with herds of elephants, leopards, buffalo, deer and sloth bears roaming wild. About four hours from Nuwara Eliya or Galle, cram in a half-day tour in your own private jeep on a trip to or from the coast. And keep an eye open for mongooses, bandicoots, foxes, water monitor lizards and even crocodiles.

Horton Plains

The best way to explore Sri Lanka's highest plateau is by walking the 10km loop that takes in misty lakes, waterfalls and thick forests. The showstopper of the Plains is World's End (a 3,700 ft sheer drop that offers fabulous views of the tea estates below). Get there early morning or the view is often obscured by mist. Mountain bikes are readily available for hire, and there are plenty of tea plantation bungalows to rest weary feet.

Ella

One of the best ways to spend a morning in Ella is to tackle the short walk up to Little Adam's Peak, which is a very gentle hike. Count on around two hours return, then head back into this backpacker town and dine like a king at Chill Cafe, home to hearty curries and delicious fish baked in banana leaves. Take the train to Ella from Nanu Oya near Nuwara Eliya, a stunning journey that winds past waterfalls and through neatly-clipped tea estates.

Tea plantations

West Coast

From Negombo (just 37km from Colombo) to Mirissa (155km from Colombo), the beach destinations lining the west coast each have their own highlights and character.

Bentota

With its large five-star resorts, exclusive boutique hotels, and picturesque beaches, Bentota is breathtaking. Apart from swimming, body-surfing or diving, you can jet-ski, windsurf, or enjoy a romantic river safari on the river and lagoon. Its shallow, safe conditions are perfect for families.

Madu Ganga River Safari

The scenic beauty of the Madu Ganga is best enjoyed on a boat trip, the perfect vantage for watching monkeys eat fruit in the trees, water monitor lizards gliding slowly through the river, and cormorants, egrets and kingfishers waiting patiently on the banks. There are around 64 islands, from a tiny speck with a deserted shrine to one housing 250 families connected to the mainland with a very long footbridge.

Madu Ganga

Kosgoda Turtle Hatchery

The sight of newly-hatched sea turtles scrabbling out of their sandy nest chambers on a beach and scuttling towards the open sea is a joy to watch. Visit Kosgoda to see the eggs being buried in the sand and the baby turtles released into the sea at night.
kosgodaseaturtle.org

Moonstone mines

There is a string of mines along the west coast, each claiming to be the only genuine moonstone mine. They are all a bit of a tourist trap but you can watch the process of digging, sieving, washing and polishing these beautiful white stones – before being led to the souvenir shop.

Hikkaduwa

One of the most famous beach resorts on the west coast, it's renowned for its diving and coral reef, which can be viewed by glass bottom boat. This is the place to watch fishermen hauling in their catch of the day. The nightlife here is great too.

Sri Lanka
Places to stay

Amaya Hills

Cultural Triangle

Amaya Hills

Nestled in the picturesque hilltops of Kandy, this is an idyllic escape from the hustle and bustle of the city. From the stunning open lobby to the cliff-top swimming pool, this is an affordable hotel with a five-star setting. You'll wake up to wispy mountain mists, feast on lavish breakfast buffets and modern interpretations of Sri Lankan cuisine, and then end the day with cocktails under a canopy of stars. amayahills.net

Back of Beyond

Enter through a small clearing in the jungle thicket and you'll arrive at the doorstep of this rustic eco-retreat – just walking distance from Sigiriya. A back-to-nature experience with a charm of its own. backofbeyond.lk

Elephant Corridor

You can certainly leave your worldly cares behind at this collection of super-luxury villa suites set in a sprawling wilderness near Sigiriya. Enjoy the ultimate one-on-one pampering with your own garden and plunge-pool. Spot elephants from your balcony, or venture out to enjoy archery or horse riding. The hotel is so spacious that you can travel around the site by bike But, if you can afford the romantic suite, complete with indoor pool, who needs to go further than the front door? elephantcorridor.com

Jim's Villas

As a refreshing alternative to some of the larger hotels, stay in one of two villas on a 50-acre organic farm with mountain views. Birdwatch on the balcony, take a dip in the pool, or wander through the spice garden. See the 'real' Sri Lanka – from a breakfast of traditional egg hoppers on your balcony to the harvesting of nuts by skillful pickers. Located midway between Dambulla and Kandy, it's less than an hour's drive to most attractions in the Cultural Triangle. jimsfarmvillas.com

Heritance Kandalama

This tranquil jungle retreat ticks all the right boxes for a luxurious grown-up getaway: no gimmicks, simply stylish rooms, elegant bars and sophisticated dining 'experiences' set within a hotel that peeps out from a canopy of lush green vegetation. Float in the infinity pool while gazing across at Sigiriya Rock, unwind in your Jacuzzi bath without the fear of being seen (except maybe by the local monkeys), and end the day with a cocktail on the terrace – just look out for the bats! There are bountiful buffets of Sri Lankan and international dishes from dusk til dawn; book the flame-lit cave dinner or champagne-fuelled breakfast on a barge. heritancehotels.com/kandalama

Heritance Kandalama

Heritance Kandalama

Mt Lavinia

Hill Country

Ceylon Tea Trails
Colonial charm meets Ceylon chic in these lakeside restored planters' bungalows, with timbered ceilings, panelled libraries, claw-foot baths and bay windows. Enjoy all the mod cons in a 'non-hotel' atmosphere, while being served gourmet meals by your own personal butler no less. teatrails.com

Jetwing St Andrew's
Relive the Raj at this bolthole that's close to the heart of Nuwara Eliya. Enjoy an elegant high tea on a manicured lawn; sip a stiff brandy by the blazing fire, or feast on a hearty English breakfast. At the end of the day, come back to a hot-water bottle between the sheets – after all, it can get chilly at 3,100ft.

jetwinghotels.com/jetwingstandrews

 If you take the train to Ella, it's worth a night's stay at the 98 Acres Resort & Spa (resort98acres.com), an historic tea estate with a handful of luxury thatched villas with mind-blowing views across emerald Ceylon tea plants towards Little Adam's Peak. For a budget break, book into Mountain Heavens guest house.

West Coast

Chaaya Tranz Hikkaduwa
At the heart of a coastal city best known for its surfing, snorkelling and nightlife, this lavish resort has all the allure of a desert island by day and the energy of a beach party by night. Dine in the speciality crab restaurant, unwind in the the rooftop spa and make a splash in the freshwater pool. chaayahotels.com/chaayatranz

Heritance Ahungalla
Secluded, stylish and so seafront you're almost in the water, this sprawling resort is a tropical hideaway. From the signature infinity pool that blends effortlessly into the Indian Ocean to the toes-in-the-sand beach dining, this is impressive without trying to impress. Beautifully isolated just north of Hikkaduwa, there's simply nothing to do but swim, snooze in the shade of palm trees, and sip Arac cocktails made from a heady blend of local coconut juice under the stars. The perfect recipe for a relaxing beach break. heritancehotels.com/ahungalla

Mount Lavinia
An enchanting British Colonial heritage hotel, located on a breathtaking beachfront. The rustic setting and live calypso band of the Seafood Cove, which serves the catch of the day, sets the mood for a blissful escape from the modern world. mountlaviniahotel.com

Heritance Ahungalla

Handpicked hotel
Up, up & away!

Heritance Tea Factory
heritancehotels.com/teafactory

Distance from Mattala
2.5 hours

It's easy to feel like you're in a far corner of the earth at this converted tea factory in the Hill Country.

There's something as relaxing about staying on a tea plantation as there is in drinking a cup of the 'brown stuff'. Perhaps it's the tranquillity of the scene – the sweeping fields of green, speckled with the colourfully dressed tea pickers. Or maybe it's the fresh mountain air, best enjoyed on a post-breakfast walk before the mist rolls in. Either way, a short break at the Heritance Tea Factory is certainly good for your health.

This beautifully converted tea factory, high above the popular hill country town of Nuwara Eliya, invites you to enter a nostalgic world of scones, pitch n putt, and hot-water bottles slipped between the sheets. The experience begins as you are greeted by turban-wearing doormen serving spicy-sweet tea and warm towels. While the unrelenting drive from the airport up narrow hill roads seems to last an age, one glimpse of the views from the lobby – at Sri Lanka's highest point of 6,850ft above sea level – and all is forgiven and forgotten.

Time for a brew?
While tea factories are not known for their outstanding beauty, the original machinery and industrial decor adds charm to the hotel; from the ride in the original factory lift up to your room to the grinding engine in the lobby, you feel part of living history.

The 'wow' factor of the rooms is definitely the view – a sea of green through huge windows – and the bowls of fresh tea leaves next to the kettle are a nice touch. (The best views are from the corner deluxe rooms).

It is, after all, all about the tea here. You can learn about the tea-picking process at the miniature tea factory; there's even the chance to pluck your own tea and have it bagged and ready for you to take home. Every day starts with steaming cups of tea at breakfast, poured in fine china cups in a converted tea sifting room. There's then afternoon tea by the roaring log fire, and even a selection of tea-inspired cocktails to enjoy as the sun sets on the terrace.

Stay, but never leave
Far from being a gimmicky resort, the Tea Factory is quite simply a destination in its own right – the main point being that once you arrive here, there is no need to leave, (at least, not for two or three days). Join the morning or afternoon nature trail through tea plantations and a Hindi village, stopping for a chat with the shy but friendly tea pluckers along the way. Burn off some steam with the family in the miniature maze, putting green and the children's play area. Or, for the ultimate hit of heaven, book a massage at the Six Senses spa.

Getting there
Fly to the new Mattala Rajapakse International airport – it's a hilly but rewarding 2.5 hour drive to the hotel. Or, fly to Colombo and combine with a stay in Kandy.

There's nothing like relaxing with the perfect cup of tea up high in the mountains – the perfect breath of fresh air

All aboard!
Dinner is a grand affair, with a choice of international and Sri Lankan dishes. But, for an experience like no other, check in to TCK 6685 for 'meals on wheels'. This gourmet adventure is six courses served by white-glove clad 'attendants' in railway uniform on a restored railway carriage – complete with sound effects and some rocking motion. It's bizarrely good.

Old Town of Galle

Sand, surf and turf

Explore the south coast

Getting there
Fly to either Colombo or the new Mattala Rajapakse International Airport – it's a 2.5 hour scenic drive to Galle either way.

Jetwing Lighthouse

Elephant trekking in Yala National Park

Grab a driver and head to the south coast for the perfect blend of beach bliss and bush breakaway.

It would be easy to pick a beach resort on the south coast and never leave, but those who do may regret it. From surfing to sun lounging, whale-watching to walking, there are too many distractions to ignore – and Galle is the gateway to them all. Lay down roots in this historic port town – which is a smooth 2.5 hour drive from Colombo on the new highway – and do as little or as much as you please. But please do something!

Begin with an early 5am start to go whale-watching with the eco-conscious Raja and the Whale from the palm-fringed picturesque Mirissa harbour; it's best to go November to April. Back on shore you can refuel on fresh clay-oven fired pizza at the picturesque Wijaya Beach restaurant. There's just time for a snorkel in the clear waters before making the 40-minute trip back to Galle. Stop en route to see the stilt fishermen and the sugary white sands of Unawatuna, one of the country's best beaches.

Begin your second day with a morning stroll in Galle around the fort's ramparts, before exploring cinnamon warehouses and beautifully restored Dutch villas, then sampling local street food – fresh pineapple, roti and king coconuts. Finally, rest weary feet at Mama's Galle Fort Roof Cafe.

What next? Well, Midigama is the best surfing spot along the south coast, with a couple of reef breaks that are ideal for beginners, and the hollow, shallow and unpredictable Ram's Right for the pros. The best time to grab the surfboard is November through to April.

If you prefer a walk on the wild side, head to the Yala National Park, famous for the elusive leopard, sloth bear and Asian elephant. It's a four to five-hour drive, or worthy of an overnight stay at the nearby rustic chic wildlife resort, Cinammon Wild (cinammonhotels.com), if you have the time.

Jetwing Lighthouse

Flippers on!

Around Galle there are some of the country's best dive spots, run by official PADI centres. Spotting bright corals and exotic fish is easy and there is the opportunity to go both cave and wreck diving.

Room with a view

The Jetwing Lighthouse hotel in Galle scores on location. The sweeping ocean view from the terrace really stops you in your tracks. There are also uninterrupted views of the ocean from the chic, uncluttered, spacious suites; with roomy balconies and elegant bathrooms, there's just the right combination of pampering luxury and understated elegance. There are two outdoor pools, tennis courts and a spa, making it an idyllic retreat for stressed-out city folk. And with spacious gardens and a stretch of untouched coastline for romantic walks, there's always a private corner.

The bars and restaurants conjure up a lost era of colonial times – think whirring fans above, and cocktails or steaming mugs of tea served by serene sarong-clad staff. The ambience is welcoming and relaxed and, above all, it's tastefully different; most certainly a recommendation for a luxurious long weekend getaway. jetwinghotels.com

Africa

Africa

The Great Pyramids of Giza

Egypt

The birthplace of civilisation and the pharaohs, this North African country's history is unrivalled. But there's even more to Egypt than that, with the Mediterranean and Red Sea, sand and sunshine.

Flight time
4 hours to Alexandria
3 hours 50 minutes
to Cairo

Door to door
30-90 minutes by car
from Cairo airport to
the city centre.
45 minutes from
Alexandria airport to
the city centre.

When to go
January to December

No matter how short your time is in the UAE, a visit to Egypt is a must. The North African country is brimming with fascinating history – not only is it the first land to create civilisation, and is the birthplace of the pharaohs, it also boasts influences from the ancient Greeks and Romans. History aside, you can enjoy snorkelling trips to both the Mediterranean and Red Sea, take a Nile cruise, or dive straight into the street life.

Egypt's capital, Cairo is the largest city in Africa and the Arab world; its chaos, air pollution and constant buzz – not to mention insane traffic – is renowned. While the pyramids and gorgeous mosques are essentials for first timers, look beyond the pharaohs to see the 'real' Cairo: watch the sun set high above the smog at Mokattam

cliff, enjoy the great flavours of shisha in one of many streetside cafes, or board a felucca, a traditional Nile sailing boat.

For a complete contrast, Alexandria is a pleasant Mediterranean city, still influenced by Europe with its Parisian-style buildings. There are enough sights in this modern beach city to keep history buffs busy, and the cooler climate tempered by balmy ocean breezes is a welcome relief in the summer.

Sun worshippers and divers will appreciate the Red Sea resort of Sharm El Sheikh, where the water activities are second to none, and the mix of hotels makes it suitable for anyone from solo travellers to families with young children.

While the choice for an Egyptian holiday is essentially beach or pyramids, there's plenty more to see in between.

A new dawn for tourism

At the very mention of Egypt as a holiday destination many travellers will ask – is it safe? Since the overthrowing of President Hosni Mubarak's rule there have been various disturbances across the country, but it is safe in many places. The Red Sea resort of Sharm El Sheikh remains one of the safest places – in fact it's the perfect time to visit before tourists start returning in their hordes. It's best to avoid areas where protests are more likely, including the Presidential Palace and Tahrir Square in Cairo, as well as Ibrahim Mosque in Alexandria. In short though, Egypt is very much 'open for business'.

Egypt
Essentials

Stay close to home and enjoy a mix of ancient marvels and modern-day chaos on a weekend break.

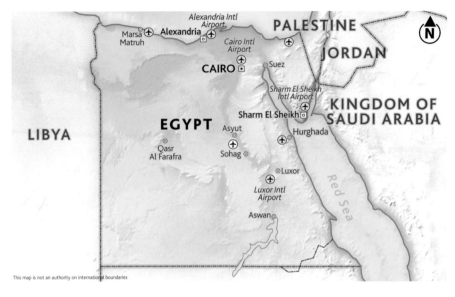

This map is not an authority on international boundaries

Getting there
Fly from Dubai to Alexandria with Air Arabia Emirates and flydubai. Fly from Dubai or Abu Dhabi to Cairo with Egypt Air, Emirates and Etihad. There's only one way of getting to Sharm El Sheikh from Dubai, and that's via Cairo with Egypt Air.

Visas
Most nationalities can obtain a tourist visa on arrival for $15 (Dhs.60). GCC nationals do not require a visa.

Time
Two hours behind the UAE.

Climate
Cairo remains mostly dry with temperatures ranging from 19°C in the winter to 45°C in the summer. Alexandria has a humid Mediterranean climate, while Sharm El Sheikh gets very hot in August.

Language
Arabic; English is widely spoken.

Currency
Egyptian Pound (EGP). 100 EGP = Dhs.52

Vaccinations
Hepatitis A, Hepatitis B and Typhoid.

Best for... budget breaks
Travelling to Cairo, Alexandria or Sharm El Sheikh doesn't need to break the bank. From all-inclusive holidays offering affordable luxury to city hotels with easy on the wallet rates, Egypt is within your reach. And, with flights starting at Dhs.860, you can afford to pack up and go at the last minute. It's smiles, salaams and thumbs-up signs all round.

Fairmont Nile City

The Sphinx

Pyramids of Giza

Lose yourself in the historical wonders of Alexandria and Cairo, or unwind on the beaches of Sharm El Sheikh – all just a weekend away.

Cairo

Cairo needs to be seen for what it is: nearly 11 million people who hustle, travel, eat, cook and chat across the city, at nearly every hour. The best option is to gradually wade into it – taking a guided tour on the first day, exploring the quiet areas on your own the next, and finally ploughing through the most crowded parts.

Egyptian Museum

Unfortunately, it's not as grand as it used to be as many pieces have gone missing over the years. However, Egypt's famous museum is still worth a visit. Housing around 165,000 artefacts, the highlight is the treasure of King Tutankhamun.

Egyptian Museum

Pyramids of Giza

The oldest of the Seven Wonders of the Ancient World, the pyramids are another tick for the bucket list. Just 30 minutes away from Cairo is this ancient complex of unbelievable architectural achievements. Cheops – also known as the Great Pyramid of Giza – is the oldest and largest of the three pyramids, which was built as a tomb for fourth dynasty Egyptian Pharaoh Khufu over a 10 to 20-year period. Originally 480-odd feet high (it's lost a few inches over the years, but is no less impressive for it), the Great Pyramid was the tallest man-made structure in the world for over 3,800 years. Few have managed to climb it, but entering the pyramid is a must-do on any trip to Cairo (you'll have to leave your tour guide at the door though as they are not allowed in). No visit would be complete without standing at the foot of the Sphinx, the enigmatic symbol of Egypt – nothing can quite prepare you for this.

Khan El Khalili

Cairo's most gorgeous bazaar features maze-like alleyways surrounding the 12th century El Hussein Mosque. Arrive before 11am and the crowds should be thin enough to imagine what these dark, claustrophobic walkways looked like hundreds of years ago. Novelties and hand-made jewellery line most of the store shelves, but spend enough time exploring and you'll eventually stumble on one of the dusty antique shops that lie on the outskirts of the maze.

Pearl of the Med

Explore Egypt's two largest cities in a short break. Located on the Mediterranean coast, Alexandria (p.106) is an easy three hour road trip from Cairo.

Khan El Khalili

River Nile

With no sun to slow its residents, Cairo's streets are best observed after dusk. Post-work strolls are a tradition, and the banks and bridges of the Nile are usually packed, especially in the summertime. This is the best time to walk and check out some of the city's best known landmarks, such as the Maspero television building, Cairo Tower, Cairo World Trade Centre and the Opera House. Hop on a Nile dinner cruise to enjoy views of Cairo's illuminated skyline.

Hammam & koshari

Although not vast, Egypt is home to some interesting dishes, including hammam (stuffed fried pigeon), macarona bel bashamel (macaroni with beef and bechamel sauce), mahshi (stuffed vegetables with rice, including courgettes, aubergines, tomatoes and vine leaves) and mombar (sausages stuffed with rice). If you don't fancy trying something too out-of-the-ordinary, then street food-style dishes are for you. Koshari is a carb-laden dish – comprising pasta, rice, lentils, chickpeas and fried onions, mixed together with tomato or chilli sauce – that you can enjoy for less than Dhs.10, while the always-crowded Gad restaurants are home to some of the best foul and falafel sandwiches.

Got room for more? Then try grilled corn, or one of the country's freshest drinks, sugarcane juice.

Bars & clubs

While not as hectic as Dubai or Beirut, Cairo is home to a vibrant nightlife scene. If you don't mind dressing up, then go and explore the beautiful people at either Club 35 at the Four Seasons Cairo; Tamarai in Nile City Towers; or Amici Zamalek at the New President Hotel. For live music and a laidback dress code, then Cairo Jazz Club is the order of the day for casual drinks and good music. Another place with a chilled atmosphere is O Bar at Fairmont Nile City, perfect for dining and partying. To book tickets, visit ticketing site tazkarty.net.

Egypt
Highlights

Sharm El Sheikh

Sharm El Sheikh

Sharm El Sheikh is a world away from the typical city life of Cairo or Alexandria. Known as the crown jewel of Egypt's Red Sea resort towns, it is all about the sunbathing, swimming and snorkelling – its turquoise sea is dotted with stunningly coloured coral reefs and 1,200 species of marine life – with a few activities and fantastic nightlife thrown in for good measure. For any boat trips or land tours, book with a reputable agent, such as Viator (viator.com), CityDiscovery (city-discovery.com), or through your hotel's concierge service.

Ras Mohammed

Ras Mohammed

Egypt's first marine park, which is located at the southern tip of the Sinai Peninsula, is one of the country's most popular dive and snorkelling sites. World-famous coral reefs, wreck diving, fantastic snorkelling and a rich array of marine life awaits. And if that's not enough, there are some stunning beachfront walks too.

Tiran Island

There are options aplenty to escape the desert and enjoy the Egyptian sun. Catch a boat trip to Tiran Island and you can be snorkelling in crystal-clear blue waters and sunbathing on white sandy beaches. There are also a number of shipwrecks amongst the coral for adventurous divers to explore.

Soho Square

For all-round family entertainment, Soho Square is one of the most popular hangouts in Sharm El Sheikh. The largest social spot in the Red Sea region, it is home to everything from shops to bars and restaurants, and sport facilities to nightclubs. The promenade features a dancing fountain, Shisha Island and a children's arcade.

Ibiza of the Middle East

Sharm El Sheikh's nightlife scene is on par with that of Dubai's – and even rivals it. Not only are the clubs open for longer, they are also a little more liberal, which probably explains why a number of Ibiza institutions have set up shop in the city. Notable venues include Pacha (with its year-round open-air rooms and poolside dance floor), Space and Privilege – each hosting plenty of big-name DJs, such as Bob Sinclair.

Desert safaris

While this excursion might be too similar to those available in Dubai, a trip into the desert in Sharm El Sheikh is still tonnes of fun. Take a two-hour quad biking trip at sunrise or sunset to truly appreciate the landscape; in the evening head across the dunes to a Bedouin camp for a traditional barbecue under the stars.

Moses' Mountain & St Catherine's Monastery

This day trip may be a long and tiring drive in the desert heat, but it's well worth it. Located around 230km from Sharm El Sheikh is the place where Moses received the 10 Commandments. Visitors can trace the footsteps of the prophet to the historic site – it's not steep, but it is 500 steps to the summit – as well as visit St Catherine's Monastery, which is believed to have been built on the site of the Burning Bush.

Open water

Interested in scuba diving in the Red Sea? Try and complete a PADI course beforehand in the UAE, as you'll have more tours to choose from. If not, you can learn while there, or simply stay above the water and hire snorkelling gear from your hotel.

Egypt
Places to stay

Fairmont Nile City

Cairo

Fairmont Nile City

For a hotel a little closer to the city centre, Fairmont Nile City is a great choice for travellers who are looking for something fancy (rooms are around Dhs.600 per night). Not only are the rooms and location impressive, there are a number of places to eat, drink and dance the night away, including O Bar. fairmont.com

Four Seasons Cairo, Nile Plaza

With Cairo's downtown area only a 10-minute drive from the hotel, the Four Seasons is one of the best-placed properties in the city. Featuring panoramic views of the Nile, the hotel includes luxury spa facilities and an outdoor landscaped pool. Predictably, rooms do not come cheap (around Dhs.1,500 per night). fourseasons.com/caironp

Guardian Guest House

For spectacular views of the Pyramids and the Sphinx without breaking the bank balance, you can't beat a stay at this budget guest house. Local excursions and horse riding activities can be arranged by staff, plus there are barbecue facilities and a spacious sun terrace that overlooks the beautiful Giza area. guardianguesthouse.com

Mena House Hotel

Fancy waking up to a view of the pyramids? This luxury five-star property (rooms are less than Dhs.1,000 a night) is surrounded by 40 acres of green gardens and has a spa, fitness centre and a pool. menahousehotel.com

Wake Up! Cairo Hostel

If you're backpacking or on a budget trip, head to the Wake Up! Cairo Hostel, which is one of the best in the city. Located in Downtown Cairo, near the Egyptian Museum, this hostel offers one, two or three-bed rooms with either an en suite or shared bathroom. Prices start from around Dhs.70 per night. wakeupcairohostel.com

Looking for a hotel stay out of the ordinary? Head to the Cairo Marriott (marriott.com) and its legendary Omar Khayyam Casino. Located in the capital's Zamalek district, the hotel was originally built as a palace in 1869. You'll enjoy great views of the Nile, one of the city's largest outdoor pools, and a rather delicious afternoon tea.

Africa Egypt

Spend big and enjoy aperitifs looking out onto the pyramids at Mena House

Mena House Hotel

askexplorer.com

103

Four Seasons Alexandria

Rixos Sharm El Sheikh

Alexandria

Helnan Palestine Hotel

It's not the closest property to the city centre, but Helnan Palestine is popular with guests wanting to stay in Al Montazah. Set on 350 acres of greenery, the five-star property features an outdoor pool and private seafront terrace. Ask for a room that overlooks the palace, which was the residence of former presidents. helnan.com

Paradise Inn
Le Metropole Hotel

Located in Raml Station, this mid-range hotel is housed in an 18th century building with classical decor, and offers views of the Mediterranean. What it lacks in modern amenities, it makes up for in charm. The Bibliotheca Alexandrina is within easy reach.
paradiseinnegypt.com/Metropole

If travelling to Alexandria from Cairo, get the hotel's concierge to book your train tickets. There have been numerous stories of late regarding tourists being sold incorrect fares and then refused a refund. Alternatively, coach companies such as Super Jet run regular services between the cities; it's 2.5 hours each way.

Sharm El Sheikh

Four Seasons Resort Sharm El Sheikh

Super luxurious, this Red Sea diving resort has the lot: four pools, five restaurants, three lounges and a spa. There are plenty of diving and snorkelling activities available on site, with the Sinai Blues Dive Centre running daily excursions. Simply do not miss one of astronomer Nader Kobaissy's twilight stargazing sessions. Fascinating for the little ones – and grown-ups too! fourseasons.com

Karma Hotel

A three-star property with rooms that start from around Dhs.80, Karma is fantastic value for money. Situated about 2km from the public Marhaba Beach, the hotel features an outdoor pool, a tennis court and a bar. A shopping mall is less than half a kilometre away. (Check hotel booking sites for prices).

Rixos Sharm El Sheikh

This new kid on the block opened following the launch of Rixos The Palm in Dubai. Located in the heart of Sharm, the hotel wows with a location that overlooks the entrance to the Gulf of Aqaba and the Tiran Island. All rooms come with a balcony or terrace overlooking the sea or garden, plus there's a private beach, swimming pool, six restaurants and five bars. rixos.com

Four Seasons Resort Sharm El Sheikh

Four Seasons Alexandria

Alexandria the Great

A weekend in the city

Tale of two cities
It's just a three-hour road trip from Alexandria to Cairo, so you can see two vastly different cities for the price of one airfare.

Kom ash-Shuqqafa Catacombs

A trip to Alexandria is a welcome break from the hustle and bustle of Cairo. Stay at the iconic Four Seasons, visit the largest library in the world, and marvel at the Mediterranean city's past.

Egypt's second largest city couldn't be or feel more different than that of Cairo. It is often overlooked as just another town; however, its atmosphere and food is less Middle Eastern, more Greek and Italian.

Signature stopover

In recent years, the Four Seasons hotel (fourseasons.com/alexandria) in San Stefano has become the poster image for Alexandria, setting new standards of luxury in the vibrant city. Here, you will be enchanted by the marble baths, private beach, sea-view balconies, infinity pool and award-winning spa, which are of course a huge draw for the more well-heeled tourist.

Be sure to make time to sample the variety of bars and restaurants on offer; the hotel's restaurants are popular with guests and walk-in residents alike, and its Friday brunch at Kala – which features a variety of international cuisine – is always fully booked. Another place to check out is Fresca, where you can sample the popular Egyptian street dessert of the same name (two thin wafers stuck together with fig jam – so simple, yet so good).

Pearl of the Med

Not only can you see most of Alexandria's breathtaking historical sites independently, a tour of the city can easily be done in just half a day. Visit downtown's catacombs of Kom ash-Shuqqafa, the largest known Roman burial site in Egypt and one of the Seven Wonders of the Middle Ages. Walk for just five minutes to reach Pompey's Pillar, a 25-metre granite column built to honour Emperor Diocletian, who freed the besieged city and brought food to its people. Not far away is the well-preserved Roman amphitheatre in Kom El-Dikka, a fascinating open air museum.

Kom El-Dikka amphitheatre

Summer nights

For a relaxed dinner on the beach, don your flip-flops for the Siwa experience at the Four Seasons, where dishes are cooked in an underground oven warmed by a wood fire.

City highlights

Want to visit a library that keeps at least one copy of every book published in the world? Bibliotheca Alexandrina harks back to the city's role as a seat of learning in ancient times, and features four museums, a planetarium, eight academic research centres, and various art galleries.

You can enjoy the great outdoors in the coastal district of Montazah, from walks through the beautiful gardens of Montazah Palace to banana boating off the coast. There's a small choice of hotels here, and anyone with an interest in royal relics will love the Al Haramlik Museum.

At the other end of town is a 15th century fort, Citadel of Qaitbay, which was constructed on the ruins of the Lighthouse of Alexandria. While the fort is not very well maintained, it is the go-to place for the city's seafood restaurants.

Bibliotheca Alexandrina

Africa

Wenchi Crater Lake

Ethiopia

From the ancient castles and churches to the ruggedly beautiful countryside and mountain ranges, Ethiopia is a country of unexpected wonders.

 Flight time
4 hours

 Door to door
1 hour by plane or 9-13 hours by car from the airport to Gondar and Axum; 30 minutes by car from the airport to Addis Ababa city centre

 When to go
September to March

Ask most people what images come to mind when you mention Ethiopia and common responses would be barren deserts, hardship and famine; while that may be the popular media portrayal of Ethiopia, it couldn't be further away from the truth. In reality, the landscape is filled with lush green farmlands, rolling plateaus and large freshwater lakes that are home to flora and fauna not found anywhere else in the world. Plus, unlike some other African nations, Ethiopia is relatively safe for travellers, as long as you stick to the interior region and major cities.

There's a little something for everyone in Ethiopia. Up north, the monolithic rock churches of Lalibela, castle complex at Gondar and stelae fields of Axum are a treat for history and culture buffs. The trekking

trails of the Simien and Bale Mountain National Parks, rising over 4,000m, should challenge the hardiest of adventurers. Down south, peaks are substituted for valleys – the Great Rift Valley no less – and serene lakes that are frequented by flamingos and over 900 species of birds. For a truly unique experience, the Omo Valley, in the deep south, offers a fascinating insight into 15 ethnic tribes that have been shielded from the modern world for generations. Adventurous types might like to pay a visit to the Danakil Depression, an otherworldly landscape of bubbling sulphur lakes and an active volcano.

Wherever you decide to travel, your trip to Ethiopia is sure to be unlike any other. And now's the time to go, before it becomes a staple on every traveller's wishlist.

Cradle of civilisation

Ethiopia's status as the cradle of civilisation was first cemented in 1974 when the remains of 'Lucy', a 3.2-million-year-old skeleton, were found near the Awash Valley. Lucy's discovery was significant as it was the first ever complete specimen of an upright-walking, two-legged human ancestor. Since then, archaeologists have found numerous other fossils along the Rift Valley, including the recently discovered remains of 'Ardi' dating back 4.4 million years; the closest we've come to finding the missing link. So, it's only fitting that we return to our ancestral home for a short break!

Ethiopia
Essentials

SUDAN

YEMEN

☐ Axum

● Simien

⊙ Gondar

DJIBOUTI

Gulf Of Aden

Dese

Dire Dawa
Intl Airport

SOMALILAND

Nek'emte
☐⊙

ADDIS ABABA
☐⊕
⊕⊙
Dire Dawa

Addis Ababa
Bole Intl Airport

Jima ⊙

ETHIOPIA

☐ Great Rift Valley Lakes

SOUTH
SUDAN

SOMALIA

Jinka
⊙

Bitata
⊙

KENYA

This map is not an authority on international boundaries

Escape the madding crowd to uncover the less than well trodden tourist trails of Ethiopia's beautiful and mysterious land.

Getting there
Fly from Dubai to Bole International Airport in Addis Ababa with Emirates, Ethiopian Airways or flydubai, from Dhs.1,005 return.

Visas
Aside from Kenyans and Djiboutians, all nationalities require a tourist visa to enter Ethiopia. It can be issued on arrival, or at an Ethiopian consulate in your country of residence for a fee of US$20.

Time
One hour behind the UAE.

Climate
Ethiopia enjoys a moderate climate with average temperatures ranging between 24°C and 28°C. The dry season is October to May, and the rainy season is June to September.

Language
Amharic; English is widely spoken.

Currency
Ethiopian Birr (ETB). 10 ETB = Dhs.2

Vaccinations
Hepatitis A & B, Malaria, Polio and Rabies, Typhoid and Yellow Fever.

Great for... natural beauty
Ethiopia may not be the most well-known holiday destination, but the staggeringly beautiful landscape, with its rolling hills, tranquil lakes and wild valleys, will make you glad you took the trip. Make the most of your holiday by visiting one of the national parks in southern Ethiopia and prepare to be wowed.

Stelae fields of Axum

The capital of Ethiopia and its surrounds can be rather overwhelming to first-time visitors, but persevere to discover its hidden treasures.

Addis Ababa

Sitting at 2,400m overlooking the Abyssinian plateau is Addis Ababa, the thriving capital of Ethiopia. Its position in the middle of the country makes it the perfect base camp for day trips around the rest of Ethiopia.

City tour

From the outset, the crowds and scale of Addis, as it is sometimes simply known, can be intimidating for a first-time visitor. The best way to come to grips with the city is to go on a city tour with a local guide to help get your bearings straight. There are various organised half-day or full-day tours that can be booked through your hotel. However, for a more personal touch, you should opt for a walking tour with a local private guide toursbylocals.com

Mount Entoto

The highest point in the city, Mount Entoto offers stunning panoramic views over Addis. Former King Menelik II clearly thought so too, building his palace (which is open to the public) on top of the mountain. Private taxis tend to overcharge for the trip up so make sure you negotiate the fare beforehand with your driver. Alternatively, you could follow in the footsteps of Olympic gold medallist and Dubai Marathon winner Haile Gebrselassie, who trained by hiking up the Mount Entoto trail every morning.

Mercato

Mercato is a vibrant and busy (bordering on chaotic) open air market in Addis spread over 100 hectares with more than 2,000 stalls selling everything from pots, pans, spices, souvenirs, clothes, coffee – you name it! A word to the wise: travel light and keep your valuables close, as there have been numerous instances of pickpocketing.

National Museum of Ethiopia

The well-maintained National History Museum separates its exhibits into four sections: Palaeontology, where the star attraction among the fossils is 'Lucy', the 3.2 million-year-old remains of one of our early ancestors; Archaeology, which houses finds from Ethiopia's early history to the 16th century; Ethnography, where you can learn about Ethiopia's tribes and traditions; and Modern Art, which features paintings and sculptures from contemporary artists. addisculturetourism.gov.et

From A to B

The easiest way to get around Addis, or out of the city on a day trip, is to hire a local driver who knows the roads. Staff at your hotel should be able to put you in contact with a private driver. Typically you would agree on a set day rate and then pay for the fuel used to get to your intended destination.

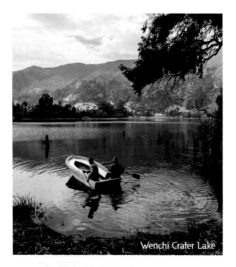
Wenchi Crater Lake

Addis Ababa

Coffee is big business in Ethiopia and the nation's coffee ceremony is there for the partaking. Green coffee beans are roasted over lit coals then ground, poured into a jebena (coffeepot) and brought to the boil at least three times. This ceremony is less about sipping coffee and more about bonding with the locals.

Debre Zeyit

Located 45 minutes away from the city, Debre Zeyit (also known as Bishoftu) is a resort town that is surrounded by seven crater lakes. Its relatively close proximity to the international airport and the variety of accommodation options make it an alternative base camp for visitors who want to skip the more crowded capital Addis for excursions around the country.

Wenchi Crater Lake

One of the most picturesque views in Ethiopia, Wenchi is an extinct volcano at an altitude of 3,400m that is home to hot springs, farms, waterfalls and a beautiful lake all set within its caldera. Dotted around the lake are mini islands, one of which is the site of a 16th century monastery that can be accessed via a short boat trip. There are a number of trekking trails ranging from an easy 4km walk from the rim of the crater down to the lake to a more strenuous 16km hike that covers all locations of interest around the crater. Wenchi is a four-hour drive from Addis and can be done as a day trip, or as a more comfortable overnight trip staying at one of the lodges near the crater.

Spicy suppers

Thanks to the liberal use of local spices, Ethiopian cuisine is anything but a bland experience. Some of the must-try dishes are: wat, a slow cooked stew made with chicken, lamb, or beef; tibs, sauteed meat with a blend of herbs and spices; and injera, a spongy flatbread similar to a pancake that is served with most meals. Kitfo – finely chopped lean beef seasoned with spices and usually served raw or rare – is an acquired taste but worth sampling. Remember, an Ethiopian meal is a very hands-on affair, so if you require cutlery you'll need to ask for it and be prepared for the odd stare and occasional arched eyebrow in your direction. Meals are a communal experience too, with everyone sharing a selection of dishes.

Hippos on Lake Awasa

Lake Abijata

The South

The Great Rift Valley, with its freshwater and alkaline lakes, is far removed from the madding crowds of the city – and at 270km away it's a perfect two day trip. If you prefer a more natural travel experience, then Ethiopia's south beckons.

Lake Ziway
The largest of the Rift Valley lakes, Lake Ziway offers the best bird watching experience with over 70 species easily visible just by walking around the shores. Common sights include the white pelican, yellow-billed stork, griffin vultures and black egrets. Five islands are dotted around Lake Ziway, one with an ancient monastery, and these can be explored by a short boat excursion.

Lakes Langano, Abijata & Shala
Grouped together based on proximity, Lake Langano has been developed for tourism and offers watersports, resorts and eco lodges, making it a nice base if you want to explore the Rift Valley lakes over a few days; Lakes Abijata and Shala, on the other hand, are designated as protected areas and frequently visited by a variety of bird species including greater and lesser flamingos. A hot spring is located on the north-east corner of Lake Shala and is a popular attraction with local residents over the weekend.

Lake Awasa
Awasa may be the smallest of the Rift Valley lakes but it supports more aquatic life than any of the others, making it an important commercial spot for the nearby city of Awasa. Beautiful lakeside resorts offer a welcome stop to visitors who want to rest the night before heading onwards to the Bale Mountains or the Omo Valley. The resorts, including Haile Resort, also offer boat rides around the lake, as well as guided excursions to spot the herds of hippos.

Safaris & spas
Lake Abaya, the longest of the Ethiopian Great Rift Valley lakes, is the place to go for boat safaris and hiking routes. Then relax in nearby Arba Minch, which boasts natural hot springs and spas thanks to its volcanic origins.

Flamingos on Lake Abijata

Bale Mountains National Park

Further south is the second highest plateau range in Ethiopia – an important nature reserve for Ethiopian flora and fauna thanks to its mix of plains, woodlands and bush land. The park offers visitors a number of walking, trekking and driving paths, making it very easy to access any peaks or valleys with minimal effort. It's a seven hour drive from Addis, and there are plenty of lodges and campsites to make a short break out of it. balemountains.org

Omo Valley

Nothing that you've experienced in Ethiopia can prepare you for the Omo Valley. This valley is home to 15 ethnic tribes, with a population of 200,000, who have lived, and continue to live, a life disconnected from the modern world. The tribes are known for their colourful clay body paint and long, intricate headdresses. A fascinating add-on to any visit to the lakes if you have a few extra days to spare. Book an organised tour in advance. omovalley.com

Out of hiding

Southern Ethiopia is the place to see the country's most elusive and magnificent wildlife, including the Abyssinian lion, Ethiopian wolf and gelada baboon. Visit the Nechisar National Park to spot zebras, monkeys, jackals and crocs.

Rift Valley

The North

Forget time machines: a trip around the famed northern historical circuit, and arguably the most popular tourist route in Ethiopia, will take you on a journey all the way back to 600BC.

Axum

Axum is best known for its stelae fields and archaeological remains of the Axumite Empire dating back to 600BC. The fields consist of tall granite obelisks that historians assume were used by Axumite rulers. Indiana Jones could have saved himself some trouble by visiting Axum as the Ark of the Covenant is allegedly housed in a chapel right here! Jokes aside, the Chapel of the Ark of the Covenant is said to contain the legendary ark but unfortunately can only be viewed by the High Priest of Axum, the sole custodian of the artefact,

Gondar

Visiting Gondar feels like stumbling into medieval Europe. The main attraction, a castle complex known as the Royal Enclosure, is often referred to as the Camelot of Africa. Also known as Fasil Ghebbi, the Royal Enclosure is surrounded by a 900m wall and contains six castles, three churches, stables and a palace dating back to the 16th and 17th centuries. Today, the fortress city is a UNESCO World Heritage Site.

Lalibela

If you could visit just one site in Ethiopia, this UNESCO World Heritage Site would be it. The town of Lalibela is known for its rock-hewn churches that have been carved into the earth, below ground level, and surrounded by trenches and courtyards. Much of its history – when and how these churches were built – is shrouded in mystery, adding to the overall mystique of Lalibela. Interconnected via a series of underground tunnels, these are still used for religious ceremonies; the most mesmerising being the Ethiopian Christmas celebration, when tens of thousands of white-robed pilgrims from all over Ethiopia make their way to Lalibela to offer their blessings.

Simien Mountains

Commonly referred to as the Grand Canyon of Africa, the Simien Mountain range is a stunning landscape of river beds, rolling plateaus and peaks topping 4,000m. The National Park on the western side of the range comprises a series of camps and trails. You could cover the entire park by car in a day, but that would be a disservice to the beautiful vistas. A number of trekking options exist, ranging from an easy overnighter to a three to four-day intermediate hike and an eight to 11 day option for adventurers wanting to ascend to the highest peak. Highlights include watching birds of prey soar on the thermals over terrifying drops of up to 1,000m.

Axum

Underground churches, Lalibela

Time difference

Time behaves somewhat differently in Ethiopia. The clock begins at sunrise, our 6am, so one hour after would be 1am, our 7am and so forth. The rule of thumb is to deduct six hours from our clock to find out what the equivalent Ethiopian time is. Avoid confusion by checking if the time referred to is 'habesha' (Ethiopian) or 'ferengi' (foreign).

Royal Enclosure, Gondar

Addis Ababa

Arequ Guesthouse

Arequ is a family run B&B guesthouse filled with charm, character and warm hospitality. Located just five minutes from the airport, it's an ideal place to stay if you're going to be out on day trips and just need to come back to a comfortable bed at night and a home cooked breakfast in the morning.
arequbandb.com

Sheraton Addis

From the perfectly manicured grounds and grand lobby to the personal butler service and pool that features soft underwater music, everything about the Sheraton Addis screams luxury. Rooms range from standard and suites to private three-floor VIP villas. Be sure to visit the spa at the Aqva Club for some pampering after a day of sightseeing.
sheratonaddis.com

The South

Haile Resort

Owned by Haile Gebrselassie, the Olympic gold medallist runner has spared no expense in building his hotel. The extensive list of facilities include a large pool complete with waterfall, mini golf course, cinema hall, three restaurants, lakeside bar, spa, walking track and a state-of-the-art fitness centre – said to be designed by Haile himself.
haileresort.com.et

Midroc Zewed Village

What the Midroc lacks in upmarket rooms, it makes up for in location and beautiful woodlands. The grounds also attract a wide range of wildlife, so don't be surprised if you wake up one morning and find a group of vervet monkeys waiting to greet you outside the bungalow. A popular resort amongst locals, it's best to book in advance.

Sheraton Addis

Arequ Guesthouse

From traditional lodges in the African wilds to mountain-top views of ancient churches, Ethiopia has it all

Go green

Nowhere in Ethiopia does eco-tourism better than the Bishangari Lodge. All the lodges have been designed using natural materials and traditional techniques, and solar power and biogas are used for energy. Additionally, the environmentally-friendly lodge recruits 98% of its staff from the local community.

Axum

The North

Bete Abraham Inn

Managed by the church, the proceeds from this hotel go towards supporting Lalibela's many priests so if you would like to pay it forward this would be the best opportunity to make a difference. This hotel, with its colourful frescoes, is located at the southern end of Lalibela. Rooms come equipped with basic amenities and tours around the area can be arranged by the hotel.
beteabrahaminn.com

Consolar International Hotel

Located on the road to the airport, next to the Pantaleon Monastery, the Consolar International Hotel ranks well on amenities and services and is aimed at the business traveller. A complimentary airport shuttle and good restaurant and bar make this hotel one of the better choices in Axum.
consolarhotelaxum.com

Goha Hotel

The Goha is located on a hill about 1.5km from the town centre. For those that don't mind the half-hour walk to reach the town or paying for a taxi, the Goha Hotel is a nice place for enjoying a good meal and great views over the castles of the historic city of Gondar. Plus, every Friday and Saturday, you can enjoy live entertainment in the form of traditional music and dance.
gohahotel.com

Mountain View Hotel

For the best views over Lalibela and the rock-hewn churches, look no further. Rooms are comfortable and clean and come with private balconies. The rooftop terrace bar, perfect for sundowners, and a restaurant with international trained chefs will satisfy the most demanding of diners. The hotel also assists in organising tours, finding local guides and hiring minibuses – leaving you more time to relax!
mountainsviewhotel.com

Handpicked hotel
The perfect balance

Radisson Blu Addis Ababa
radissonblu.com/hotel-addisababa

Distance from airport
20 minutes

Located 20 minutes away from the airport and set in the heart of the city, the Radisson Blu is a welcome and affordable haven away from the Addis crowds.

When booking a hotel for a city break you generally want one of two things – a central location from which to soak up the sights and sounds of the city, or an affordable base camp for day trips around the region. The Radisson Blu in Addis Ababa ticks both boxes with its city centre address and budget-friendly accommodation that leaves you wanting for little during your stay.

The Radisson Blu is something of a restful haven at the heart of this historic and chaotic city. Set along a wide tree-lined street, near to the UN Conference Centre, Menelik II's Palace and Meskel Square, you are also just walking distance from the city's cosy espresso bars and bustling outdoor markets. And, while this isn't a hotel to luxuriate in and be dazzled by, it *will* cater to your every city break need.

Transfers to and from the airport are taken care of, there's complimentary high speed wi-fi in all rooms (a rarity in the city), and free late checkout up to 6pm if you're catching a late flight. The Radisson's Grab & Run takeaway breakfast – tea or coffee in disposable cups along with fresh fruits and pastries – is perfect for an early day trip before breakfast is served, or if you don't have time for a sit-down meal.

The spacious rooms have all the mod cons you'd expect from a modern hotel, and are everything you need after a long day on the tourist trail – most importantly a comfy bed!

The finishing touches

Feeling peckish? There's Verres en Vers, a French brasserie-style restaurant that serves breakfast, lunch and dinner buffets along with an a la carte menu that's arguably one of the best French offerings in Addis. For a bit of pampering, the hotel's Rainforest Day Spa offers a range of affordable massages and treatments, perfect after a tiring day out trekking or driving along Ethiopia's bumpy roads. And, in between all that, plan your itinerary over a cappuccino at Tomoca, which serves Ethiopia's finest coffee.

Striking the perfect balance between form and function, the Radisson Blu Addis Ababa is the perfect base for a weekend break.

Further afield

Kuriftu Resort and Spa is set on the edge of a mountain overlooking a crater lake, with some stunning views over Lake Tana. This luxury eco lodge, just 45 minutes from the airport, is well-known for its spa. (kurifturesortspa.com)

Out of
this world

Explore **the hottest place on earth**

Getting there
The only way to
visit this intimidating
landscape is an
organised tour with
a travel company. Try
wildfrontierstravel.com

When it comes to extreme travel destinations, there's nowhere like the Danakil Depression, with its searing temperatures, bubbling lava lakes and active volcano.

Imagine an other-worldly landscape of raging volcanoes, boiling sulphur springs and basins with salt flats; that's what you'll find at the Danakil Depression, the hottest place on earth. Sitting mostly below sea level in the Afar region of Ethiopia, this is one of the harshest landscapes on the planet and one of the most tectonically active areas, too. It's home to the legendary Erta Ale, one of the the most active volcanoes in Africa. There's a lava lake at its summit, which can be reached by foot or camel, in a journey that takes up to four hours. Needless to say, a gentle afternoon stroll it is not!

Live on the edge

However, if you like your holiday with a liberal helping of extreme adventure, then Danakil is the perfect destination. Daytime temperatures exceed 50°C, there is little to no shade to be found outside of your vehicle. and security can be an issue given the area's proximity to the Eritrean border. Tours must be taken with a registered tour company who will provide two Jeeps, a local guide and armed security to ensure your safety. You'll have to be self-sufficient when it comes to food and water, and you'll need to take camping and cooking gear since there's no accommodation or firewood in the region.

Take the challenge

If you're ready to brave the trip (and enjoy the subsequent bragging rights) be prepared to travel. It's a one hour flight from Addis to Mekele with Ethiopian Airlines, and then a four-hour drive to the Berahile, which offers good access to Dallol, Lake Asale and Erta Ale. Grab a window seat on the flight to Mekele as the mountain views are amazing.

Sulphur pools

Erta Ale volcano

Salt caravans

Berahile is situated around 120km from Mekele along the salt caravan route to Lake Asale. The route attracts a stream of salt caravans, with an estimated one million camels passing through annually.

Africa

Lake Nakuru

Kenya

It's all about the great outdoors, whether you lounge on glorious beaches in the coastal city of Mombasa or head inland to gaze at the wonders of the animal kingdom.

 Flight time
5 hours

 Door to door
30 minutes by car to Nairobi city centre; 1 hour flight or 5 hour drive from Nairobi to Masai Mara

 When to go
December to March, June to October

Kenya is the heart of East Africa, where you'll find one of the highest concentrations of wild animals on the planet. This corner of the globe is blessed with awe-inspiring scenery and incredibly varied natural beauty. From its wide, dry plains and lush, green forests, to its picture-perfect tropical beaches, the landscapes alone are breathtaking, never mind the stupendous wildlife that calls these vistas home. These include, of course, the Big Five. Traditionally the most coveted of game sights, all five species are here, doing what they have done for thousands of years: the magnificent lion, undisputed king of the African plains, the underestimated Cape buffalo, the extraordinary, galumphing African elephant, the elusive leopard and the lonesome, critically endangered rhinoceros.

For a more relaxing break, it's not all binoculars and safari shorts – Kenya's position on the Indian Ocean blesses its palm-fringed shores with white sand, warm, clear waters and a pleasantly balmy climate. The coastal towns of Mombasa, Malindi and Lamu are a fascinating blend of Swahili and Arab culture that enjoy a uniquely African beach holiday vibe, and some spectacular marine life is waiting to be explored amongst the coral reefs that stretch the length of Kenya's coast. But a trip to Kenya is more than a safari or a beach holiday, it's a chance to experience the spirit of Africa in all its guises – a vibrant culture, a perennial smile and a laid-back pace that will see all of life's worries melt away with a simple 'hakuna matata'.

Born to be wild

There is a whole host of safari companies that make adventure tourism in Kenya's famed national parks, from the wilderness of Masai Mara National Reserve to the heights of Mount Kenya National Park, easily accessible, even for those on a shorter timeframe. Safari camps and lodges vary from the rough and ready to uber-luxurious five-star options. Witnessing an alpha lion stalk across the dusty plains in the dawn light, or a herd of elephants cross a crocodile-infested river under the hot African sun, or simply sipping sundowners while the animal kingdom gathers at the watering hole below – these exhilarating experiences can be enjoyed in just a few days in Kenya.

Kenya
Essentials

From beach to bush, Kenya's varied landscape can bring you relaxation, adventure, or a heady mix of both.

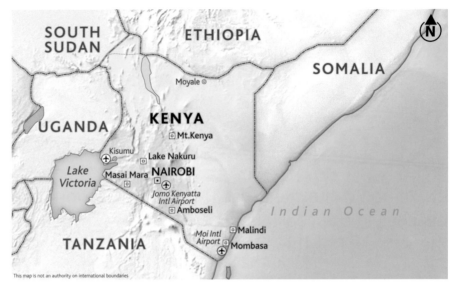

SOUTH SUDAN
ETHIOPIA
SOMALIA
Moyale ⊙
UGANDA
KENYA
⊡ Mt.Kenya
Kisumu
⊕ Lake Nakuru
Lake Victoria
Masai Mara
NAIROBI
⊕
Jomo Kenyatta Intl Airport
⊡ Amboseli
TANZANIA
Moi Intl Airport
⊡ Malindi
⊕ Mombasa
Indian Ocean

This map is not an authority on international boundaries

Getting there
Fly from Dubai, Abu Dhabi or Sharjah to Jomo Kenyatta International Airport in Nairobi with Air Arabia, Emirates, Etihad and Kenya Airways. Flights start from Dhs.1,495. RwandAir flies direct from Dubai to Mombasa.

Visas
Most nationalities need a tourist visa to enter Kenya, which is granted on arrival for US$ 50. Visit immigration.go.ke for details.

Time
One hour behind the UAE.

Climate
A pleasant climate all year round, averaging around 25°C. Evenings in the higher altitudes of the national parks can feel quite cool.

Language
Swahili and English.

Currency
Kenyan Shilling (KSh).
KSh 100 = Dhs4.32.

Vaccinations
Hepatitis A, Hepatitis B, Malaria, Meningitis Polio, Typhoid and Yellow Fever.

Best for... wildlife
Every year, from around June to September, more than two million herbivores make the 800km journey from the Serengeti in Tanzania in search of grazing ground. The enormous herds of the Great Migration are an incredible sight, and predators are hot on their tail to catch something tasty from this all-you-can-eat buffet.

Masai Mara National Reserve

See the Big Five against the beautiful backdrop of Kenya's game reserves with time to explore the country's vibrant capital.

Masai Mara

Kenya's most famous safari destination is incredibly popular for good reason. Covering a 1,510sqkm area in Southwestern Kenya, it is part of the enormous Mara-Serengeti ecosystem that stretches down through Tanzania. The sweeping Mara plains are home to thousands of mammals, ballooning to millions during the Great Migration. Sightings of lion, giraffe, elephant and hippo are pretty much guaranteed, while leopard, hyena and cheetah may be spotted on the prowl for wildebeest, zebra and gazelle.

Getting there

Accessed either by road or by air, it is a five-hour drive from Nairobi through the breathtaking Great Rift Valley (although the route involves some pretty bumpy tracks on approach to the reserve), or there are several companies, such as Safari Link, that run flights from the capital (Wilson Airport), taking around an hour. Several of the lodges have their own runway. Flying in is an experience in itself and, considering the time and discomfort that is cut from the journey, it's worth the extra spend.

Pick your spot

There are two distinct areas of the Masai Mara National Reserve. The Mara Triangle, which is strictly regulated to protect and conserve the wildlife, is accessed mainly by plane. The main, and more relaxed, part of the reserve is easier to reach from Nairobi by road and can therefore get quite crowded with white vans all vying for the best photo opportunity.

Safari drive

The classic safari experience, a safari drive with an experienced guide can get you hair-raisingly close to all manner of beasts. All tour companies, lodges and camps will arrange excursions into the bush, from early morning starts to watch the animals hunt for their breakfast, to late afternoon drives in the gorgeous light of an African sunset. Just don't forget your camera!

maasaimara.com/safaris

Nature calls

Camping in a national park, whether in a tiny two-man or the most luxurious of tented resorts, is a noisy experience. While the cackle of hyenas, strange yap of the zebras and unceasing thrumming of the cicadas makes for a fantastic soundtrack to the evening, it is not conducive to the most restful night's sleep. Earplugs are recommended!

Walk on the wild side

Several conservancies and ranches on the outskirts of Masai Mara National Reserve (as it's not allowed inside the park) can arrange for a walking safari with a specially trained Maasai guide. It is a thrilling way to get up close and personal with nature, and learning about the bush and its inhabitants from somebody who calls the landscape home is fascinating.

Up, up and away

Floating lazily over the savannah in a hot air balloon as an array of wildlife go about their morning is pretty special. With a bird's eye view you can gain access to areas even the toughest 4WD can only dream of reaching. It is particularly recommended during the Great Migration, when the plains are packed with animals as far as the eye can see. Some companies lay on a special Champagne breakfast in the Mara upon landing – it's a seriously stylish safari.

Horse riding safari

Dreams of thundering across the plains with a herd of zebra might just be realised on an African horseback safari. It's a chance to get off the beaten track with a calmer, more secluded and natural experience of the African wilderness. On the back of a horse, a shallow river can be easily crossed and narrow gorges make for fantastic exploration.

Meet the Maasai

Visiting a local Maasai tribe in their village is an experience well worth trying. You will meet Maasai families and be invited to take a nose around their homes. They'll tell you about their culture, food and traditions, and you'll learn what it's like to make a livelihood while sharing a neighbourhood with some of the deadliest predators in the world.

 Stay in Nairobi on arrival, then catch an early flight to Masai Mara in time for an afternoon safari drive. Spend two or three nights, before returning to Nairobi in the morning. The schedule for domestic flights goes by 'Africa time', and is quite relaxed, so leave time to account for a delayed return to Nairobi, and for the transfer between Jomo Kenyatta and Wilson Airport.

Giraffe Manor

David Sheldrick Wildlife Trust

Game for it?

Meaning 'barbecued meat' in Swahili, Nyama Choma is Kenya's favourite dish. The meat in question is often tastily grilled goat, but Nairobi's most famous grillhouse, the appropriately named Carnivore, also has more exotic cuts on its huge barbecue pit, including ostrich, crocodile and, wait for it, camel!

Nairobi

With a thriving cultural scene, world-class watering holes and wild Africa on its doorstep, Kenya's cosmopolitan capital has plenty to keep visitors busy.

Nairobi National Park

With the city's skyscrapers as a backdrop, Nairobi National Park is a bizarre 'safari' experience, but the animals wander freely around the open plains. There are no elephants, but there are many other species that will tick the boxes.

Nairobi National Museum

For a culture fix, Nairobi National Museum is a great place to learn about Kenya's rich history, from pre-colonial times to the melting pot of cultures that is modern-day Kenya. There are some great geological and natural history exhibits and a contemporary East African art gallery.

Langata Giraffe Centre

The African Fund for Endangered Wildlife's centre works to protect Rothschild giraffe, and at their centre the giraffes can be fed from atop a platform. Spend a night next door at Giraffe Manor (see p.134).

David Sheldrick Wildlife Trust

This elephant orphanage on the edge of Nairobi National Park works to rehabilitate young elephants and rhinos. It is open to visitors for one hour each morning, but for a more intimate experience, sponsor an elephant on the trust's website before arriving. As well as helping conserve an endangered species, you can take part in the evening feed. sheldrickwildlifetrust.org

Kitengela Glass Shop

There are several tourist markets in Nairobi for grabbing last-minute souvenirs, but for something more special, Kitengela Glass Shop has some wonderfully unique designs that are handmade using recycled glass.

Hiring a driver

The easiest way to get around Nairobi, or out of the city on a day trip, is to hire a local driver who knows the roads. Staff at your hotel should be able to put you in contact with a taxi driver; just be sure to agree on a reasonable price depending on how far you are going and how much of the day you need them.

Mount Kenya

And... relax

Out of the city

A day or overnight trip from Nairobi will take you through the Great Rift Valley, one of Africa's geological wonders and a habitat that transcends time. Views from the escarpment before descending are breathtaking, as the valley suddenly drops thousands of feet, affording views for miles.

Lake Naivasha

The lake itself is home to hundreds of hippos, and a trip on a long boat can get you pretty close to one of Africa's deadliest beasts. It is also a wonderful place to watch fish eagles swooping in and catching their prey. Drop by Elsamere Conservation Centre where you can enjoy 'Kenya's best afternoon tea' and learn about Joy Adamson, whose experience raising an orphaned lion cub inspired the film *Born Free* and a legacy of wildlife conservation. Other lodges on the shores of the lake include Lake Naivasha Sopa Resort and Camp Carnelley's, which does great food.

Mount Kenya National Park

Nanyuki, at the base of Mount Kenya, is where views of the rugged peaks of Africa's second highest mountain, reaching 5,199m, can be enjoyed from afar. The town is also a good base for hiking trips into the national park, which is rich with wildlife. There are several resorts on the outskirts, including eco-conscious Segera Retreat (segera.com). A popular stop-off on the way is Trout Tree Restaurant, where you can eat super fresh fish straight from the trout farm – in a tree.

Hell's Gate National Park

A fascinating hiking destination, Hell's Gate is the only national park in Kenya that visitors are allowed to explore on foot – and yes, there are lions! The volcanic landscape is cinematic, having inspired Disney animation *The Lion King*, with wonderful gorges, basalt towers, geysers and hot springs. Biking and camping are also possible.

Amboseli National Park

A five-hour drive south of Nairobi – or a quick and more comfortable flight transfer – Amboseli is set in the shadow of Africa's highest and most iconic peak, the volcanic cone of Mount Kilimanjaro, on the Tanzanian border. All of the Big Five species can be found here, and there are, of course, several luxury retreats, such as Amboseli Serena Safari Lodge (serenahotels.com), as well as some more humble dwellings from which to base a safari trip and enjoy romantic views of snow-capped Kilimanjaro.

Segera Retreat

Kenya
Places to stay

Kichwa Tembo

Masai Mara

Karen Blixen Camp

The height of safari comfort, each luxury tent at this eco-camp has a view over the magical Mara River. Guests can watch Africa's greatest show from the comfort of an armchair, with hippos, giraffes, elephants and more all coming to the river to play. Romantic meals can be taken right in the bush. karenblixencamp.com

Keekorok Lodge

A large lodge, Keekorok has comfortable rooms and chalets, all with patios overlooking the reserve or the swimming pool. It is more affordable than some of the more luxurious camps and lodges in the Mara, but still an indulgent safari experience. wildernesslodges.co.ke

Kichwa Tembo

This family-friendly camp sits in the path of the annual Great Migration on its own private concession overlooking the Sabaringo River. The camp is run by &Beyond, who work hard on conservation and sustainability with local communities. They also run nearby Bateleur Camp, for a truly luxurious and exclusive safari experience. andbeyondafrica.com

Mara Explorers Camp

An African safari doesn't have to blow the budget, and if you're willing to forgo the private butler or even a hot shower, there are many more affordable options. Staying in a basic permanent safari tent with just a Maasai warrior for protection can add to the wilderness experience and give you a true sense of adventure. maraexplorers.com

Riverside Camp

Owned and run by Maasai, Riverside is a great budget option, which does have flushing toilets and running water. riversidecampmara.com

Kichwa Tembo

 Park fees can change quite often, but are currently around US$ 70 for adult foreign nationals. The more upmarket accommodation will have all fees included in the package, but if you are doing a more budget safari, check what is included in the price as other costs can include vehicle fees, driver hire, and ranger hire.

Sankara Nairobi

Giraffe Manor

Nairobi

Ole-Sereni

For a herd of wildebeest sweeping majestically across the plain, you'll be better off in the Masai Mara during the Great Migration. But for some wildlife spotting in the city, the Ole-Sereni overlooks Nairobi National Park, where there are a few wildebeest, plus giraffe, zebra and lots more species. The hotel is conveniently close to Jomo Kenyatta International Airport.
ole-serenihotel.com

Sankara Nairobi

This five-star haven of luxury in the upmarket Westlands area is something of an expat hangout. The hotel's rooftop pool is a glam yet chilled place to have an evening drink and serves tasty bar snacks. As a base for exploring the capital, Sankara Nairobi is a pretty plush place to start, and genuine works of modern East African art create a sense of place. sankara.com

Tribe

A trendy boutique hotel in Nairobi's Diplomatic District, Tribe is attached to The Village Market – a smart leisure and retail complex where you can pick up some souvenirs and Maasai handicrafts. Impressive examples of local Kenyan art adorn the interior, lending a cultural touch to this otherwise polished hotel. There's also a spa, well-stocked library, rooftop bar and heated pool surrounded by waterfalls and gardens.
tribe-hotel.com

Giraffe Manor is a boutique hotel in a colonial manor in Nairobi. A herd of giraffes live onsite and wander freely around the grounds, often poking their heads in the windows to see what food they can forage from the breakfast table. Book early!
giraffemanor.com

Sarova Whitesands Beach Resort & Spa

Tamarind Village

Comfortable, spacious apartments with between one and three bedrooms, that take inspiration from Mombasa's colonial past and Swahili heritage. Each apartment has a peaceful veranda overlooking the creek and the Old Town, and activities and watersports can be arranged. tamarind.co.ke

WaterLovers Beach Resort

This small boutique hotel is actually 35km south of Mombasa's Moi International Airport, on the beautiful Diani Beach. The resort's eco-tourism policy gives it a rustic, African feel, and it is home to a family of Colobus monkeys. As well as well-equipped suites, there is a villa that accommodates up to eight people. waterlovers.it

WaterLovers Beach Resort

Island charm

The island of Lamu is a heavenly place to escape to, steeped in Swahili culture. Walk through narrow alleyways and admire traditional architecture, and relax on its quiet, pristine beaches. It is best reached on a domestic flight from Nairobi or Mombasa.

On the coast

The Driftwood Club

A small but wonderfully rustic, family-run place on Watamu Beach, a couple of hours north of Mombasa in Malindi. It has comfortable thatched beachfront cottages, authentic food and a blissfully laid-back atmosphere. It's the perfect place to lose yourself 'in the moment'. driftwoodclub.com

Sarova Whitesands Beach Resort & Spa

This sprawling resort within Mombasa Marine Park has five outdoor swimming pools, three restaurants and a late night beach bar. Glass bottom boats are available for exploring the marine life, and watersports on offer include sailing trips and jet ski hire. There's also an onsite PADI certified diving school. sarovahotels.com/whitesands

Journey into the wild

Explore **Lake Nakuru National Park**

Bird's eye view
Sunrise is when the animals are at their most active – a wonderful time to go hot air ballooning. Visit kws.org for details.

Huge flocks of brilliant pink flamingos are the highlight of Lake Nakuru National Park, but there's every chance you'll see leopards and white rhinos too.

If you've ever sat at home watching *National Geographic* and dreamt of spotting leopards as the dusty African wind blows in your face, then a safari adventure in Lake Nakuru is definitely for you. Days spent tracking wild creatures in their natural habitats, evenings around the campfire re-living the day's adventure, and nights spent listening to nature's own symphony – it's truly magical.

Where the wild things are

While smaller and quieter than many of the other national parks, Lake Nakuru should not be overlooked. Here you can watch a sea of flamingos feeding in the shallows, before taking flight in a frothy cloud of pink. As well as being a birdwatcher's paradise, a slow-paced game drive through Lake Nakuru will bring you within touching distance of some mesmerising creatures – water buffalo grazing on shallow slopes, an African eagle perched in the trees, and giraffes poking their towering heads out of the taller branches.

Both black and white rhino are most likely to be spotted at the water's edge, although the former are harder to spot, and there's a herd of hippos in the northern part of the lake. The park is best explored in the gentle sun of the late afternoon. You can circle the lake clockwise by car, then drive to the top of Baboon Cliff for a stunning sunset view.

No safari would be complete without seeing at least one of the Big Five – and there's every chance you'll see the elusive leopard here. The best place to see these spectacular creatures is high up in the branches of the fever trees that line the shimmering lake; just keep your eyes peeled for the leopard's tail dangling below the branches as he escapes the heat of the day.

Plan your trip

From Lake Nakuru take an unforgettable drive through the Great Rift Valley to a tented camp in the Masai Mara for more safari fun.

African adventure

It's a three-hour car journey along some of Kenya's better roads from Nairobi to Lake Nakuru; while you could do the trip in one day, it would be pretty exhausting. Alternatively, you can take a 25-minute flight from Nairobi (airkenya.com). Once in the park there's a small choice of cottages and suites vs tented camps, all of which organise game drives, horse riding and birdwatching tours.

While not five-star luxury, the rooms at Lake Nakuru Lodge (lakenakurulodge.com) have all mod cons – and a front door. For style and substance, the chalets at Sarova Lion Hill Game Lodge (sarovahotels.com) are divine. To live the safari dream though, stay under the canvas at Flamingo Hill Camp (flamingohillcamp.com). But be warned: there are no fences – it makes a late night dash for the loo a heart-racing experience!

On safari

From the 3am laughs of hyenas outside your tent to the early wake-up calls of baboons on your balcony, there's never a dull moment in Lake Nakuru. And whether you enjoy sundowners on the terrace or bush tucker by the fire as rhinos and gazelles graze nearby, nothing quite beats going 'into the wild'.

Barefoot on the beach

Sunbathing in Mombasa

Kenya is full of surprises. It's not all big cats and dawn game drives – there's smooth white sandy beaches too. Lots of them. Head to the bustling island city of Mombasa and you'll find a string of luxury hotels hugging the powdery white shores of the Indian Ocean. This is where temperatures hover around a perfectly balmy 30°C (with tropical downpours around April and May, and October and November). There are no early wake-up calls or bumpy roads to travel – just lazing in a hammock, snorkelling crystal clear waters, and deep sea fishing. That's as hard as life gets here.

A melting pot

Away from the sprawling beach resorts, wooden dhows you'd expect to see in the Arabian Gulf, 16th century European defensive forts and British colonial architecture all sit side by side against a backdrop of urban, cosmopolitan Africa. But, while the city's buzzing nightlife, famous restaurants and historical sights are all worth exploring, it is Mombasa's idyllic beaches that are the main draw.

Fly direct
RwandAir is currently the only airline to fly direct from the UAE to Mombasa, leaving from Dubai three times a week. rwandair.com

Kenya's picture-perfect stretch of palm-fringed shoreline attracts divers, adventurers and beach bums alike.

Watamu Beach

Further up the coast towards Malindi, a scenic journey of around two hours, is Watamu Beach. The diving and snorkelling around here is excellent, and it is an important turtle breeding area, thousands of which lay their eggs from January to April. If you'd rather not swim, there are plenty of glass bottom boat and fishing trips available.

 During the rainy season, from April to May and October to November, hotel rates on Kenya's coast drop quite a bit, and there are fewer travellers around. The rains often only last for a few hours and can be quite pleasant.

Back to nature

Shimba Hills National Park is an easy day trip from the Mombasa area. This wildlife park is home to a healthy elephant population, as well as some rare species of antelope and the colobus monkey.

Nyali Beach

Mombasa's Nyali Beach has been a popular destination for decades. Beachside resorts are well-established along its stretch and a wealth of watersports are on offer from many of the hotels. The Voyager Resort offers total relaxation on the doorstep of an 18-hole golf course, casinos and a crocodile sanctuary. Kitesurfing has become increasingly popular around the world, and Mombasa's reef-protected shallow waters, soft sand and good winds make it a great place to learn. You're only a short taxi ride from several top-class restaurants too.

Diani Beach

Around an hour south of Mombasa, Diani Beach is well worth the journey from the city. Away from the urban action, life on Diani Beach is slower and more peaceful. It's the place to go for a truly relaxing beach holiday with some of that legendary African hospitality. Exclusive beach resorts with all the trimmings, eco-resorts and more rustic, budget-friendly accommodation are all available, as well as some options for wellness and activity retreats.

Africa

Intendance Bay, Mahe

Seychelles

This sunny slice of the tropics offers a dreamlike setting that's as far removed from mass tourism – and the rest of the world – as you can get.

Flight time
4 hours 40 minutes

Door to door
15 minutes by car from the airport to central Mahe; 1 hour ferry ride to Praslin, where you can get a 30-minute boat trip to La Digue

When to go
April to September

Sometimes you're just looking for some respite from the circus of city life – a more relaxed type of holiday where you can, quite simply, get lazy. The Seychelles offers just that – with all the laidback tempo of an uncrowded desert island. There are few travel destinations that evoke the image of an island paradise as much as the Seychelles, and with good reason. Lush unexplored jungles, powdery white-sand beaches and an azure ocean teeming with marine life create the overall impression of a modern-day Eden.

The Seychelles is made up of 115 tropical islands (you can stay on 15 of them) scattered through the Indian Ocean, 1,000 miles east of Africa. You can hop between these tropical islands – some hilly and granitic, others low-lying and coral-based – in a light aircraft or by boat across coral seas. Flight transfer times from the mainland airport vary between 15 minutes and one hour, depending on which island you are visiting, so you can make the very most of a short break.

The largest of the islands is Mahe, but the smaller Praslin and La Digue have just as much to offer. There is plenty to do at the many luxury, villa-based resorts such as swimming, snorkelling, diving, tennis, and yoga. But the Seychelles is all about relaxing on the sunny beaches, feeling the warm tropical water lapping against your toes, and playing at being Robinson Crusoe with a tropical cocktail in one hand, a book in the other.

The great escape

Proving that you don't need to travel far for utter seclusion, the Seychelles offers quiet beaches and isolated resorts less than five hours from the UAE. One of the most environmentally-conscious nations in the world, this cluster of islands is practically one large nature reserve. There's an abundance of spectacular fauna and flora to be found in its sprawling reserves and national parks. Stroll around the Botanical Gardens of Mahe; listen to the soundtrack of exotic bird calls on Praslin; and admire the rare giant plodding Aldabra tortoises on Cerf Island. For pure and natural fun, both above and below the water, this is Mother Nature's very best work.

Seychelles
Essentials

The lush jungles, abundant oceans and pristine beaches of the Seychelles are all the antidote you need to busy city living.

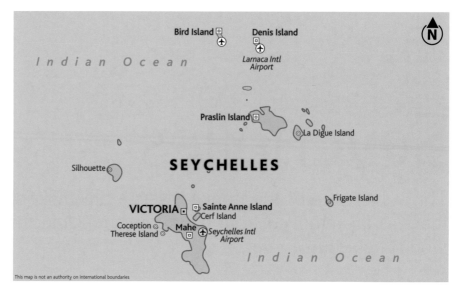

Bird Island
Denis Island
Indian Ocean
Larnaca Intl Airport
Praslin Island
La Digue Island
SEYCHELLES
Silhouette
Frigate Island
VICTORIA · Sainte Anne Island
Cerf Island
Coception Therese Island
Mahe
Seychelles Intl Airport
Indian Ocean

This map is not an authority on international boundaries

Getting there
Fly from Dubai or Abu Dhabi to Seychelles International Airport on Mahe with Air Seychelles, Emirates and Etihad Airways, from Dhs.3,800 return.

Visas
All nationalities can enter the Seychelles; all you need is a valid passport, return or onward ticket, proof of accommodation and sufficient funds. For more information, email info@immigration.gov.sc.

Time
Same time zone as the UAE.

Climate
The weather is always warm in the Seychelles, ranging between 24°C and 32°C with the hottest months falling between December and April.

Language
English, French and Creole.

Currency
Seychelles Rupee (SCR). 10 SCR = Dhs.3.

Vaccinations
Hepatitis A, Hepatitis B, MMR (Measles, Mumps, Rubella) and Typhoid.

Great for... family getaways
The Seychelles' luxury resorts are small pieces of paradise not just for honeymooners but increasingly for family holidays too. Enjoy some good old-fashioned family time and swim, paddle, kayak and snorkel. Then, book the little ones into a kids' club if you fancy some time to yourself; most resorts offer excellent childcare facilities.

Vallée de Mai, Praslin

Petite Anse Bay, Mahe

The glorious sandy beaches of the Seychelles don't just exist in glossy brochures – this place screams 'get me there now!'

Mahe

As the largest island in the Seychelles archipelago and the home of its capital city Victoria, Mahe is the island that most travellers flock to. Although Victoria has its own low-key charms, including a vibrant local arts scene and a national museum, for the majority of holidaymakers it's Mahe's natural beauty that is the biggest draw. The lush, mountainous interior contrasts wonderfully with the powder-white beaches and azure water; head for the hills for a gentle stroll or jungle hike, or explore the coast to discover the best sunbathing and snorkelling spots in the Seychelles.

Beau Vallon

If searching for entertainment outside of your resort, head for Beau Vallon, a town in the north-west of Mahe. There are low-key beachside bars and restaurants where you can sample traditional Creole cuisine. Driving along the coast, you'll pass quiet, picturesque beaches; all you have to do is pick your patch of sand for the day. Many have market stalls selling fresh tropical fruit.

Mission Point

This popular viewpoint is close to the remains of Mission Lodge, a former missionary settlement. You'll find it high up in the green hills of the island; time your visit with the early evening and enjoy views of a Seychelles sunset.

Morne Seychellois

The beauty of the Seychelles is not limited to the beaches. There are several nature trails to explore in the Morne Seychellois National Park, where hikers can tackle winding trails, steep slopes and the country's highest peak (905 metres). It's not an easy climb to reach the highest slopes, but you'll be rewarded by gorgeous panoramic views.

Victoria

Known for being the smallest capital in the world, Victoria boasts a number of museums, churches and art galleries. However, most places close on Saturday morning and don't re-open until Monday.

Vallée de Mai, Praslin

Vallee de Mai

This nature reserve is a UNESCO World Heritage Site on the island of Praslin and is estimated to be 650 million years old. Here, you can marvel at a host of rare indigenous flora and fauna including the symbol of the Seychelles, the Coco de Mer tree, and its national bird, the black parrot. Some resorts, including the Four Seasons Seychelles, organise trips to this tourist attraction.

Pick of the beaches

If you're visiting Praslin on a romantic holiday for two, then Cote D'or is the perfect choice of beach, being both beautiful and secluded. This stunning stretch of silver sand and turquoise water is made for sharing with that special someone.

Pearls of Praslin

Not only is the Black Pearl Ocean Farm a great place to learn more about the Seychelles' interesting history of pearl harvesting, you can also buy a pretty memento of your trip at the Black Pearl Shop next door.

Praslin

The second-largest island in the Seychelles provides the perfect balance between the relative busyness of Mahe and the quaint but quiet La Digue. Praslin's most popular attractions can be found either by the sea or under it. In fact, some travellers argue that the beaches of Praslin – such as the stunning Anse Lazio, with its crystal clear water, silky white sand, and dramatic granite boulders – are even superior to those of larger Mahe. Praslin is also a great base for a spot of island hopping with two of the best snorkelling spots in the Seychelles – Ile Felicite and Ile Cocos – located within easy reach. You can fly from Mahe to Praslin with Air Seychelles (airseychelles.com).

Fish market, Victoria

Feeling peckish? The day's catch can be on your table for lunch

Curieuse Island

Bird Island

La Digue

La Digue is the smallest of the three main islands in the Seychelles, and is also known for being the quietest. There are no cars on the island, although you can hire bicycles for exploring the area. La Digue is also renowned for having some of the Seychelles' loveliest beaches which, coupled with its beauty and seclusion, makes it extremely popular with visitors in search of a romantic break. There are plenty of stunning stretches of coastline to choose from, but one of the finest has to be Anse Source D'Argent.

Flora and fauna

This peaceful island is home to a wide array of flora and fauna, including the black paradise flycatcher, one of the rarest birds on earth. You can also expect to see beautiful orchids, blossoming hibiscus and sweet-smelling vanilla vines during your travels.

Black parrot

Taste of the tropics

Influenced by French, Indian, Asian, African, Malagasy, and their own local cultures, the people of the Seychelles cook up exotic Creole dishes. Think croissants for breakfast, grilled fish with ginger for lunch, exotic coconut curries, and evening BBQs on the beach.

Island hopping

In such a vast archipelago, there are plenty of other areas worth exploring. Some of the lesser known, quieter islands are perfect for a day trip. The waters surrounding Ile Felicite and Ile Cocos, which can be reached off the coast of La Digue, are teeming with marine life and offer superb snorkelling opportunities. Alternatively, for the ultimate in seclusion and exclusivity, head for one of the smaller islands that boast their own private resort or lodge.

Bird Island

The perfect eco-tourism destination, with a sole hotel, Bird Island Lodge. Some of the species that you might see include green turtles, giant tortoises, dolphins, manta rays and whales. birdislandseychelles.com

Curieuse Island

The unique appearance of Curieuse Island is due to the presence of red earth intermingling with rich green vegetation. Here you'll find Coco De Mer plants that are endemic to the Seychelles, takamaka trees, large Aldabra tortoises and green turtles.

Sainte Anne Island

Just 5km from Victoria, this is the largest island in the Sainte Anne Marine National Park and is home to the exclusive all-inclusive Sainte Anne Resort & Spa. beachcomber-hotels.com

The Anse Major range, Mahe

Seychelles
Places to stay

Kempinski Seychelles Resort

Mahe

Le Meridien Fisherman's Cove

Banyan Tree Seychelles

The site of this enchanting resort that overlooks the picturesque Intendance Bay was originally bought by iconic British actor Peter Sellers and the Beatle, George Harrison, in the 1970s, who intended to use it as their own island home. Today, it's a luxury resort with a beautiful selection of villas, from hillside havens overlooking the ocean to beachfront spa properties with their own steam rooms and massage pavilions.
banyantree.com

Kempinski Seychelles Resort

This stunning resort in Baie Lazare in the south of Mahe is perfect for a romantic break with its flawless beach, luxurious rooms and hillside spa. There are plenty of ways to stay active, from snorkelling off the beach to cooling off in the Olympic-length swimming pool. Round off your day with a sumptuous meal at l'Indochine.
kempinski.com

Le Meridien Fisherman's Cove

Nestled in the western-most tip of Beau Vallon, Le Meridien Fisherman's Cove is an idyllic haven that is perfect for sunworshippers, thanks to its expansive white sand beach and oceanside swimming pools. The lush gardens make you feel as though you have escaped to a tropical island, and the popular restaurant Le Bourgeois serves up delicious Creole cuisine while you soak in glorious views of the Indian Ocean.
lemeridienfishermanscove.com

Sunset Beach Hotel

This is boutique accommodation in the heart of vibrant Beau Vallon that doesn't sacrifice luxury or style. There's a secluded, pristine beach where adventurous guests can borrow snorkel equipment to explore the coral reefs that teem with marine life just offshore, or simply sunbathe on the sand.
thesunsethotelgroup.com

Sunset Beach Hotel

Photo courtesy of Banyan Tree Hotels & Resorts

 Although the Seychelles is usually associated with five-star luxury, it is possible to enjoy a holiday on a more modest budget. There are plenty of quaint, affordable self-catering facilities and guesthouses. Try exploring your options in the busier areas of Mahe such as Beau Vallon. At Beau Vallon Residence (beauvallonresidence.sc), it is possible to find a room for Dhs.240-380 per night – but these book up fast.

The Islands

New Emerald Cove Hotel

Located on the beautiful island of Praslin, the New Emerald Cove Hotel is built in its own private cove at the beautiful Anse La Farine beach. What truly sets this luxurious resort apart is the fact that it is only accessible by sea, making you feel as though they you're on your own secluded private island. There's plenty to do within its vicinity, from big game fishing to trekking and excursions, but it's the snorkelling and diving off the main reef directly in front of the hotel that is out of this world. You can choose to do everything, or simply relax and do nothing at all. emerald.sc

Raffles Praslin Seychelles

This stunning island getaway is the first purpose-built Raffles resort, as well as being home to the first Raffles signature spa. Take your pick of 86 luxurious villas, many of which boast spectacular views of the Indian Ocean and nearby Curieuse Island. It's the perfect resort for adventurous holidaymakers, with plenty of attractions nearby including the UNESCO World Heritage Site, Vallee de Mai, and Curieuse Marine National Park.
raffles.com/praslin

Photo courtesy of Banyan Tree Hotels & Resorts

La Digue Island Lodge

This attractive boutique hotel is a laidback alternative to the usual resort chains. The lack of traffic on the island – there are no cars, only bicycles and ox-drawn carts – adds to the air of peaceful seclusion that makes you feel like you've stepped back in time. The charming A-frame chalets and the beautiful Anse Reunion beach add to the island romance. ladigue.sc

Bird Island Lodge

Bird Island Lodge is the sole hotel on the stunning wildlife reserve of Bird Island. A 30-minute flight from Mahe International Airport, it is a truly private paradise – with no phones or TVs on the island, it allows you to truly unwind and get back to nature. There's a pristine 5km white-sand beach, plus plenty of opportunities for spotting exotic wildlife from dolphins to turtles.
birdislandseychelles.com

Cerf Island Resort

Holidaymakers who long for an Eden-esque paradise should look no further than this island getaway. Boasting just 24 luxurious villas, the peace and luxury of this resort make it perfect for a romantic break. Cerf Island is 1km long, and you'll find that its convenient location at the entrance to the Sainte Anne National Marine Park means there's incredible offshore diving and snorkelling if you're up for exploring the underwater playground. cerf-resort.com

New Emerald Cove Hotel

Sunset Beach Hotel, Mahe

Handpicked hotel
Paradise found

Four Seasons Seychelles Resort & Spa
fourseasons.com/seychelles

Distance from airport
30 minutes

Four Seasons Seychelles Resort & Spa

Lose yourself in your own private Eden of lush greenery, flawless beaches and peaceful seclusion.

The Four Seasons Seychelles is as elusive as it is exclusive. Although the journey from Mahe International Airport takes just 30 minutes, the drive into the island's interior feels like you're leaving the world behind. Comprising 67 villas and suites nestled on stilts in the lush, green hills of Petite Anse Bay, the overall impression is that you've arrived at your own Eden — albeit one with its own private infinity plunge pool.

The influence of French colonial and traditional Creole elements can be seen in the white-washed timber, wooden floors and vivid blues of the rooms. There are plenty of places for soaking up the sun, as well as room for a candlelit dinner if you'd rather order in than eat out. In many ways, there's no reason to ever leave your villa.

The best of the beaches

As tempting as it would be to hide out in your hillside haven, you'd miss the resort's biggest draw: the beach. Even the best photographs can't do it justice; the beach is a riot of vivid colours — silky-soft white sand, luminous blue waves and slate-grey granite boulders, all set against emerald-green hills overlooking the Indian Ocean. There are plenty of sun loungers and umbrellas where you'll be served iced water and fresh juice — there's even sunscreen on hand.

If you fancy something more energetic than sunbathing, there are kayaks, stand up paddleboards and snorkelling equipment on offer to help you explore the bay, and an on-site marine expert holds regular guided snorkelling tours of the offshore reef.

For lunch, Kannel, the beachside restaurant nestled among the cinnamon trees next to the hotel pool, serves up a delicious Grill of the Day: try their incredible fish tacos (accompanied by the Cocktail of the Day if you're feeling in the holiday mood).

Dining and unwinding

For whiling away the late afternoon hours, there's no better place to go than the resort spa. From the beautiful relaxation room overlooking the ocean, to the range of natural, luxury products and soothing signature treatments (see below), a spa visit is a great way to transition into holiday mode or treat yourself at the end of your stay. An afternoon of pampering will leave you glowing and refreshed for the evening.

When it comes to dining, ZEZ may be the most romantic place in the Seychelles, with its soft lighting, sea views, and delicious cuisine. For a truly romantic experience, book a table in the open air, and dine under the stars while being caressed by the ocean breeze: the perfect end to a day in paradise.

Every Saturday, the Four Seasons celebrates Creole culture with an evening of traditional food, drink, music and dance

The star of the spa

The resort spa has a number of signature treatments, but the star of the show is undoubtedly the Hilltop Fusion. Customised for each individual, this 60-90 minute massage uses the spa's new Yii-King range, an organic collection based on a 4,000-year-old holistic healing philosophy. Medium to firm pressure melts away tension and quiets your mind.

Sainte Anne Marine Park

Life on the ocean wave

Exploring tropical reefs

Free as a bird
Staying on La Digue?
Hire a bike, throw
your snorkel gear and
a picnic in the basket,
and head to a
secluded beach.

Stay close to the water to discover the pride and joy of sunny Seychelles.

With more than 100 islands, crystal-clear waters, an array of marine life and warm temperatures all year round, the Seychelles is the perfect destination for watersports lovers, whether you're hoping to delve into the deep or happy to drift along the surface.

Dive straight in

The Seychelles is one of the best diving destinations in the world, if you're up for taking the plunge. Fisherman's Cove Reef is a popular site with novice divers, with many a Hawksbill turtle to see; and dives down to 45m at Shark Bank are rewarded with sightings of huge grouper, barracuda and stingrays. Both sites are accessed from Mahe. The shallow waters and abundant coral reefs have meant there are many shipwrecks to explore for divers. The most spectacular is the oil tanker Ennerdale, which is about 30m deep, eight miles north-east of Victoria, and home to whale sharks (in season).

From the top

Snorkelling is a great option for those who wish to explore the world beneath the waves but without getting in too deep (no pun intended). You don't need a boat trip to find a great snorkelling spot (although the marine parks listed right are well worth the excursion). Many hotels including the Four Seasons Seychelles and Sunset Beach Hotel have excellent coral just off the beach.

Visit from May to September for the best windsurfing conditions. Most islands cater to surfers of all levels; check out wannasurf. com for a complete rundown of spots. What's more, the warm calm seas of the Seychelles are perfectly suited to stand up paddleboarding (SUP). As you gently paddle along, you can soak up the rays, glimpse some of the sea creatures and experience a challenging full-body workout.

Port Launay

When to go

The best times to go diving or snorkelling are from March to May and September to November, when the water is calm, the temperatures are warm, and visibility is at its best. However, June to August is the best time to spot whale sharks.

Baie Ternay

Located off Mahe's coast, this is regarded as the finest marine park in the Seychelles; you could be lucky enough to see eagle rays, reef sharks and turtles, depending on the season.

Port Launay

The snorkelling and diving conditions in this stunning marine park are excellent, and there are also a number of pristine, secluded beaches for soaking up the sun.

Sainte Anne

The first marine park to be set up in the Seychelles, this park extends over six islands including Cerf Island and Ile Cachee. It's especially well known for its population of green turtles.

Silhouette Island

The largest of the marine parks, Silhouette Island has been designated as a protected area since 1987. It's known for the dramatic granitic rock formations that slope steeply and teem with marine life.

Eurasia

The Old City walls, Baku

Azerbaijan

Don't be quick to rule out this eastern European backwater. It's a unique getaway where flame-shaped skyscrapers stand alongside medieval fortresses and donkeys battle with luxury 4WDs.

Flight time
2 hours 55 minutes

Door to door
30-40 minutes by taxi from the airport to Baku city centre; 30-40 minutes by bus

When to go
March to October

No longer the Baku of beyond, the cultural capital of Azerbaijan is rapidly changing and fast becoming a rather surprising party town. It's close enough to pop over for a weekend, is scattered with affordable accommodation and is a journey into the unknown – if you like that kind of thing.

Alternately called the Paris of the East and the Next Dubai, the oil-rich Baku is well poised to become the Middle East's next big luxury travel destination. Culturally, its main claim to fame is the well-preserved Old City, a maze of honey-coloured limestone streets dating back to the Arab conquest that's full of mosques, caravanserais (traditional roadside inns) and madrasas (religious schools), surrounded by 13ft-thick walls. Once the sun sets, its urban nightlife, array of ambient jazz clubs, and world-class ballet performances bring this modern, cosmopolitan hotspot into its own. Take a trip over to the capital between late May and early June, and you can soak up the sounds of the annual Jazz Festival – the open-air brass, bass and drum performances in Fountain Square are nothing if not unique.

A short distance away from the capital are mountainside villages, fascinating ruins, and rural communities that still live a traditional lifestyle – all of which are perfect for a day trip out of the city. From the beauty of the High Caucasus mountain range in the north to the lush tropical regions of the south, and back to the breakneck pace and exciting buzz of modern-day Baku, Azerbaijan offers a unique, culturally rich way of life.

Off the well-worn tourist path

Sometimes it's just better to explore a path less travelled. And, while some of us may have seen Baku in the Bond movie, *The World is Not Enough*, or as the host of Eurovision 2012, it has largely stayed out of the tourism limelight. That's why now is the time to explore this ex-Soviet city and its surrounds – before everyone else does. This is a land of the weird and wonderful – from a quirky miniature book museum to mud volcanoes and fiery mountains – and where else can you drink sweet tea in cave-like dining rooms, party 'til dawn at Chevalier, and bathe in oil. Intrigued...?

Azerbaijan
Essentials

GEORGIA

RUSSIA

Nabran

Zagatala

Guba

Caspian Sea

Ganja
Intl Airport

Ganja

ARMENIA

AZERBAIJAN

Sumqayit

Heydar Aliyev
Intl Airport

Absheron
Peninsula

Baku

Istisu

TURKEY

Nakhchivan

Lankaran

Lankaran
Intl Airport

IRAN

This map is not an authority on international boundaries.

N

With its handsome old buildings and cobbled streets, a city break to Baku is like a romantic trip to an open air museum.

Getting there
Fly from Dubai or Abu Dhabi to Heydar Aliyev International Airport with Azerbaijan Airlines, Emirates, flydubai, Qatar Airways and Turkish Airlines from Dhs.1,300 return.

Visas
All visitors to Azerbaijan, except Turkish, Georgian and CIS nationals, must obtain a single or double entry visa (valid from three to 90 days) prior to arrival in the country. Apply online at evisa.mfa.gov.az.

Time
One hour ahead of the UAE.

Climate
Azerbaijan has a seasonal, Mediterranean-like climate with hot, dry summers (25°C-35°C) and fairly mild winters (3°C-10°C).

Language
Azerbaijani; English is not widely spoken.

Currency
The new manat (AZN).
1 AZN = Dhs.4.7.

Vaccinations
Diphtheria, Hepatitis A and B, Malaria and Tetanus.

Best for... nightlife
Baku is 'the next big thing' after Beirut, with clubs including X-Site and the kitschy Chevalier; some of the more trendy clubs have a high minimum spend, so be prepared. There's a big jazz scene in Azerbaijan where, more than anything, the locals listen to mugham jazz, a fusion of jazz and folk music.

Ateshgah Fire Temple

Government House

Climb Maiden's Tower, eat lunch at Fountain Square, walk along the Boulevard and listen to jazz until the early hours. And that's just one day...

Baku

The capital of Azerbaijan is a city within a city: Old City (Icheri Sheher), nestled within the modernised Downtown district. Ancient history and culture live on in the monuments within Old City (p.174), the caravanserais, tandoor bakers, and inevitable carpet shops. In Downtown, designer boutiques jostle for seafront space with luxurious hotels, and high-rises tower over museums from the Soviet era.

Old City

The Boulevard

Enjoy an afternoon stroll along this three-kilometre promenade, which runs along the seafront in Downtown Baku. Admire the architecture, sip coffee in one of the many cafes or enjoy the thrills of the antique carousels, bumper cars and Ferris wheel with the family. The Boulevard is home to the International Mugham Centre, a musical fountain, the world's second-highest flagpole and the Park Bulvar shopping mall.

Martyrs' Alley

This sombre monument to those killed when the Soviet Army invaded Baku in 1990 has become a cemetery for other war heroes. A maze of walkways leads to the eastern edge of the park, with great views over Downtown, or take the funicular (railway) down the hill. Further south are terraces of graves; it feels every inch like a war cemetery. At the end of the rows of graves is a lookout point and a teashop, and there's an eternal flame burning in memory of unnamed martyrs.

Azerbaijan History Museum

Also in Downtown is one of Baku's best museums. Housed in the former residence of oil baron Zeynalabdin Taghiyev, this mansion is truly unique with traditional exhibits on the ground floor and Taghiyev's renovated residence upstairs. It is worth paying extra for a guide to get the full experience. Don't miss the sitting room, which is completely covered in tiny mirrors.

Baku city centre

Culture & heritage

There are a number of other large museums in Baku's Downtown area, which offer a good flavour of different aspects of Azeri culture. An impressive Soviet-era pseudo-Greek acropolis houses an interesting Carpet Museum, which charts the history of Azeri carpet-making and includes over 1,000 rare and beautiful rugs from Azerbaijan, as well as knotted and flat weave carpets from all regions. A guided tour (AZN3 extra) helps to put the designs in context and to explain the significance of their symbols. In the same building are the Theatre Museum and Museum of Independence; less compelling but worth a visit nonetheless.

Fountain Square

This crowded square in Downtown, with its sounds of cascading water and children's laughter, is a nice place to enjoy the beautiful fountains or people-watch from its shady benches. Many people come to here just to stroll or hang out. The square never closes and is typically at its busiest around 9pm, which is dinnertime for most Azeris. A favourite beefburger joint, Sunset Cafe, is located just off the square, as is MUM, a large Soviet-style department store that sells all kinds of items from gold to Russian dolls.

Traditional bazaars

There are two well-known flea markets, Gentjilk and Airport Bazaar. The latter is bigger, housing hundreds of vendors and selling everything from teapots to car tyres – at rock bottom prices. The name is somewhat misleading: this market is nowhere near the airport, and while you can find just about anything, you won't find much of an aeronautical variety.

Reigniting Baku

Baku Flame Towers is a striking new addition to the skyline of Baku. The three flame-shaped towers, clad in orange and blue-tinted glass, include a Fairmont hotel – which opened in July 2013 – as well as homes and offices.

Carpet Museum

Fountain Square

Don't be surprised to pay 5 AZN (Dhs.24) for an espresso in a nice cafe in Downtown. Prices are on the up!

Azerbaijan
Highlights

The Boulevard, Baku

Maiden's Tower

Paris has the Eiffel Tower, Athens has the Acropolis – and Baku has the castle-like structure of Maiden's Tower, an architectural landmark that's shrouded in mystery. Shaped like a giant key, its walls, built in the 12th century, have survived the Mongol invasion and endless wars between the Ottoman, Persian and Russian empires. It's worth the perilous climb up the spiral staircase to the top, where you'll be treated to Baku's dramatic panoramic views, and the odd gust of strong wind.

Palace of the Shirvanshahs

Palace of the Shirvanshahs

Built by the Shirvan Kings in the 15th century, this huge complex, in a relatively quiet corner of the Old City, contains a two-storey palace, a minaret-topped masjid, a mausoleum and a bath house. Although not as large or ornate as other palaces, it's nevertheless a striking place, and the view of the palace's curved, coloured walls set against the Caspian Sea is very photogenic, particularly at sunset.

Miniature Book Museum

As the name suggests, here you can find tiny books in a number of languages, with 3,700 fingernail-sized books displayed. Check out the smallest book in the world – a 3.5 millimetre by 3.5 millimetre book made in Japan – using tweezers and a magnifying glass. It's located near the Palace of the Shirvanshahs within the Old City and admission is free.

Azeri dining

Resting places for both people and animals in travelling caravans, caravanserais usually had an open interior courtyard with small rooms around the outside. Some of Baku's historic caravanserais in the Old City have been turned into restaurants. The atmospheric Karavan Saray restaurant, just up the hill from the Maiden's Tower, captures the ambience of medieval times perfectly; The Mugham Club, located among colourful carpet and souvenir shops, is the top pick for traditional mugham music.

Maiden's Tower

Absheron Peninsula

This spit of land jutting out into the Caspian Sea with Baku at the centre can be covered in a day trip from the capital. Drive beyond the eyesores of pylons, oil derricks and pools of oily waste to discover a trail of natural wonders.

Ateshgah Fire Temple

Heading east on the peninsula, you pass through Surakhani with its Ateshgah Fire Temple. Once the site of an ancient Zoroastrian fire-worshippers' temple, the main structure seen today was built by pilgrims from India in the 18th century. It's actually a complex composed of an outer ring of small cells and a stone shrine in the middle of a courtyard. The temple was constructed to venerate the eternally burning fire found there. The central, castle-like structure has jets of natural gas on the four corners of the roof – which are very photogenic when lit, with flames shooting into the sky.

The Caribbean it is not, but the Absheron Peninsula is dotted with a number of beach resorts – if you fancy a Baku-style seaside escape

Gobustan National Park

The Gobustan petroglyphs at this park are an absolute must-see if you can find your way on the bumpy roads. These ancient carvings dating back to the Stone Age are carved into the rock faces of cave dwellings; the number of individual etchings is thought to be in the thousands, and it's a designated UNESCO World Heritage Site. The caves are located above the town, past a group of gigantic boulders, nestled into the sides of dry, tumbleweed-strewn mountains. The site also features an area of bizarre gurgling mud volcanoes, one of the largest and most dense in the world. The site is a little off the main track, but it's worth the effort to see the bubbling mud.

Yanar Dagh

For a surreal experience, take a 30-minute taxi drive north of Baku to Yanar Dagh, or Fire Mountain. It's this type of feature that inspired Azerbaijan's ancient name, which roughly translates to 'The Land of Fire'. As the name implies, you'll find a fire at the base of a hill, about a kilometre from Digah village. This raging fire in the hill is about 15 metres long and the fire is continuously fed by a seep of methane gas from cracks in the soil. Flames jet out into the air up to three metres. You can sit and stare at the hypnotic flickering flames while you drink tea at a cafe, and it's particularly striking at night.

To Absheron and back

There are very few road signs to direct you to the key attractions outside Baku, so it's best to take a taxi. There's still a likelihood you'll get lost, but if so just grin and bear it, and admire the unusual landscape of rusting oil rigs, Soviet-era factories and the flocks of buffalo.

Yanar Dagh

The Greater Caucasus

The North

A two-hour drive takes you to northern Azerbaijan, which is home to the breathtaking Greater Caucasus range, mountain roads and lush valleys.

Besh Barmag Daghi

North from Baku is an impressive rock mountain, which looks out across the dusty plain lining the coast of the Caspian Sea. The walk can be a little difficult and in the warm months it can be hot, yet it's worth it for the stunning views of the landscape. You can also visit a mystical menagerie en route, so it makes for an interesting day trip.

Caucasian mountains

True escapism

Take a hike to the mountain village Xinaliq, where shepherds speak their own language and the only attraction is a one-room museum. It's the land that time forgot.

Guba & Nabran

The awe-inspiring Greater Caucasus range is home to the highest peaks of Azerbaijan. In Guba, you can explore a fascinating history, ancient culture and beautiful environment. The city's bazaar is a hive of activity, the genocide museum is enlightening, and the cascade of waterfalls on the Gudialchay River at Tangaalti Gorge are mesmerising; there are also a few working synagogues to explore. The largest tourist zone, Nabran, offers a more traditional vacation – there are numerous beaches, picturesque bays, and a somewhat varied nightlife.

Sheki

Sheki is a gem of historical and natural beauty, and offers an authentic Azerbaijani experience. It's a charming town to explore, with inviting shops and curiosities to poke through at almost every turn. Be sure to try the sweet halva from one of the confectionary shops. Streets wind along, offering a chance to discover some of the many mosques and buildings dotted around. Nestled between the surrounding mountains, Sheki also provides some excellent exploring and hiking possibilities just beyond the town's limits.

The West

Along the Baku-Ganja highway lies a region of long, green plains and mountain ridges, where time seems to stand still.

Mingachevir

This young city on the shores of a reservoir is a centre of activity: the Ateshgah teahouse/disco is home to an odd giant spiderweb and spider; the Kur River is a picturesque setting for an afternoon stroll along Mingachevir's boardwalk; and the promenade features carnival rides for children and scenic spots to drink tea or have a beer. Pop-up kiosks serve kokteyl (a tasty milkshake), and there's a good choice of eateries with signature Azerbaijani cuisine on the menu.

Seasonal appeal

So, when is the best time to visit Azerbaijan? Well, spring has beautiful blossoming trees and cool temperatures; summer is action-packed with street performances and art exhibitions; the autumn air is crisp for walking and hiking; and winter is the perfect time to ski in the mountains. The choice is yours...

Naftalan

If you're willing to bathe in chocolate-brown gloop, give an oil bath a try. Naftalan, south of Ganja (whose name, appropriately means 'oil buyer'), features famous oil baths advertising miraculous healing powers. The baths' skin-cleansing properties have been touted since the medieval era and you can try all sorts of treatments and oils at the Naftalan Sanatorium.
naftalan-booking.com

The Tears of Kapaz

Lake Goygol and its mountain passes are amongst Azerbaijan's most beautiful natural treasures. Mount Kapaz is the crowning glory – and below it lie the seven lakes known as the Tears of Kapaz, created nearly 1,000 years ago when an earthquake shook the mountains so violently that inconceivable hefts of rock were heaved into the river valley below, creating seven lakes. Lake Goygol ('Blue Lake') is the pearl of these tears. It's an area of stunning natural beauty.

The South

There are vacation spots aplenty in this greener region, well-known for its beautiful mountain views and local produce, as well as peaceful national parks.

Istisu (natural hot springs)

Just four hours south of Baku there are numerous places that feature hot water springs that bubble up from beneath the Talysh Mountains. Both Masalli and Lankaran have baths you can enjoy for just a few manat. The Masalli baths are a little more up to date, with individual rooms and hillside spots where you can sit drinking tea. The Lankaran Istisu, a 15-minute taxi ride from the city, is a little more rustic, but you can choose the optimum temperature of your steamy sauna by testing the water first. In both cases, you'll need to bring your own towels.

Azerbaijan
Places to stay

JW Marriott Absheron Hotel

Baku

Excelsior Hotel Baku

Excelsior is Baku's most grandiose, swanky hotel, located a little way out of the city centre, and a favourite of the city's wealthy set. It's a plush affair, with ornate, decadent interiors and luxurious rooms. It features an amazing indoor swimming and fitness area, complete with a running track, outdoor pool and spa.

excelsiorhotelbaku.az

Fairmont Baku Flame Towers

Located in one of Baku's iconic Flame Towers, this hotel offers unparalleled views of the city. From the 20-foot glass chandelier in the lobby to the contemporary art adorning the walls, the Fairmont Baku simply oozes luxury and style.

fairmont.com/baku

JW Marriott Absheron

This upscale hotel is the city's latest addition to its futuristic skyline and historic buildings. Stylish and spacious rooms with panoramic views of the Caspian Sea, luxury bathrooms and a magnificent indoor pool — just 100 metres from Freedom Square.

jwmarriottbaku.com

Landmark Hotel Baku

This high-storey, five-star hotel in the heart of the city has good-sized rooms and a 10th-floor swimming pool. The Sky Bar on the 19th floor serves up cocktails with some of the best views in town, while sushi fans can get their fix on the 21st floor at Seto; Shin Shin is a good spot for Asian fare.

Old City Inn

A small but friendly option right in the Old City, this hotel has just 12 rooms and is a characterful place to stay. There are great views from the top of the building — and with so much on your doorstep, wining and dining choices in the vicinity are plentiful.

oldcityinn.com

Probably the most attractive Old City hotel is the Sultan Inn Boutique Hotel (sultaninn.com). Its rooftop bar is a great spot to take visitors for a cocktail overlooking Maiden's Tower, and there's a good business lunch served here too.

The quirky three-star Fawlty Towers hotel is good for a budget break

Excelsior Hotel Baku

JW Marriott Absheron Hotel

Excelsior Hotel Baku

Guba

Out of Baku

AF Hotel Aqua Park

Located 21 kilometres south of Baku, the AF Hotel holds one major attraction – its Aqua Park. Featuring four swimming pools, plus water slides for adults and kids, and private beach access, it's a popular spot for day trippers from the capital. Accommodation is offered in standard hotel rooms and self-catering suites, and there are a number of restaurants and a bar on site. afhotel.az

Guba Olympic Complex

Just 90 minutes from Baku, and set in the old land of forests and rivers, mountains and lakes, is this traditional collection of furnished apartments, classic-style villas and a 60-room hotel. It's well-designed and comfortable accommodation, with all the essentials for a short stay – satellite TV, a 24-hour bar and room service. gubaolympic.az

Within a two-hour drive of Baku, in just about any direction, there are numerous spots where you can pitch up your tent and enjoy the great outdoors. Shirvan, on the southern road to Lankaran, is a good area for exploring and camping, with beaches and mud volcanoes, but it gets very hot in the height of summer, even with the sea to cool you down. Alternatively, heading north-west towards Sheki or Ganja, you can pick a picturesque spot along the way.

Keravansaray Hotel

This superb converted caravanserai is enough reason to visit Sheki. While they're certainly not luxurious, the rooms have wonderful arched brickwork ceilings as well as sitting areas, basic bathrooms and western loos. There's hot water in the showers but not in the sinks. Prices vary considerably between rooms for no apparent reason; book ahead, especially for single rooms.

Qafqaz Riverside Hotel

This peaceful resort is located on the banks of the Damiraparan river, in northwestern Azerbaijan. Escape Baku 220km away and soak up the spectacular views of snowcapped mountains and dazzling emerald green forests all around. There's a choice of rooms, suites and modern villas for all budgets, with a spa and outdoor swimming pool to enjoy at your leisure. qafqazriversidehotel.com

River Side Hotel

A tranquil four-star establishment on the banks of the River Kur is tranquil, where the rooms are basic but comfortable, service is helpful, and amenities are plentiful. From here, you can get a great view of the river, the boardwalk and the mountains behind the city. And if you're lucky, you'll be in town on a day when the competitive rowers are training for their annual crew races, giving you a bird's eye view! riverside.az

Qafqaz Riverside Hotel

Tale of two cities

Explore Icheri Sheher

Fountain Square, Baku

Walking tour
You can stroll the tiny streets in around three hours; when you get tired, pop into a tea shop for a genuine Azeri experience.

For anyone who enjoys exploring a city by foot, a wander through Baku's meandering cobblestone alleys is a joy.

Baku is a tale of two cities – one inside the other, like a kernel nut inside its shell. Downtown, the Soviet-built city, surrounds Icheri Sheher, the old inner city that dates back to at least the early centuries AD. For anyone looking to indulge in some history, a walking tour inside the citadel wall of the Old City is a must.

The Double Gate area (Gosha Gala Gapisi in Azeri) is a common taxi pick-up and drop-off point, and is a good place to start. As you pass through the Double Gates, head west (turn right) toward the Shirvanshahs' Palace. Walking downhill in a southerly direction will take you to the Maiden's Tower (p.164). As you walk through this atmospheric area, it's likely that you'll hear traditional Azeri mugham music, along with the click and slap of dice being thrown by local men huddled along the street playing nard (Russian backgammon); you'll probably also smell the delicious aroma of cooking shashlik (barbecued lamb kebabs).

Many of the streets and building walls have neutral earth tones, with splashes of colour courtesy of the decorative carpets displayed outside cave-like shops. Artists frequently depict the Icheri Sheher in their art, with the bold colours representative of the lively Old City. There's very little traffic in this part of town, so you get a real sense of what life must have been like during medieval times.

Interesting attractions include mosques, caravanserais (roadside inns), bathhouses and carpet shops, but there are few signs to distinguish one building from another. Look out for the Juma (Friday) mosque, one of the Old City's most significant buildings, which was built in the 15th century.

Icheri Sheher, Old City

Roadside inns

Some of Baku's historic caravanserais have been turned into restaurants. The Mugham Club, an old caravanserai that's located among colourful carpet and souvenir shops, west of the Maiden's Tower, is the top pick for traditional mugham music.

In the market for a carpet

The Old City is a great place to while away a few hours shopping for carpets. Shop vendors will invite you to sit and drink piping hot tea from tulip-shaped glasses as they unroll their wares. If you do intend to buy, cash is the preferred method of payment, and be sure to ask about export certificates as antique carpets are export-restricted. Whatever you're after, haggle!

Preserving the past

There are several bathhouses, or hammams, in the Old City, such as the Haji-Bani Bathhouse (16th century) near the Maiden's Tower; bathing, massages, tea and hookah pipes are all part of the ritual. While ancient buildings abound, elegant European-style mansions sprang up in Baku during the oil boom between 1870 and 1920. Reassuringly, efforts are underway to preserve their original features. Some beautiful examples of turn of the century architecture and oil boom mansions include Baku City Hall, the Mukhtarov Palace, the Taghiyev Palace and the Ismailiyya Palace, all just outside the walls of the Old City.

A night on the town

Partying in Baku

City centre, Baku

Holiday to the end
Catch the 3.10am
flydubai flight back to
Dubai, and you have
one extra evening to
enjoy Baku's nightlife
before heading home.

Perhaps the most surprising thing about Baku is its cosmopolitan nightlife and restaurant scene – who knew that such a backwater could be such a party town?

Whether you want an upmarket cocktail and a glorious view, or a pint and sport on the big screen, you will find it all in Baku's bar scene while, among the restaurants, you can find everything from capital kebabs to superior sushi. Here's where to go to get the best of everything.

Eat Azeri

Azeri cuisine is excellent when prepared properly and in a restaurant with enough custom to ensure a wide selection of dishes are available. 'Plov', a rice dish mixed with various condiments, is called the 'king of meals' in Azerbaijan. For an authentic experience, order plov at Kohna Shahar in the Old City, which is furnished in the traditional style with old carpets, ottomans, vintage crockery and musical instruments. Another traditional restaurant in the Old City is Karvansara, where two medieval caravanserais behind the Maiden's Tower have been transformed into an inspiring oriental restaurant. It's also worth a trip out to the original Bah-Bah Club, 4km from Baku city centre on the coastal highway towards the airport. Some of the best national cuisine is prepared by award-winning Lankaran native, Shahhussein Kerimov, at the Old City Restaurant near the south-western Old City gate that leads onto the Boulevard.

Alfresco dining

For unbeatable everyday Azeri food in the great outdoors head to Sultan's in Downtown, where you can sample Azeri fine dining on the (small) terrace at Zeytun, on the third floor of Park Bulvar. Chinar in Downtown offers the last word in cocktails and Asian fusion cuisine (the team have links to London's Hakkasan restaurant), which can be enjoyed on the terrace. Occo restaurant is another chic option for Downtown dining.

Dress to impress

Although you're unlikely to be turned away for being dressed inappropriately, Baku is very much home to a culture of dressing up, so be sure to tuck in that (ironed) shirt and polish up your shoes before a night out.

All-singing, all-dancing

The beautiful medieval caravanserai setting of the Old City's Mugham Club would be among the most atmospheric dining venues in town, even without its excellent food and nightly song-and-dance shows. Or, if you want to take your karaoke to another level, book out the Sultan Suite at the Boutique Palace Hotel, complete with infinity mirrors, in-room Jacuzzi, private hammam and laser light projections, as well as state-of-the-art karaoke with access to some 20,000 songs.

In the mix

The best places to go for cocktails are the bars in the big hotels. For perfectly-mixed drinks with killer vistas, look no further than the Azza Bar at ISR's Radisson; the Mirvari Bar above the Park Inn (where you can also get good sushi); or up on the new terrace at Shin-Shin at the Landmark.

Occo restaurant

Íkos village

Cyprus

Bask in year-round sunshine, explore archaeological wonders, take a hike in the wilderness, enjoy lazy long lunches – and be back in the office by Sunday.

Flight time
3 hours 50 minutes

Door to door
Airport to Limassol is 40 minutes by car; 1 hour 40 minutes to Paphos

When to go
January to October

As countries go, Cyprus wins the prize for the smallest country with the biggest cultural heritage. This picture-perfect island, said to be the birthplace of the mythical Aphrodite, is all glittering golden sands, sparkling azure seas and archaeological ruins – and what's more, it's got a cracking climate too. The summers are perfect for catching up with some much-needed R&R on the beach, while the winters are mild enough for mountain walks and skiing on the slopes.

The charming coastal towns of Limassol, Paphos and Larnaca are dotted with many mosaics, temples and tombs – and charming tavernas too. The island is also home to the magnificent Troodos Mountains – a string of stunning peaks where majestic monasteries and quaint villages cling to the hillsides. It's seriously breathtaking.

There's plenty of variety, from the neon-lit nightlife of Ayia Napa to the uncrowded beaches of Limassol. Explore nature trails through the pine forests of the Troodos Mountains, drive along rollercoaster-like paths, and discover mythology and archaeology in a land made colourful by thousands of citrus trees.

It's a little under four hours from Dubai, and whether you put down roots in one of the many seafront hotels in Paphos or in Limassol, there are plenty of day trips right on your doorstep. In fact, you're only ever a short stroll or drive away from stunning history, beautiful beaches, rugged mountains or vibrant nightlife.

As befitting an island steeped in the mythology of the Greek gods, Cyprus is divine – even for those on mortal budgets.

Lay down the beach towel

Why sweat it out on the beaches of the UAE, when it's cooler and less humid in Cyprus? For the easiest beach holiday, fly to Larnaca on the east side of the island and stay in one of the hotels overlooking the half-mile beach. It's hard to do anything but relax on the sandy beaches of Limassol, which has the longest coastline of the island. For the best beaches – think golden sands and calm, crystal waters – head to Coral Bay, just north of Paphos. And, for a beach break with a burst of adrenaline, try sunbathing and bungee jumping at Nissi Beach in Ayia Napa.

This map is not an authority on international boundaries

Troubled times spell a window of opportunity for a bargain break in Cyprus – where soaking up the sun and culture is as hard as it gets.

Getting there
Fly from Dubai or Abu Dhabi to Larnaca airport with Emirates (daily) and Etihad (Monday, Wednesday, Friday), from Dhs.2,000 return.

Visas
Many nationalities can enter Cyprus for a period of up to 90 days without the need for a travel visa, including travellers from the UK, Canada, Australia and the US. To check your visa requirements, visit mfa.gov.cy.

Time
One hour behind the UAE.

Climate
Cyprus has a Mediterranean climate with hot, dry summers (up to 36°C) and cold winters (lows of 5°C).

Language
Greek and Turkish are the official languages, but English is widely spoken.

Currency
Euro (EUR).
1 EUR = Dhs.4.7.

Vaccinations
Hepatitis A and B.

Best for... seasonal attractions
Enjoy sampling some of the region's finest wines (many of which are free!) at the Limassol Wine Festival from 30 August for 11 days. Escape for a spring break to Larnaca in May/June, when the Kataklysmos family festival brings fireworks and funfairs to the seafront. Or hit the slopes of Mt Olympus, covered in a blanket of snow January-March.

Lofou village

Sometimes the best way to escape the present is to revisit the past, which is beautifully preserved from coast to coast.

Paphos

There are ancient secrets around every corner of this UNESCO World Heritage Site – with its treasure trove of mosaics and archaeological discoveries – but it still has two feet firmly in the modern day too. There's no better way to soak it all up than with a chilled beer, Cypriot coffee or feast of just-caught seafood in one of the many tavernas that dot the scenic harbourside.

City tour
George's Fun Bus is a great day out on a funky and fun tour bus. You are entertained all day with the witty humour of your guide and taken to many memorable places in and around Paphos such as Adonis Falls, before ending the day with a BBQ and live music.

Almyra Hotel

Tombs of the Kings

Aphrodite Hills Resort

Can you dig it?
Paphos is a hot bed of the remains of theatres, fortresses, tombs and palaces that are either fascinating for historians or just fun to explore for the rest of us, including Kourion, the Medieval Fort and Tombs of the Kings (see p.195). Archaeological sites within the town include Agia Solomoni Christian Catacombs. From ground level, the white cloths hanging from the branches of a tree as you drive into Paphos are intriguing, but venture below and you'll discover an underground complex of tombs that is both unexpected and beguiling. And the secret behind the sacred tree? It is believed to cure whoever hangs an offering, in this case a white cloth, from its branches.

A round of golf
The magnificent Aphrodite Hills Resort golf course, overlooking the site where Aphrodite is said to have been born, is the perfect mix of challenging pot bunkers, manicured fairways of lush Bermuda grass and generous tiered greens. Tee off amongst indigenous olive and carob trees, but just don't let outstanding views over the Mediterranean put you off. And, with a 130m gorge dividing tees at the par 3, the 7th hole is the perfect opportunity to put your skills to the test. For those who prefer the 19th hole, golf widows included, skip straight to the Anoi pub for some light refreshments. aphroditehills.com

Mezze for two

Who knew that a journey into the past could be so exhausting? Reward yourself and reflect on the monumental sights you have seen with a humungous mezze at Aqui Cafe Bar overlooking Paphos' picturesque bay.

Paphos Harbour

Coral Bay beach

Sun, sand and sea

Thanks to the buckets of sunshine in Cyprus, it's nearly always a good time to enjoy the picture-perfect beaches at Coral Bay, just 14 miles north of Paphos. This large horseshoe-shaped cove is ideal for families in search of safe swimming and soft sand. To complement its fair share of sunbeds, parasols and inflatables, there are several sea-facing restaurants where a seafood mezze of sardines, red mullet and octopus is the perfect ending to a day in the sun.

On the water

Paphos has plenty of boats, all bobbing beautifully on a waterfront lined with tavernas. There are glass bottom boats that cruise along the coastline to the famous Vera K shipwreck, where you can spot tropical fish without getting soaked. For a more entertaining trip, the Jolly Roger pirate ship cruises out from Paphos to Coral Bay, then anchors for a spot of swimming and snorkelling. paphosseacruises.com

Animal attractions

Family fun is plentiful, not least at one of Paphos' newest attractions, Paphos Zoo. There are feathered friends including parrots, toucans and eagles, plus antelopes, zebras, gazelles and giant 150kg tortoises. Just a short drive from Paphos' centre, you'll find the Lara Beach Turtle Conservation Station – a serene stretch of sand where, if you're lucky, you can find leatherback or green turtles scurrying across the sand. September is the best time for viewing.

Partying in Paphos

Quieter than Ayia Napa, and livelier than Limassol, Paphos has some great bars, cafes, pubs and clubs. The Hollywood Music Bar on (would you believe it) Bar Street, the themed Flintstones Bar, and the legendary Harry O's are all worth checking out. For late night partying, Escape Beach Club, Rainbow Club (which only opens around 2am) and Robin Hood Club all make for awesome nights out.

Limassol Old Town

Limassol

Funky beachside bars complement candlelit tavernas, modern architecture and ancient ruins vie for attention, and luxury hotels line the water's edge in this cosmopolitan beachside town that's just half an hour from the airport.

Old Town

For those who love to 'potter', the narrow streets and authentic shops of Limassol's picturesque old town beckon. Admire ancient architecture, shop for souvenirs at the Cyprus Handicraft Centre, eat afelia (pork cooked in red wine and coriander seeds) and kleftiko (slow-roasted lamb with herbs) in a traditional taverna, and collect seaside souvenirs from the touristy but very charming Sponge Shop.

At the heart of the old town is Limassol Medieval Castle, surrounded by a cluster of restaurants; To Frourio, for one, is just as popular for its 18th-century historically listed building as it is for its mezze. The Folk Art Museum is a wonderfully preserved traditional building that houses a collection of Cypriot folk art dating back two centuries. And another refreshing pit stop is Draught at the Old Carob Mill complex, an ultra-fashionable spot where massive copper vats line the wall and in-house ale is brewed. The shaded museum exhibits here offer a great respite from the midday sun too.

Best of the beaches

The dark sandy beaches of Limassol are safe and shallow, and stretch for miles. A couple of miles from the main town is Lady's Mile, a sandy beach that is especially safe for children; Pissouri is great for scuba diving and snorkelling; and Kourion is a stony beach with dramatic ruins on the clifftop above. Look out for the hanggliders and windsurfers. There is a paved coastal path, a highway for joggers, that runs along the coast from Limassol, with several trendy cafes to enjoy along the way.

Molos

Breathe in the fresh sea air along the Molos seafront promenade, which traces Limassol's shoreline for over a mile. Whether walking or jogging, there are plenty of distractions along the way. Unmissable is the open-air Sculpture Park with works by Cypriot, Greek and international artists. There's no need to rush; leave plenty of time to enjoy the sea and port views from one of the many cafes and bars along the route.

 Limassol Carnival is the island's liveliest, with 10 days of parties and parades beginning eight weeks before Orthodox Easter Sunday. It's the best place to pick up an Easter 'flaouna' – shortcrust filled with a cheese, egg and mint filling.

Eat like a local

The Phiti Tavern in a small mountain village is perched high above the town of Polis, where the owner's Sunday lunch is legendary among locals and expats alike. Course after course of dips, salads and grilled meats is followed by the best roast pork, slow-cooked for seven hours with olive oil and local herbs.

Cyprus Wine Museum

Learn all about the wine production of Cyprus, with the wonderful guide Maria to fill your head with knowledge. See medieval drinking cups, ancient wine presses and an interesting video to satisfy your thirst for knowledge. Top it all off with a trip downstairs to the wine cellar for the fun part – tasting some of Cyprus' finest wines, including Koumandaria – a sweet dessert wine made from sun-dried grapes. There's no pressure to buy a bottle but it almost seems rude not to!

Santa Marina Retreat

Want to burn off some energy? This family-friendly activity centre offers a range of outdoor pursuits at a stunning hilltop location. Practise your aim at archery, get in the saddle for horse riding or test your head for heights on the challenging Sky Trail. Just a few miles from the coast, landlubbers can brush up on tennis, climbing and rollerblading; for the less adventurous there is a small petting zoo, horse museum and cafe.

Nissi Beach, Ayia Napa

Ayia Napa

Azure waters, sandy beaches, lively nightlife and multi-star hotels. Ayia Napa has all the ingredients for a holiday in the sun. Set in the far eastern end of southern Cyprus, this 'party capital' is well-loved for sun, sand and sea by day and clubbing by night. The holiday fun continues at Europe's largest waterpark, the Greek-themed Waterworld. The more traditional attractions include the 16th century Venetian monastery and Cape Greko National Park – but for most, this destination is all about the 'here and now' rather than the past.

Larnaca

Just a few minutes from the airport, this seaside town is worth the diversion to or from your hotel. There are several archaeological sites including the beautiful 18th century Kamares aqueduct, the rare sixth-century mosaics of the Angeloktisti church, and Choirokoitia. The nearby Lefkara village, known for its lace and silverware, and the Stavrovouni Monastery perched on a rocky 750m-high ledge are both scenic stops. And don't miss the scores of flamingos and wild ducks on the Larnaca salt lake, best admired as you walk the nature trail along its shores.

Medieval Castle, Old Limassol

Troodos Mountains

A day to spare?
Pop into the cosmopolitan capital city Nicosia to visit the Cyprus Museum for an enlightening journey through the country's history. Alternatively, lie back in the old Turkish bath at Omeriye Hamam and enjoy a centuries-old tradition. While not on the top of the list of places to visit, Nicosia is a capital city with heart.

Troodos

Any trip to the Troodos Mountains, with its scented forests, magnificent monasteries and picturesque villages, is like a breath of fresh air.

From the top
It's just a stone's throw from the beaches and coastal resorts but the pine-covered Troodos region is worlds apart. Take hairpin bends on mountain roads past cherry blossom trees, citrus groves and hillside villages towards the highest peak, Mt Olympus at 1,952m. The views are spectacular and, on a clear day, you can see right across to northern Cyprus. But it's the journey up there that fascinates the most.

Call of the wild
The world stands still at villages such as Omodos where locals play backgammon, narrow cobbled streets are lined with dainty stores selling local produce, and old women sit on corners sewing delicate lace cloths. Sip strong Cypriot coffee at a cafe overlooking the glorious monastery. Before leaving, go to George's Bakery for Turkish bread, carob coated nuts and soujoukkos (a snack made of grapes with almonds). A quick side trip to the artists' village of Lania is a must.

Explore mountain life on a nature trail across the Troodos forest. One of the best is the Caledonian Falls route – a gradual walk though forest paths, across mountain streams, past waterfalls and ending at the Trout Farm. The ultimate reward, aside from the views, is lunch here, where trout is a speciality. There are also plentiful clearly marked hiking and biking routes (head to Porto Platres to hire your wheels), to enjoy the year-round mild climate. Or wrap up warm for the ski season between January and March.

Wine tasting
For something more sedate, join a tour of the many wine villages, tasting reds and whites along the way, but save the best for last – the sweet dessert wine of Koumandaria. And then soak it all up with visits to a Byzantine church with frescoes painted in cobalt blue, red and gold; the shoemaker museum in Spilia or the folk museum in Omodos.

Byzantine church

Le Meridien Limassol Spa & Resort

Paphos

Anemi Hotel Apartments

A stylish boutique hotel with bright and airy rooms, modern kitchens and a large swimming pool with a furnished terrace. It's just 200 metres from the sandy beach, and great value for money if self-catering, with plenty of restaurants and bars nearby.

anemihotelcyprus.com

Aphrodite Hills Golf & Spa

Luxurious but casually elegant, this is the perfect getaway for anyone wanting to just relax; for sports enthusiasts looking for a golf or tennis holiday; or even for an idyllic Cyprus wedding. It's a high-class haven, with a Cypriot Village Square offering a great selection of restaurants and bars, a spa with thermae facilities, golf course, and a live programme of alfresco musicals.

aphroditehills.com

Capital Coast Resort

Enjoy all the perks of a self-catering holiday with the comforts of a hotel stay at this beachfront resort. You can make yourself at home in the modest but contemporary suites, but take full advantage of the spa with hammam, swimming pool and rooftop bar. For a dip into some culture, it's walking distance from the Tombs of the Kings.

capitalcoastresort.com

Thanos Hotels

The three most opulent resort hotels in the area – the Annabelle, Almyra and Anassa – are owned by one of the island's wealthiest families. The Annabelle offers old-school glamour set within six acres of lush gardens on the Paphos harbour front. Almyra is its more stylish yet unpretentious neighbour with a small beach, plenty of alfresco dining offerings, chill-out terraces with daybeds, and private villas with rooftop terraces. The Anassa, near Polis, is a majestic resort with all the charm of a traditional Cypriot village.

thanoshotels.com

 If you prefer beaches, bars and big beats, the Napa Mermaid Hotel in Ayia Napa (napamermaidhotel.com.cy) is one of many hotels along the main strip. Located 100m from Grecian Beach, its boutique rooms are great value for money. It's an idler's idyll by day, and at night takes on a life of its own.

The holiday villas at Aphrodite Hills are fantastic for families, and the welcome pack is worth every penny

Almyra Hotel

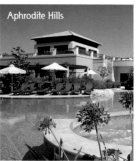
Aphrodite Hills

Almyra Hotel

Amathus Beach Hotel

Limassol

Amathus Beach Hotel

A wonderfully lavish hotel that has its own private beach, eight bars and restaurants, a huge kids' pool and a luxury spa, so there is no great reason to venture outside. Grand or not, it's often the little things that mark out a good hotel – and the Amathus comes up trumps with smooth white bedlinen, fluffy towels and the Amathus ruins just 1km away.
amathus-hotels.com

Crowne Plaza

Just 2km from the Old Town, this contemporary and affordable hotel is perfectly located for exploring the island – and enjoying Limassol's nightlife. The choice of Cypriot and Italian restaurants, recently renovated rooms, and the clean, sandy beach make this hotel stand out from the rest.
limassol.crowneplaza.com

Old meets new

If you feel the need to explore, Limassol's historic old town is about 15 minutes' drive away from the main beach resorts; for lively clubs and bars, the main strip of Limassol is just a five-minute taxi journey.

Sailor's Rest, Limassol

Le Meridien Spa & Resort

Luxury for parents, a paradise for kids, this self-contained five-star resort has two huge boasts: some of the largest rooms on the island, and a Penguin Village for children. There's a mini football pitch, bouncy castle, swimming pool, mini amphitheatre and climbing frames, as well as themed activities. Grown ups are pampered with a variety of restaurants, a maze of swimming pools, and beautiful gardens leading to the sandy beach.
lemeridienlimassol.com

Troodos

The Library Hotel

Located in the foothills of the unspoilt Troodos Mountains, the delightful 11-suite mansion is the perfect base from which to explore Kalavassos, a rural village. It's a great place to relax, eat appetising Greek food, sample local wine, enjoy country walks, unwind in the hotel's mud steam bath, or read a book or two.
libraryhotelcyprus.com

Troodos Hotel

At one with nature, this cosy family hotel is at the heart of Troodos Square, 1,725m above sea level and just 5km from the island's highest peak – Mt Olympus. Find yourself a spot at the bar or beside the roaring log fireplace, and relax with your favourite drink while admiring the views.
troodoshotel.com

NEXT TO THE TURQUOISE WATERS
OF THE MEDITERRANEAN SEA...

A PRIVATE PARADISE LYING ON 100,000m²
OF EXQUISITELY LANDSCAPED GARDENS
AND OUTSTANDING FACILITIES IS
WAITING TO BE DISCOVERED...

CYPRUS'S ONLY INTERNATIONAL FIVE STAR CHAIN HOTEL ON THE BEACH

Le **MERIDIEN**

LE MERIDIEN
LIMASSOL SPA & RESORT
N 34° 42' E 33° 10'
T +357 25 862 000
enquiries@lemeridienlimassol.com
lemeridienlimassol.com

Handpicked hotel
The real deal

St Raphael Resort, Limassol
raphael.com.cy

Distance from airport
45 minutes

Yes, you can have your ice cream and eat it at St Raphael, where one price covers just about everything.

An 'all-inclusive resort' is often a dirty phrase, one that conjures up images of plastic wristbands and forced group activities – but that's not always the case. The rather charming St Raphael Resort in Limassol has ripped up the rulebook: instead of house beverages and the same recycled buffet every night, guests can eat at up to six restaurants, pick from a menu of drinks – and not face a shocking bill at checkout.

Under one roof

Slap-bang on Limassol beachfront, St Raphael is a playground for watersports enthusiasts, who can kayak, pedalo, windsurf and snorkel; at extra cost, there is a diving school. If all that seems too much, simply relax on the sandy stretch of beach, in the gardens or by one of two swimming pools. There's quiet, kid-free zones and sun loungers are aplenty, so no need to creep out at 4am and 'reserve' one!

Beat the heat while enjoying a drink at the swim-up bar in the relaxed main pool, or make more of splash in the family pool. There's a water slide, toddler pool, kids playground, and the poolside Splash – a 'come as you are' cafe with tables just splashing distance from the pool where snacks are served without any fuss. And isn't that just how it should be. As well as a kids' club and indoor games room, there's bingo, quizzes, archery and daily shows in the outdoor 'theatre'. So there's never time to say 'I'm bored'!

For those who want to get down to the serious business of relaxing, simply hand in your towel token at the spa and unwind in the Jacuzzi, sauna and indoor pool – or go for a spoil and book a treatment. There are aromatherapy and waterbed massages, but go for the ultimate: a chocolate mud wrap.

Breakfast is particularly lavish (take full advantage of the sparkling wine, fresh waffles and Cypriot cheese) in the sea-facing Octagon restaurant. Throughout the day there's food for all tastes, from sand between your toes casual dining at Seashells to a pile-your-plate-high buffet at the Octagon. Once the sun sets, dress up for dinner at the Phoenician, which serves a mezze of Mediterranean delights with all the theatrics of an open kitchen. Keeping it more casual is the Palladium, where buffet tables groan under the weight of dishes varying from BBQ to carvery, with a side helping of belly dancing or a live pianist.

Rest your head...

With so much going on, the rooms are almost an after-thought. Spacious and light, modern but basic, their wow factor is the view of the sea and marina from the roomy balconies. If travelling with a family it's well worth upgrading to the new executive suites with a separate area for bunk-beds and a huge balcony with sun loungers and table.

St Raphael is not exclusively an all-inclusive hotel, but with so much on offer, why not? After all, enjoying meals without the Euro signs helps you to forget about the outside world – which is exactly what a vacation is supposed to do, right?

Lookout point

A five-minute walk from the hotel, next to the marina, is the stylish Sailor's Rest, where families play card games over a cappuccino and couples snuggle on the sofas with a glass of fizz. Not to be overlooked is the menu of lobster tagliatelle and prawn saganaki, cooked with ouzo and feta cheese.

Stroumbi village

A journey through time

Drive from Limassol to Paphos

Behind the wheel
It's easy to hire a car and explore at your leisure, especially as most sites are well signposted. Remember to drive on the left!

Kourian archaeological site

Tread the dusty footsteps of Cyprus' past to discover 10,000 years of history.

"It's an archaeological paradise". In the words of a passionate guide, one who has been leading tours of the island for over 20 years, Cyprus serves up some of the best ancient sites. No other country does history quite like it. It is after all the home of the Greek goddess Aphrodite. That said, it's no surprise that UNESCO has named Paphos, Choirokoitia and 10 of the Byzantine churches of Troodos as World Heritage Sites.

Time travelling

There are so many paths leading you back to the glorious past, but if you plan to centre your holiday along the south coast, then a good starting point for a day trip is the route from Limassol to Paphos. Leave the modern city behind to find the Medieval Castle of Old Limassol, where, legend has it, Richard the Lionheart married in 1191.

Move on to Kolossi Medieval Castle where a trek up the spiral staircase is well worth the views from the top. And to quench your thirst at the bottom, there's a charming cafe serving fresh orange juice.

The Greco-Roman Kourian archaeological site, a city kingdom dating back to 2BC, is a must-see. It has amazingly well-preserved floor mosaics, and is also under the cover of sun-shielding roofs. Add the dramatically situated hilltop and sea-view ruins of a Roman amphitheatre, and you've got great archaeology! (All for just 1.70 euros). You should also visit the Temple of Apollo – though if you are a real follower of history, don't touch its altar, as the punishment was being thrown into the sea from the cliffs!

Pass citrus groves, stopping only to stock up on fresh strawberries and oranges at the roadside fruit stalls – it's a fitting alternative to the service station snack stop. The House of Efstolias and the Sanctuary of Apollo Hypates are good places to stretch the legs.

Apollo Temple

Home of mosaics

End your journey at Kato Pafos Archaeological Park, with sites from prehistoric times to the Middle Ages. It's a vast site so, if time is limited, just head for the mosaics in the House of Theseus.

In the footsteps of kings

A must-see is Aphrodite's Birthplace – a rock jutting out of the ocean waves just yards from a scenic beach. The story goes that anyone who swims in the water surrounding the rock will become 10 years younger. If you prefer to stay on dry land, it's a stunning photo opportunity – whether from the road or on the beach – and the cafe opposite beckons for lunch and souvenirs.

The final destination on this route is Paphos, where remains of ancient villas, palaces, theatres, fortresses, tombs and Roman mosaics are quite literally scattered across the city. Just outside Paphos is the Tomb of Kings – a collection of monumental underground tombs carved out of solid rock that date back to 3BC. The sun-scorched ruins remain one of Cyprus' most famous sites and, with lots of steps, nooks and crannies, it's just plain fun to explore.

Eurasia

Ananuri

Georgia

From the charming Tbilisi capital to the snow-capped mountains of the Caucasus, Georgia is a fascinating and rewarding destination for anyone looking to step off other well-beaten tourist trails.

Flight time
3 hours 20 minutes

Door to door
20-45 minutes by car from the airport to Tbilisi city centre

When to go
March to September

Bordered by the Black Sea, Russia, Turkey, Azerbaijan and Armenia, there are few places in the world as enigmatic as Georgia. It's a bizarre mix of Asia and Europe with a heavy Soviet Union influence and all just a three-hour or so flight from the UAE.

A deeply complicated history has given Georgia a wonderful heritage of architecture and art, from its sublimely perched old churches, fort ruins and cave cities atop mountains to its stunning holy and green valleys peppered with stunning vineyards as far as the eye can see. Georgia is one of those relatively untapped countries that offers a gorgeous canvas to hike, horse ride, walk, raft and meander through.

Just as unique are its proud, rowdy, cultured people who may not be able to speak English, but will certainly try to invite you for dinner or suggest the best places to eat a meal. In fact, its cuisine is a hidden gem that most travellers haven't tried before. Blessed with a relatively warm climate and outstanding organic produce, the country is home to some of the world's most inventive and original food traditions. Georgia claims to be the birthplace of the dumpling as well as wine connoisseurs and cognac specialists, and it's a place where guests are considered a gift from God, creating a warm welcome unlike any other. Whether you just spend a few days in Tbilisi with its intriguing mix of the dreary and the exotic, or you head into the wilderness for an adventurous escape, one thing's for certain – a short break to Georgia will be a journey you'll never forget.

A long weekend

Focus on Tbilisi, the intriguing capital of Georgia with its unintelligible curly writing, its 20ft statues of its celebrated poets, its neither eastern nor western sense of place, and buildings showing a few signs of its heavily beaten-up past. Within hours, you'll have fallen in love with this alluring city. Indulge in delicious Georgian cuisine with locals such as Khinkali dumplings and cheese pies and wash it all down with a bottle of Georgia's finest ale, Natakhtari. Then, take a day trip to the spectacular David Gareja cave monastery, before spending the evening in vineyards of Sighnaghi 'town of love' toasting to new friends made.

RUSSIA

⊕ Sukhumi

Black Sea

K'ut'aisi ○

GEORGIA

Tbilisi Intl
Airport   Sighnaghi

TBILISI ⊡⊕

○ Batumi

Batumi Intl
Airport

TURKEY   ARMENIA   AZERBAIJAN

This map is not an authority on international boundaries

N

Welcome to
Georgia – an
enigmatic and
rewarding
destination
that's perfect
for adventurous
travellers.

Getting there

Fly from Dubai to Tbilisi airport with
flydubai, which flies direct three times a
week (Tuesday, Thursday, Saturday) from
Dhs.933 return. Emirates flies via Istanbul
and Baku, and Qatar Airways flies via Doha.

Visas

Passport holders from Canada, European
Union, Japan, Lebanon, the United States of
America, and citizens of all GCC countries
do not require visas. Visit mfa.gov.ge.

Time

Same time zone as the UAE.

Climate

The Greater Caucasus mountain range
protects the nation against cold air from
the north. Average temperatures in summer
reach up to 22°C. The winter average is 3°C.

Language

Georgian; Russian is widely spoken and
English is limited.

Currency

Georgian Lari (GEL). 10 GEL = Dhs.22.

Vaccinations

Hepatitis A and B.

Best for... outdoor adventures

Georgia's Svaneti, Kazbegi and Tusheti
regions are filled with remarkable walking
and hiking routes. Get your adrenaline
pumping by rafting on Georgia's rivers,
horse riding through towns, paragliding in
its skies or bungee jumping off its bridges.
One thing's for certain, there's never a dull
moment in Georgia.

Adjara region

Peace Bridge

There's more to Tbilisi than meets the eye. Head out, get lost and explore this charming Caucasian capital and beyond.

Tbilisi

Tbilisi is the beating heart of the South Caucasus and it's where Georgians travel to for action and excitement. The city packs both history and modernity into a smallish valley that's flanked by dramatic hillsides on either side of the Mtkvari River. The capital is striving to move into the 21st century after a tumultuous political past and the streets are bustling with pedestrians, construction debris and the constant tooting from well-worn cars. But there's a charm to Tbilisi that begs to be explored; hidden, cobbled streets open up to beautiful green parks, and dimly lit basements hide some of the liveliest and best restaurants in the country. It's unique and pulsing, and well worth a visit.

Old Town

Most visitors gravitate towards the Old Town as it's the most picturesque and interesting part to explore. Situated in the shadow of the Narikala Fortress, the Old Town is an assortment of twisting alleys full of hidden courtyards and tumbledown houses, with outrageous wooden balconies that lean at precarious angles. Shisha cafes, restaurants, hostels, and boutique stores stand side by side with graffiti-covered walls, derelict buildings, churches and synagogues. While away your time at the base of the fortress and watch the locals go about their day. Religion unites its people and you'll find Sioni Cathedral packed on the weekends.

City views

The bow-shaped pedestrian Peace Bridge acts as a symbol of Tbilisi's strive towards modernity. The glass and steel footbridge over the Mtkvari River offers a unique view of Metekhi Church, Narikala Fortress, Mother Georgia and the statue of the city's founder Vakhtang Gorgasali.

Aerial tramway

In June 2012 a new aerial tramway opened in Tbilisi. It connects the newly constructed Rike Park at the foot of the Peace Bridge with Narikala, a fortress that dominates the Old Town skyline. The journey takes you across the Mtkvari River, over the recently renovated rooftops and buildings of the Old Town, and up to Narikala Fortress in just under two minutes.

Narikala Fortress

Narikala was first built back in the fourth century when it acted as a Persian citadel. History, however, has not been kind to the fort which has been blown up, rebuilt, and blown up again more times than can be counted. Its foundations were rebuilt in the eighth century by the Arab emirs but a huge explosion of Russian ammunition that was stored inside its walls practically destroyed everything including the church within the fort, which was then only rebuilt in the last decade.

Mother Georgia

From outside Narikala Fortress entrance, you can follow the path to the statue of Mother Georgia, a huge aluminium statue of a woman holding a sword in one hand and a cup of wine in the other – the archetypal metaphor for Georgia – proudly welcoming guests but passionately defending its land.

Mount Mtatsminda

Mtatsminda is likely to be the first thing you see, especially if you're arriving into the capital at night, not so much for its green vista, but more for the 210m-high red TV mast that looms over the city like a brightly-lit Christmas tree. Alongside the mast, however, is Mtatsminda Park which spreads over the hilltop, with plenty of funfair rides and attractions, and expanses to walk. The best views are from the giant Ferris wheel that sits next to the TV mast. If you need a pit stop, head to the small outdoor cafe next to the dinosaur park which serves up delicious plates of Khachapuri cheese pies and stews.

Winning wi-fi

There are many reasons why you'll love Tbilisi, but one of them is the blanket of free wi-fi spanning across the city. From the tiny cafes right up to the five-star hotels, Tbilisi is a hotspot champion – you'll be connected almost anywhere you go.

Old Town

Weekend flea market

At weekends, Tbilisi hosts a charming flea market by the banks of the river. You can find almost anything at the Dry Bridge Market (open from 8am to 2pm), but the most interesting stalls are the ones selling Soviet memorabilia. For a few Lari you can pick up medals the Soviet state once awarded Georgian citizens for their bravery.

Georgia
Highlights

Abanotubani bath houses

Sulphur baths

Nothing quite prepares you for the experience of a Georgian sulphur bath, but a dip in the hot springs of Abanotubani is a popular pastime in the capital of this former Soviet state. A domed bathhouse – with its beautiful tiled surroundings, wreathed in the pungent smell of sulphur from the hot springs beneath the city – can be found with public (3 GEL) or private (20-50 GEL) spaces. Head down the dimly-lit staircase and you'll be shown to the bathing area. Then, strip down to your birthday suit and enjoy. You can also experience a vigorous scrub down from one of the stern-faced workers that's sure to revive you if the sulphur scent has knocked you out.

Pies & dumplings

Georgian cuisine is a delightfully hearty affair with bread and cheese a staple in every diet. Head to Marjanishvili Street and, opposite the Old City Wall, you'll find Shemoikhede Genatsvale, a traditional Georgian restaurant that's popular with both tourists and locals. Head to the basement, follow the loud music and you'll arrive in an underground lair filled with people guzzling beer and wine accompanied by a mound of tennis-ball sized dumplings (Khinkali) filled with potato, meat and mushrooms. Order Khachapuri, Georgia's ubiquitous pies – stuffed with melty curd cheese and served sliced, like a fat double-crust pizza – and you'll be happy and, stuffed, for hours.

Narikala Fortress

Luxury

No12 Boutique Hotel Tbilisi
This delightful boutique hotel is located in a quiet neighbourhood within the charming streets of the Old Town. The nine rooms are designed to complement Georgia's architecture and the balconies offer magnificent views out towards the river. no12hotel.com

Courtyard by Marriott
This is the less expensive and less formal of Tbilisi's two Marriotts and occupies a historic building close to Liberty Square. It's a favourite for business types but its central location means it's a great base for visitors too. marriott.com

Tbilisi Marriott Hotel
Arguably Tbilisi's grandest hotel, this Marriott is in the heart of old Tbilisi and is known for its elegant furnishings, including a glorious lobby with crystal chandeliers and gilded columns. The hotel has 127 rooms and is located near some of Tbilisi's museums, galleries and theatres. marriott.com

On a budget

Boombully Rooms & Hostel
The young, enthusiastic staff is the main selling point at Boombully as they often go out with their guests. There are comfortable bunks with a spacious sitting area. The atmosphere is friendly and it's a popular place for backpackers. boombully.com

Old Town Hostel
Tbilisi Old Town Hostel is situated in the heart of the city and is spread over two floors in a quiet lane, with a nice garden for sitting out in during the warmer seasons. It has two private rooms with four dorms and bunk beds. Staff here are fantastic and often help guests with tours of the surrounding area. oldtownhostel.ge

Courtyard by Marriott

The lively Rustaveli Avenue is a short walk from most hotels and hostels

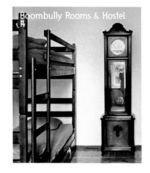
Boombully Rooms & Hostel

Tbilisi Marriott Hotel

Why Not? Tbilisi Legend Hostel is run by two experienced travellers who fell in love with Georgia and decided to stay. Located in a traditional old Tbilisi-style house, the affectionately known Why Not? hostel has been renovated with all the amenities needed for a comfortable stay. (whynothostels.com)

Handpicked hotel
Tbilisi's finest

Radisson Blu Iveria Hotel
radissonblu.com/hotel-tbilisi

Distance from airport
40 minutes

Fancy a little luxury during your off-the-tourist-trail adventure? The Radisson Blu Iveria might just be the ticket.

Sometimes you want a holiday that's relaxing; white sandy beaches, coconuts, crystal clear waters and butler service at the push of button. Other, braver times, you want a challenging vacation; language barriers, hidden gems that only you've discovered, with the occasional dramatic event to tell all your friends back home. But occasionally, you want a little bit of luxury amidst all that madness too. The Radisson Blu Iveria Hotel, Tbilisi is just that.

The towering hotel is one of the tallest buildings in town and while its Soviet-era concrete facade on Rose Revolution Square can seem quite daunting from the outside, the spectacularly revamped interior soothes the mind even after experiencing a frenzied 40-minute drive from the airport.

Cosmopolitan living

The whirling glass doors in the lobby lead you into a glass-enclosed space with stylish lounge chairs and excellent views of the city. Guests are welcomed with a broad smile; a coffee station at the entrance warms business travellers heading off for early morning meetings and bellboys ferry guests' luggage to and fro. You'd be forgiven for thinking you were in the heart of New York City rather than in Georgia.

Rooms, reached via glass elevators, are the star of the show here. Their contemporary style and futuristic decor are in stark contrast to the city's stunning Old World architecture. Glass walls with pretty etchings separate the bed headboards with the bathroom. Deep soaking tubs survey the exterior windows as do the glass shower stalls. Along the wall of glass is a complete cushioned sitting area allowing guests to take in the river views in total splendour.

Surrounding sights

The hotel is perched along Rustaveli Avenue, Tbilisi's main artery. You can't visit Tbilisi without exploring Rustaveli Avenue and the hotel's location makes it the ideal base. Named after the 12th century Georgian poet, Shota Rustaveli, Rustaveli Avenue is home to many of the city's main landmarks and attractions, including the Parliament of Georgia, Liberty Square and the Museum of Georgia. Culture lovers can enjoy watching performances at the Rustaveli State Academic Theatre or at Georgia's oldest opera house, the Tbilisi Opera and Ballet Theatre. Head downhill and you'll also reach Tbilisi's other famous spots such as Narikala Fortress and the rest of the charming Old Town area. And, while English is rarely understood, a taxi back to 'Rad-e-sson' is a request all taxi drivers recognise.

Should a full day of exploring leave you tired, head back to the hotel and hop to the spa for a little pampering, or simply gorge in Filini, the hotel's Italian restaurant. It may seem like a bit of cop out to eat Italian food when there's exceptional Georgian cuisine in the city, but you'll not be disappointed with your lazier self. The signature pizzas, live risotto stations and superb service create a wonderful experience emphasising Georgia's kind and friendly hospitality.

Getting there

Before arriving in Georgia, make sure you contact Radisson Blu Iveria Hotel, Tbilisi and arrange a private pick-up from the airport. The service costs 60 GEL and saves the hassle of trying to break down language barriers before you've even made it into the city.

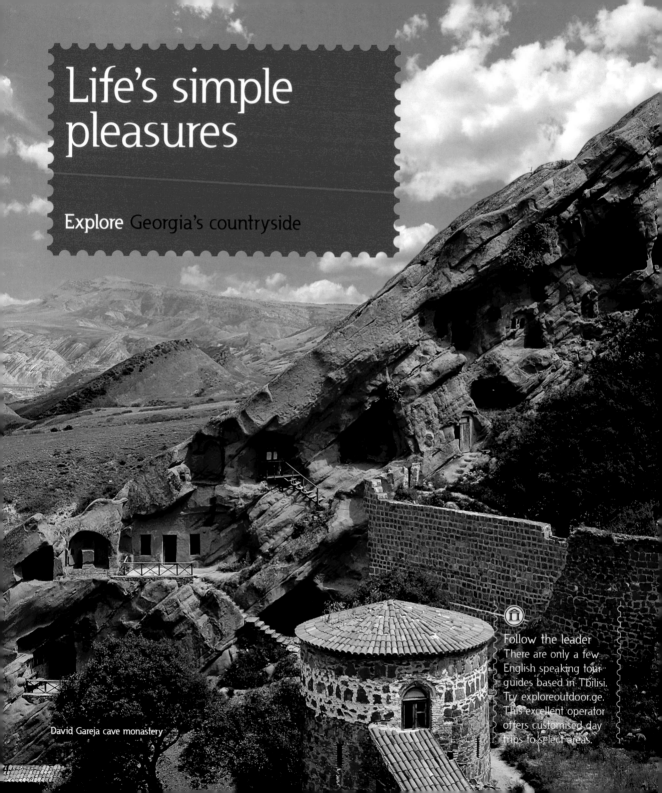

Life's simple pleasures

Explore Georgia's countryside

David Gareja cave monastery

Follow the leader
There are only a few
English speaking tour
guides based in Tbilisi.
Try exploreoutdoor.ge.
This excellent operator
offers customised day
trips to select areas.

Scale the mountains of Georgia, visit monolithic cave cities, stand on the border of two Caucasus countries, and toast to good health in a vineyard – all in one glorious day.

You'll be filled with a sense of jealousy when you choose a short break to Georgia. It seems the country is littered with travellers who've lost all sense of time. There are many ambling their way across Europe's more unique tourist routes, and there are others who are travelling towards China or Mongolia by foot with not a care in the world other than what adventure they might find themselves in next.

Unfortunately – as a short breaker – time is of the essence and with a country as vast, extreme and exciting as Georgia, an action-packed day trip is just what the intrepid explorer (on a time limit) needs.

Cave cities

Luckily, within a couple of hours' drive east of the capital lies the ancient, highly revered cave monastery of David Gareja. Located on the border with Azerbaijan, it is one of the most majestic of Georgia's sites. It was founded in the desert in the 6th century and makes for a fantastic day trip from Tbilisi. The rolling hills give way to semi-desert and soon it's like driving on the moon. There are virtually no signposts and the roads themselves are in terrible shape; often blocked by herds of sheep.

Lavra is the picturesque cave city, and the only inhabited working monastery in this desolate land. David was one of 13 ascetic Syrian fathers who travelled from the Middle East to spread Christianity in Georgia in the sixth century. Toil up the hill and you'll find more historically important abandoned monasteries hewn from caves in the hillside. Be warned, the hike is a strenuous half-hour slog but the views are staggering. The top of the hill demarcates Georgia's southern border, and it's even possible to cross a few yards into Azerbaijan – just be sure the Azerbaijani border police don't catch you.

Bodbe Convent

Walk down a steep path some 800m and you'll arrive at a tiny chapel over St Nino's Spring. You'll find a few Georgians collating holy water to drink and you can take a dip in the small pool in the chapel.

Sighnaghi

Nestled atop a vine-covered hillside in the heart of Georgia's wine country, the walled city of Sighnaghi is a hidden treasure known for its charm and beauty. Famed for its wineries, indulging in a degustation menu at one of the vineyards is a must. The local Georgian-American winery Pheasant's Tears (pheasantstears.com) makes excellent wine by the traditional qvevri method, where wine is fermented in clay pots buried underground. Alex Rodzianko, the wonderful wine expert, is happy to show you around the vineyards and storage rooms before sending your tastebuds on a Georgian wine adventure. Be prepared to sit for hours sampling Georgia's finest, toasting 'to the feet and hands that made the wine'. As the sun sets on an unforgettable day, there's time to indulge in Georgia's pride and joy liquor, Chacha, with its high alcohol content likely to set your sinuses ablaze.

Eurasia

Cappadocia

Turkey

Where east meets west, Turkey is home to ancient ruins, sublime beaches, historical wonders and vibrant cities – with the fresh scent of kebabs and tea in the air.

Flight time
4 hours 30 minutes

Door to door
20-45 minutes by car from Atatürk International Airport to Istanbul city centre; up to two hours for flights to Bodrum or Cappadocia

When to go
Spring and autumn for city breaks
May to October for beach holidays

Whether you're looking to enjoy a trendy city break, swim in the warm waters of the Mediterranean, or swap the modern world for archaeological ruins, you'll find what you're looking for in Turkey. Straddling the continents of Europe and Asia, this is a destination that's overflowing with ornate Ottoman palaces, colourful bazaars, sublime beaches, historical wonders and natural beauty.

For many, the star attraction of Turkey is Istanbul. It's widely known as a city of contrasts, where centuries-old historic attractions beckon alongside chic bars, lively nightclubs and trendy boutiques. You could easily spend your entire short break exclusively in 'the Bull', as it is affectionately known, without ever getting bored.

However, there is much to see beyond the city, particularly on the coast. Turkey is home to some of the most beautiful stretches of beach in Europe. Whether you prefer the bustling resorts of the Bodrum peninsula or the quieter coves of the Turquoise Coast, you're sure to find the perfect spot to roll out your beach towel. There are ample opportunities to explore the ocean too: opt for a sailing cruise and split your time between sunbathing on deck and snorkelling along the vibrant coast.

Further inland, you'll discover some of Turkey's biggest attractions: its ancient ruins. From the amphitheatre at the Acropolis to the temples of Ephesus, these well-preserved glimpses into the past are an absolute must-see.

Day tripper

There is no doubt that Istanbul boasts enough cultural attractions to keep even the most energetic visitor occupied almost indefinitely. In many ways, it's the perfect city break destination, with its awe-inspiring architecture, world famous landmarks, fantastic restaurants and irresistible party scene (see p.227). However, as well as being a must-see in its own right, Istanbul is also a gateway to a host of other attractions. The city is a great base from which to take one- or two-day tours, many of which are just a short flight (or ferry ride) away. As a result, even if your time in Turkey is limited, it's still easy to see plenty of what the country has to offer and be back in your hotel by bedtime.

Turkey
Essentials

Ancient ruins meet modern metropolises in Turkey – a cultural crossroads where east and west collide.

Getting there
Fly from Dubai or Abu Dhabi to Atatürk International Airport in Istanbul with Emirates, Etihad, flydubai and Turkish Airlines from Dhs.1,900 return.

Visas
Nationals of most countries do not need a visa to travel in Turkey for up to 90 days; more than enough time for a short break. Others can obtain a sticker visa upon their arrival. Visit mfa.gov.tr for details.

Time
One hour behind the UAE.

Climate
The inland areas of Turkey experience blistering hot summers and bone-chilling winters, whereas temperatures are far more moderate on the coast.

Language
Turkish; English is widely spoken,

Currency
Turkish Lira (TRY).
1 TRY = Dhs.2.

Vaccinations
Hepatitis A, Hepatitis B, Typhoid.

Best for... culture & history
Few destinations can boast as rich and varied a history as Turkey, a country that has felt the influences of Ottoman sultans, ancient Romans and Byzantine Christians. Relics of the past are not locked away in museums but instead are out in the open air, from the crumbling ruins of Pergamum to the ancient city of Troy.

in Florya!

HAVING **16** DIFFERENT THEMES AND **1** RAIN FOREST
FROM BLACK SEA TO AMAZON FORESTS,
THE WORLD'S BIGGEST THEMATIC AQUARIUM,
ISTANBUL AKVARYUM PROMISES
A UNIQUE EXPERIENCE TO VISITORS.

Istanbul & beyond

There is no doubt that Istanbul is a fantastic holiday destination, one which seems to provide inexhaustible delights. You could spend your entire short break enjoying historic sights such as the iconic Blue Mosque and Hagia Sophia by day, and whiling away the evenings as you sample the legendary nightlife (p.227). However, beyond Istanbul, a short day or overnight trip outside of the city is all it takes to discover Roman ruins, idyllic islands and architecture dating back to the Ottoman Empire.

Bursa

Bursa was the first capital of the 14th century Ottoman empire and is considered by many to be the birthplace of modern Turkish culture. An 80-minute ferry ride from Istanbul, it's home to some astounding architecture including the 14th century Great Mosque where Muslims still worship.

Cruise on the Bosphorus

One of the best options for an Istanbul day trip is a Bosphorus cruise. The Bosphorus is the 20-mile strait that runs through Istanbul, separating the two continents that have formed Turkey's cultural identity: Europe and Asia. Cruise durations can vary from under two hours to half a day, or longer, and you can even rent a private boat. It's a great way to take in some of the stunning architecture; keep an eye out for the Ortaköy Mosque and the Istanbul Modern Art Museum.

Princes' Islands

If you're looking for an escape from the hustle and bustle of the city, this chain of islands will fit the bill. Depending on which you choose, the journey is a 45-90 minute ferry ride. Heybeliada and Buyukada are both popular with locals in the know, and each offer plenty of beaches, restaurants and cafes to keep day trippers entertained. There are no cars on the islands – travel is by horse and cart, bicycle or on foot. Take a carriage ride to the beautiful restaurant Club Mavi on Buyukada for the best views.

Bosphorus strait

Bursa

Princes' Islands

Ruins at Ephesus

Historic highlights

If you're visiting Ephesus, it's a good idea to organise a tour guide to ensure that you don't miss any gems, like the library, the Temple of Artemis or the Temple of Hadrian (complete with its carving of Medusa).

Ephesus

If you're planning a two or three day trip from Istanbul visit Ephesus. Aside from Pompeii, this is the largest and most well-preserved ancient city in the Mediterranean; a walk among the intricately carved pillars and crumbling amphitheatre feels like stepping back in time. Take the 1.5-hour flight from Istanbul to nearby Izmir, and plan your journey to include a trip to Pergamum.

Pergamum

Pergamum is home to some iconic ancient ruins including the world-famous Acropolis. You could spend hours exploring this hilltop fortress and its many treasures: the altar of Zeus, the temple of Dionysus and the remains of a huge ancient library that was said to house over 200,000 volumes. Be sure to visit the Theatre of Anatolia.

Troy

A five-hour drive from Istanbul lies one of the most significant cities in Greek mythology: Troy. This UNESCO World Heritage Site is thought to be 4,000 years old. According to legend, it was here that an epic battle between the Greeks and the Trojans ended when the Greek army infiltrated their enemies' defences by hiding inside a giant wooden horse.

Troy

Pergamum

Pamukkale travertines

Explore the ancient ruins of a bygone era, marvel at a logic-defying landscape, or simply soak up the sun.

Pamukkale

To arrive at the site of Pamukkale is to feel like you've stepped onto the surface of an alien planet. A far cry from the cosmopolitan streets of Istanbul or the golden beaches of Bodrum, the land resembles a surreal world of snow-white cliffs, dramatic stalactites and pools of impossibly blue water. In fact, the name Pamukkale means 'cotton castle', a fitting title for a landscape defined by its towering white structures.

Pamukkale travertines

Rock pools & ruins

The gleaming concentric cliff terraces are called travertines – limestone deposits formed by the flow of calcium-rich mineral water – and pleasantly warm springs bubble and overflow within them. Historically, Pamukkale was the site of Hierapolis, a spa city that the ancient Romans built around the precious pools. It was thought that the warm mineral water had healing properties, a belief that continues to this day.

Today, Pamukkale is a UNESCO World Heritage Site and while tourists are welcome to visit, they do have to follow certain rules to the letter – such as removing their shoes so as not to damage the travertines. After the tourism boom of the late 20th century, an overwhelming influx of backpackers left the travertines dry, dull and damaged. Now that it's a protected site, the beautiful cotton castles have regained their former lustre and are open to visitors once more. There are also plenty of other attractions to see in the area, including the ruins of Hierapolis just a short distance away from the pools, where you'll find the fascinating remains of Roman baths, winding streets and a grand theatre.

Getting there

Flights from Istanbul to nearby Denizli operate twice a day and take just over an hour; from Denizli to Pamukkale by bus takes around 45 minutes. Day trips are available from Atatürk International Airport, which include pick-ups, tours and flights.

Nemrut Dagi (Mt Nemrut)

Nemrut

In Turkey, modern luxuries and attractions exist alongside reminders of the country's rich history, and there are countless places to see the ruins and remains of bygone eras.

Statues of kings

Perhaps the most unusual of Turkey's ruins can be seen at Nemrut Dagi (Mt Nemrut) in the incredible UNESCO World Heritage Site of Mount Nemrut National Park. At this memorable site near Adiyaman, the landscape is littered with a collection of statues: huge, enigmatic faces, some human, some animal, staring sternly from the slopes of a 2,150m mountain.

According to historians, these expressionless guardians surround a royal mausoleum that dates back to the 1st century BC. The tomb sanctuary was built by King Antiochus I Theos of Commagene, along with colossal statues of himself, lions, eagles and various gods, including Hercules, Zeus and Apollo. The magnitude of the king's undertaking was immense, considering that some of the stone blocks weigh up to nine tonnes.

Although it's widely accepted that these statues were once attached to bodies, only the profiles remain, weathered by the elements and the passing of time. Today, it is one of the most popular tourist attractions in Turkey and one that should not be missed.

Getting there

To travel from Istanbul to Mount Nemrut National Park, fly to Adiyaman. The daily flight takes just under two hours. Visit between May and October; during the rest of the year, some routes are closed.

Urfa

Combine a trip to Nemrut with a tour of Urfa, a fascinating historic town that is widely believed to be the birthplace of the prophet Abraham. A visit to Urfa feels as though you are stepping back in time, from its traditional buildings to its bustling bazaars. Don't miss the chance to visit to Gobekli Tepe, famed for being the oldest temple in the world and believed to date back to 9,000 BC.

Urfa

Try to time your visit to Mount Nemrut for sunrise or sunset, when the light really is at its most dramatic.

Fairy chimneys of Cappadocia

Cappadocia

As you arrive at Cappadocia, you'd be forgiven for thinking that you'd stumbled onto the set of a science fiction film. This surreal landscape in central Anatolia is populated by jaw-dropping rock formations: haphazard towers, towering cliffs, and ancient cave houses all connected within a labyrinthine concealed city.

You'll find this otherworldly environment in the Goreme National Park, a UNESCO World Heritage Site. On first glance, most visitors simply register the unusual shape of the landscape, the result of centuries of wind and rain eroding the tuff (hardened volcanic ash) that forms much of the valley. Closer inspection of the various towers, domes and arches, however, reveals that there are in fact homes, hotels and even churches hewn into the rock.

Cave dwellings

Some of the buildings integrated into the landscape are contemporary hotels created as more and more tourists flock to the area to see the famous Cappadocia 'fairy chimneys' (as they are known), some of which are up to 40 metres tall. However, many of the dwellings date back as early as the 4th to 13th centuries, when the Byzantine Christians carved their homes and their lives into the landscape, creating one of the largest cave-dwelling complexes in the world. Delve further into the rock formations and you'll also find stunning examples of Byzantine art within the interiors. Be sure to check out Gumusler Monastery, a 10th century monastery carved into the rock, said to be home to the only smiling Madonna painting in the world.

Hiking & biking

There are a number of ways to explore Goreme National Park. For a budget-friendly option, ask your hotel or travel company to recommend a walking or hiking trail and set off on foot. Mountain biking is also a great way to enjoy the fairytale landscape, although the terrain can be challenging. However, perhaps the best way to view it is from above, on a hot air balloon ride.

Getting there

Flying from Istanbul to Erkilet Airport in Kayseri takes just under an hour; a shuttle bus from Istanbul to Cappadocia takes around five hours, depending on the traffic.

Avoid the crowds

For a secluded experience on the normally busy Bodrum peninsula, take the short drive south to Barbaros Bay. It's a peaceful stretch of coast (with just the Kempinski Hotel Barbaros Bay) and the views are spectacular.

Bodrum

Unlike many other popular resorts, Bodrum has managed to maintain its authentic charm, from its pretty whitewashed houses draped in wild flowers to the brightly coloured boats bobbing in the harbour. And of course, there are the beaches themselves: long stretches of golden sand and sparkling ocean, each with their own unique appeal. All you have to do is pick a favourite.

Loud & lively

If you like your beaches with a generous helping of nightlife, then head for Gumbet. Once a quiet cove sandwiched between the pine-forested mountains and the sparkling Aegean sea, today it is widely regarded as the liveliest of Bodrum's beaches. As a result, Gumbet tends to attract a young crowd of revellers, although the wide selection of activities and dining options makes it popular with families, too. The beach itself is perfect for sunbathing or, if you're feeling energetic, there are watersports on offer.

Peace & quiet

If you prefer something a little bit more laidback, then Bitez could be the answer. This hidden gem is just a short drive away from bustling Bodrum town and Gumbet's somewhat rowdier restaurants and bars, but it feels like you're in another world. The Bay of Bitez boasts a crescent-shaped cove

Bodrum

with a tranquil stretch of beach overlooking the sparkling Aegean sea, sheltered by lush green hills and citrus groves.

Stunning sunsets

Bodrum peninsula's largest bay is Turgutreis, and it's also swiftly becoming one of the most popular. Once a sleepy fishing village, today this coastal town is a sought after beach break hotspot for locals and visitors alike. There are a number of pretty coves to choose from here, but the best is undoubtedly Akyarlar, with its pale shores, turquoise waters and backdrop of towering cliffs – best seen as the sun sets.

Getting there

It takes just over an hour to fly from Istanbul to Milas-Bodrum Airport, which is great news if you want a short break with the best of both worlds: the city and the sea.

 The picturesque Bodrum peninsula is perfect for a boat trip. Locals in the know recommend steering clear of tours organised by the large travel agents; instead, head to the smaller, local harbours to find an independently run boat tour. There'll be fewer people and more chances to relax with your fellow passengers.

Bodrum

Four Seasons Hotel Istanbul

Istanbul

Four Seasons Hotel Istanbul

Four Seasons Hotel Istanbul

If it's five-star luxury in the heart of the city that you're after, look no further than the Four Seasons Istanbul. Housed in a former 19th century Ottoman summer palace, some of the city's most important landmarks, including the Blue Mosque and Hagia Sophia, are just a few minutes' walk away. Be sure to try the signature Four Seasons Foot and Shoulder Massage at the luxury spa: the perfect way to unwind after a day of sightseeing. fourseasons.com/istanbul

Hotel Ibrahim Pasha

This chic boutique hotel is one of Istanbul's hidden gems. Located in the heart of the 'Old City' of Sultanahmet, Ibrahim Pasha has an enviable location close to the Hippodrome and the palace of Suleiman the Magnificent, and you can organise a private guided city tour through the hotel. The sunset views of the Blue Mosque from its rooftop are nothing less than awe-inspiring. ibrahimpasha.com

Park Hyatt Istanbul – Macka Palas

To rub elbows with the fashionable set of Istanbul, head for the Park Hyatt Istanbul – Macka Palas. Located near the trendy shopping district of Nisantasi, there are plenty of high-end shopping boutiques right on your doorstep. After a day of retail therapy, relax and rejuvenate in the luxury spa. istanbul.park.hyatt.com

Sumahan on the Water

Located on the quieter Asian side of the Bosphorus, Sumahan on the Water provides a tranquil alternative to city centre hotels. It boasts bright contemporary rooms with their own fireplaces, some of which have their own Turkish-style bath. Many also have great views of the strait, and there's a water taxi to ferry you across to the busier part of town within minutes. sumahan.com

Hotel Ibraham Pasha

Empress Zoe Hotel

It is possible to enjoy 'the Bull' without breaking the bank. Cheap and cheerful accommodation is widely available and well-located for exploring the city; check out Lush Hotel (lushhiphotel.com) or Nomade (hotelnomade.com). The low-key Empress Zoe (emzoe.com) is a great option in an enviable location.

Kempinski Hotel Barbaros Bay

Pamukkale

Melrose House Hotel

This charming boutique hotel is perfectly situated for visits to the nearby 'cotton castles' of Pamukkale, and will even arrange travel to the travertines. Be sure to try the restaurant's delicious traditional Turkish cuisine. melrosehousehotel.com

Nemrut

Zeus Hotel

Although it's located 45km outside of Mount Nemrut, Zeus Hotel is by far the best accommodation option in the area, boasting attractive rooms, a huge swimming pool and a sauna and Turkish bath, plus a souvenir shop where you can pick up a few mementoes of your trip.
zeushotel.com.tr

 Many travellers use Istanbul as a base and visit the famous fairy chimneys on a day trip. Having said that, there are a number of cool and quirky hotels, whose architecture makes use of the landscape, including Cappadocia Cave Suites (cappadociacavesuites.com) and Gamirasu Cave Hotel (gamirasu.com).

Bodrum

4Reasons Hotel and Bistro

This chic boutique hotel in Yalikavak on the Bodrum peninsula boasts stylish rooms and a large pool terrace. Its excellent location means that it's possible to take day trips to the nearby beaches, or horse riding and trekking trips in the surrounding hills, but you might find yourself simply wanting to relax in the tranquil surroundings.
4reasonshotel.com

Kempinski Hotel Barbaros Bay

This stunning hotel overlooking Barbaros Bay offers the ultimate in luxury and hospitality, as well as some of the best views of Bodrum peninsula. When you're not soaking up the sun beside the gorgeous infinity pool, enjoy a pampering treatment in the luxury Six Senses Spa; the menu includes an indulgent traditional-style Turkish hammam as well as reiki, colour therapy and shiatsu massages. kempinski.com

Sandima 37

This elegant, intimate hotel in Bodrum has just six suites, making it perfect for a romantic summer break away from the hustle and bustle of busier resorts. The restaurant boasts authentic local cuisine, and there's no better way to spend an afternoon than relaxing in the shade of the orange and lemon trees overlooking the swimming pool.
sandima37suites.com

Barbaros Bay

Anything but plain sailing

Holiday on the water

Getting there
Fly to Istanbul and
get an internal flight
with Turkish Airlines to
Dalaman – where a taxi
will be waiting for you.

A luxury cruise on a traditional gulet sailing boat is one of the most captivating ways of exploring Turkey's southern coast, and a great option for a group holiday with friends or a family break.

While many of Turkey's best attractions can be found on land, particularly in the mesmerising cities such as Istanbul and Bodrum, a luxurious cruise onboard the stunning Ecce Navigo (Latin for 'Here I Sail') offers one of the most captivating ways of exploring Turkey's southern coast.

A traditionally styled, 34-metre wooden sailing ketch becomes your home away from home with luxurious accommodation both above and below deck. A private charter carries up to 10 people comfortably within the five spacious cabins; not that you'll be staying in the cabins that much. Instead, you'll be chilling on the spacious aft deck indulging in a gourmet meal, lazing on a lounger at the tail deck or performing sun salutations with your new onboard yoga instructor on the forward deck. Anything goes onboard, and a trip can be as taxing or as adventurous as you want. Whatever your requirements, the Ecce Navigo might just be the ticket to the holiday of a lifetime.

Adventure-seekers
Experience the picturesque harbour towns of Gocek, Marmaris and Fethiye; explore the ancient city of Caunos and its lush lagoon; go hiking to see breathtaking views over the mountains; and most importantly of all, relax in tranquil turquoise bays. This is the ultimate adventure-seekers holiday but with plenty of time to enjoy the luxuries onboard.

Yoga lovers
Over the week your personal masseuse and yoga instructor will work to create the most beneficial treatments and practices for you and your group. A typical day begins with a sunrise yoga session, followed by a delicious breakfast. After that, you can simply relax in the sunshine, read a book or take a dip in the sparkling Mediterranean. If you're feeling

All aboard
Sailing trips are seen as expensive, but with a few friends onboard, the price is similar to many full-board hotels.

more active, you can go snorkelling, hiking or sightseeing. Holistic massages are also available onboard.

Family fun
It's always lovely to have the whole family together on holiday; it's even lovelier when there's a professional childminder to look after them. Kids can enjoy snorkelling and other water activities from kayaking and banana boating to wakeboarding and waterskiing all under the watchful eye of the onboard nanny. Meanwhile, grown-ups can enjoy pampering sessions and indulgent gourmet meals.

Set sail
Rates for private charters and tailored retreats onboard the Ecce Navigo start from EUR 32,500 (Dhs.154,000). For information and bookings, visit eccenavigo.com

Yoga onboard the Ecce Navigo

Hagia Sophia

City of contrasts

Sightseeing in Istanbul

Public transport
Well-connected bus and tram networks make it easy to visit Istanbul's most popular tourist attractions during your short break.

Basilica Cistern

Istiklal Caddesi

From ancient monuments to hip young neighbourhoods, Istanbul is a city of many contrasts, sure to keep the most adventurous explorers entertained at all hours.

Topkapi Palace

Istanbul is a city capable of being all things to all travellers, whether you seek historic attractions or hedonistic thrills. While Ankara is the official capital, many view Istanbul as Turkey's cultural capital, a place where ultramodern malls co-exist with centuries-old mosques and the call to prayer echoes over rooftops populated by chic cosmopolitan bars.

To see as many of the historic attractions as possible, the best place to base yourself is Sultanahmet. The so-called 'Old City', is the pulsing heart of Istanbul and where you'll find the three most prominent sites: the Blue Mosque, Hagia Sophia and Topkapi Palace.

The top three

The Blue Mosque, or Sultan Ahmed Mosque, is the star of the Istanbul skyline. Locals in the know recommend entering via the Hippodrome entrance, and taking some time to relax and admire the courtyard. However, keep in mind that it's still a place of worship for modern Muslims, and entry may be limited during prayer time.

The Hagia Sophia is a stunning example of Byzantine architecture; it has been a sixth century Christian cathedral, a 15th century Ottoman mosque and (since the 20th century) a modern Turkish museum. For 1,000 years after it was built, the Hagia Sophia was the largest enclosed space in the world, and even today its scale is impressive.

Just a short distance from the museum, you'll find Topkapi Palace, the legendary symbol of the Ottoman Empire, whose history reads more like a soap opera. Exotic stories abound of what went on within the walls of this opulent palace, populated by a cast of concubines, sultans, princes, and the men and women of court.

City highlight

The vast Istanbul Aquarium is one of the city's best family-friendly attractions. Catch a film at the 5D cinema or take part in the shark diving programme. (istanbulakvaryum.com)

As the sun sets

If Sultanahmet is where tourists get up at the crack of dawn to go sightseeing, then the hip neighbourhood of Beyoglu is the place to head when the sun goes down. It's defined by Istiklal Caddessi, a long pedestrian stretch lined with buzzing restaurants and bars. This is the place to grab some dinner, toast to a successful day's sightseeing or stay up all night – or possibly all three.

The area attracts a lively cosmopolitan crowd drawn by the vast array of nightlife, from stylish cocktail bars to shabby-chic pubs. The throng of revellers can occasionally get overwhelming, but it's easy to escape the frenetic pace of the streets by heading to one of the many rooftop bars. Check out 360 Istanbul for some of the best sundowner views.

Alternatively, head for the rooftop bars that line the Bosphorus and gaze from continent to continent across the water.

Paragliding in Serbia

Destination Europe

Discover Eastern European cities

Yerevan, Armenia

✈
Hidden gems
Be adventurous and try lesser known destinations like Skopje in Macedonia or Kiev, Ukraine. Flights to both are 5 hours 30 minutes, and well worth the trip.

When planning a short break, travelling from the UAE to some of Europe's most fascinating cities is easier than you think.

It may not seem like an obvious choice for short breaks from the UAE, but there are plenty of European destinations that are less than six hours away – suitable for an Eid break, some festive fun or even a last-minute long weekend. And, if you book with low-cost carriers such as flydubai (flydubai.com), you can enjoy the perfect getaway without breaking the bank.

flydubai flies to 60 destinations from Dubai, including several emerging European cities. Whether you want to relax in quaint parkside cafes, lose yourself in the music at a summer festival, sample some world-renowned nightlife or simply soak up the culture at traditional markets, you can find what you're looking for at an up-and-coming destination.

Yerevan, Armenia

While it's the undeniable cultural and economic heart of this mountainous nation, Yerevan can at times feel like a city on a permanent holiday. During the summer, locals saunter up and down the main boulevards stopping at park-side cafes to chat. There are cultural attractions aplenty, from the 19th century Russian edifices in the centre to the many museums and monuments. For night owls, there are dozens of theatres, concert halls, live music clubs, and restaurants; the steakhouse Baobab is a must-visit.

Where to stay: Areg Hotel (areghotel.com); Armenia Marriott Hotel Yerevan (marriott.com).

Take with you: A good book for long, lazy afternoons spent in cafes or parks.

Flight duration: 3 hours 10 minutes

Prices: Return flights with flydubai start from Dhs.1,455

Bucharest, Romania

Bucharest is the place to visit when you want to get into the Christmas spirit and shop 'til you drop. Even the staunchest Scrooge would be moved by the Christmas markets that run in Bucharest's Old Town and its surrounding areas during the holiday season. Oozing atmosphere and sparkling with lights, the markets are crammed with stalls vying to put on the biggest, brightest and prettiest displays. Warm chilled fingers with roasted chestnuts, spicy gingerbread and a hot drink while you browse. Not festive enough? Visit the huge Christmas tree in Piaa Universit ii (University Square). For a taste of Romania's nightlife and social scene, head for the restaurants and cafes that line the streets of the Historic Quarter.

Where to stay: The Grand Hotel Continental (continentalhotels.ro)

Take with you: Plenty of warm clothing! In December, average temperatures hover around 3°C.

Flight duration: 5 hours 10 minutes

Prices: Return flights with flydubai start from Dhs.1,850

Belgrade, Serbia

This fascinating city that simply begs to be explored. There's plenty to see and do: you can get in touch with your wild side at Belgrade Zoo, take a sightseeing cruise down the River Danube or escape to Ada Ciganlija, which swarms with swimmers during hot summer days. There are plenty of places to refuel and taste the national cuisine; the bohemian quarter of Skadarska has some of the best taverns and street cafes. Make sure you finish your meal with Serbian coffee and a piece of orasnica (walnut cake). Don't leave without sampling the city's famous nightlife scene, which truly has something for everyone with a choice of clubs, bars and even floating venues on the river. If it's a festival atmosphere you're after, hop on a train to Novi Sad, home to the Exit Festival (exitfest.org), one of Europe's best and most loved events.

Where to stay: InterContinental (ihg.com) or Hyatt Regency (belgrade.regency.hyatt.com)

Take with you: A decent tent and sleeping bag if you're heading to Exit Festival, or your dancing shoes if staying in Belgrade.

Flight duration: 5 hours 30 minutes

Prices: Return flights with flydubai start from Dhs.2,305

Pack your bags

If you have baggage to check in, make sure you book and pay for it at flydubai.com at least four hours before you fly. Stick to the luggage allowance, or risk being charged at the (often pricey) per kilo airport rate.

Farm in Serbia

Middle East

Bahrain International Circuit

Bahrain

Take flight to the Island of Golden Smiles and discover a cosmopolitan country that's as much a paradise for shoppers, partygoers and culture vultures as it is for racing fans.

Flight time
1 hour 15 minutes

Door to door
15 minutes by car
from Bahrain
International Airport
to Manama

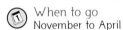
When to go
November to April

Bahrain isn't just about Formula 1. Yes, the annual Grand Prix is a huge draw for racing fans, but there's so much more to this archipelago of 33 islands.

Although it is a small country, there is still a fair amount of heritage with enough forts, museums, archaeological sites, pre-medieval shrines and mosques to charm and intrigue. As well as enjoying the high speed thrills at the Formula 1 race track, in the centre of Bahrain, you can be pampered at desert spas, lose yourself in spice-scented souks, splurge at chic shopping malls, or sip cocktails and dance the night away.

Bahrain may be the smallest of the Gulf states (being roughly the same size as Singapore), but it's nevertheless an increasingly appealing holiday spot.

The country is far more liberal than neighbouring Saudi Arabia, less developed than the UAE as a tourist destination, and its manageable size makes it easy to navigate and explore in just a long weekend. Much of the action in Bahrain is concentrated in the capital Manama – a busy, cosmopolitan city with a traditional souk area, high-rise buildings, modern shopping malls and an almost unlimited choice of international cuisine.

Time stands still at the tiny villages and towns dotted across the flat country; even in increasingly modern Manama, you are never far away from reminders of the cultural past, whether you're admiring the traditional-style architecture or hearing the call to prayer from a centuries-old mosque.

A weekend escape

Most sights are in or a short drive from Manama, the capital city, making it ideal for a short break to recharge the batteries. As it's not bursting with cultural activities, many visitors spend their time partying and shopping rather than sightseeing. But only slightly further afield you can tour the island and its archaeological sites, stopping off at Barbar, Qal'at Al-Bahrain, A'ali, Bani Jamrah and Muharraq Island along the way. While the F1 racing is the main draw for tourists – eight million turn up for the annual Grand Prix – Bahrain's weather, culture and friendly atmosphere are not to be missed. There is a wide choice of modern tourist accommodation, with many new luxury hotels on the horizon.

Bahrain
Essentials

Motorsports fans should plan their Bahrain trip for April, which is when the Gulf Air F1 Bahrain Grand Prix takes place each year.

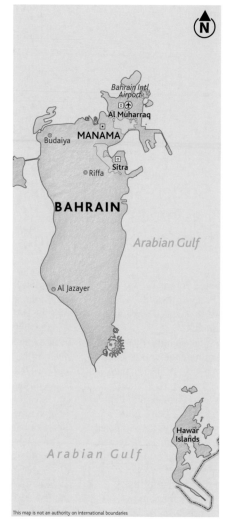

Bahrain Intl Airport

Al Muharraq

MANAMA

Budaiya

Riffa

Sitra

BAHRAIN

Arabian Gulf

Al Jazayer

Hawar Islands

Arabian Gulf

This map is not an authority on international boundaries

Getting there
Fly from Dubai or Abu Dhabi to Bahrain International Airport with Air Arabia, Emirates and Etihad, from Dhs.700 return.

Visas
Citizens of GCC countries (Saudi Arabia, the UAE, Kuwait, Qatar and Oman) do not require visas to enter Bahrain, and many non-GCC citizens can obtain a tourist visa valid for up to three months upon arriving in the country. For more information regarding visa requirements, visit evisa.gov.bh before you travel.

Time
One hour behind the UAE.

Climate
From November to April, you can enjoy warm days and cool nights; between December and February, temperatures range from 10°C-20°C. From July to September, the weather is hot and humid. Average temperatures hover around 36°C.

Language
Arabic; English is widely spoken.

Currency
Bahraini Dinar (BD).
1 BD = Dhs.9.7.

Vaccinations
Diphtheria, Hepatitis A, Hepatitis B, Rabies, Tuberculosis and Typhoid.

Best for... history & culture
Bahrain has a rich heritage that co-exists peacefully alongside modern life. Just a short drive from the ultramodern malls and hotels of Manama, you'll find everything from traditional forts and dhows to archaeological remains and burial mounds. You can learn more about Bahrain's ever-present past with a visit to the Bahrain National Museum.

Bahrain Fort

The world has been coming to see our treasures for hundreds of years.

People have come for Bahrain Fort (a UNESCO World Heritage Site), the Temples at Barbar, the 5,000-year-old Dilmun burial mounds, the old quarter of Muharraq and of course, our coveted pearls. They have stayed for the enveloping warmth of Bahraini hospitality. Start your visit at www.bahrain.com

BAHRAIN

Grand Mosque, Manama

Bahrain has one foot in the past, the other in the future – from bustling souks and modern malls to ancient ruins and pristine beaches.

Manama

The name Manama might mean 'Sleeping Place', but Bahrain's bustling capital does anything but live up to its title. This dynamic city is a playground for night owls, drawing scores of visitors each weekend in search of late night shopping, buzzing bars and lively nightclubs. During the day, there's plenty to do too, from immersing yourself in Bahrain's rich history to indulging in some retail therapy. Or, do both at the Manama Souk.

Manama Souk

A visit to this labyrinth of twisting alleyways and bustling shops is an absolute must-do. It's easy to imagine what it must have been like centuries ago, when traders

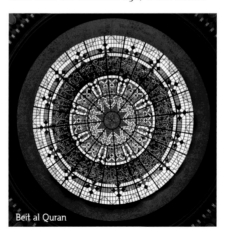
Beit al Quran

sailed in on dhows laden with goods for the markets. Today, a visit to Manama Souk remains a rich sensory experience, a riot of sights, sounds and smells, from brightly coloured fabrics to the evocative aromas of the spice souk. Be sure to practice your haggling skills – bartering over the price of your purchase is part of the experience and should help you get a good deal – and ask the local porters for help if you get a bit carried away splashing the cash.

Culture & heritage

Trace Bahrain's pearl diving heritage at the Museum of Pearl Diving or learn more about Islam at Al-Fatih Mosque. A must-visit though is Beit al Quran (meaning 'House of the Quran'). Not only is this a striking example of Bahraini architecture, it is home to rare Islamic manuscripts and stunning art. Be amazed by the beautiful engravings of Arabic calligraphy that adorn its walls, and marvel at the stained glass dome – a fascinating way to while away an hour.

Further afield

For perhaps the most fascinating (and famous) of Bahrain's cultural attractions, you'll have to head away from the city centre to Saar, near A'ali Village. Here, the surreal landscape is made up of row after row of ancient burial mounds. These intriguing remains date back to the Dilmun, Tylos and Hellenistic periods and are thought to be anything between 2,000 and 4,000 years old.

Muharraq

There's no doubt that you'll get to see at least some of Muharraq during your holiday as it's home to Bahrain International Airport. However, this island off the coast of the north-eastern tip of Bahrain, connected by three main causeways, is more than just a transport hub: Muharraq was once the capital of the country. Although it has since been replaced by Manama, it has strongly maintained its significance in the island nation, with many visitors and locals considering it to be the centre of Bahrain's cultural heritage.

Shaikh Isa bin Ali House

Shaikh Ebrahim Centre for Culture & Research

Wander through Muharraq's narrow lanes and you'll find plenty of traditional Bahraini houses. But the beautifully restored buildings within the Shaikh Ebrahim Centre for Culture and Research are your best stop for an insight into the country's heritage. From the embroidery at Kurar House to the pearling exhibition at Bin Matar House, you can take a fascinating walk through history. There are also regular art exhibitions and film screenings at Maison Jamsheer, just a stone's throw from the Centre.

Shaikh Isa bin Ali House

There's a myriad of cultural attractions and architectural wonders that make Muharraq a must-see for history lovers. The most important and impressive of these is probably Shaikh Isa bin Ali House, a stunning 19th century building that was once the home of Shaikh Isa bin Ali Al Khalifah. He ruled over Bahrain from 1869 to 1932, the longest reign of any ruler in the kingdom's history. The building is an impressive example of traditional Islamic architecture, from its spacious courtyards and intricately carved wooden doors to the ingeniously designed windtowers. If nothing else, the latter provide a welcome antidote to the Bahraini summer heat.

Beit al Quran

For history buffs

To find out more about the remains of the burial mounds and other aspects of Bahrain's rich history, visit the Bahrain National Museum. Located at the ocean's edge, this is a popular tourist attraction in itself.

Al Jassrah Centre of Handicraft

Sakhir

While everywhere in Bahrain is within an hour's drive, you really feel you are away from the city once you head south. Although it can seem pretty remote in the centre, there's plenty to see around Sakhir.

Jebel Dukhan

The rather poetically-named Jebel Dukhan means 'Mountain of Smoke' and is derived from the hill's appearance on humid days, when its peak becomes surrounded by a smokey haze. It's home to a number of mysterious caves and, at just 134 metres above sea level, it is also the highest point in Bahrain. Despite its relatively modest size, the views from the top of Jebel Dukhan are still rather impressive, and it's a popular spot for picnicking when the weather is pleasant.

Tree of Life

The famed Tree of Life is just a short distance south-east of Jebel Dukhan. Also known as Sharayat Al Hayat, this famous acacia plant takes its name from its ability to thrive in the middle of the otherwise barren desert landscape, despite the apparent lack of an obvious water source. What's more, in contrast to the typical acacia tree lifespan of 150 years, the Tree of Life is estimated to be at least 400 years old. It's worth going to see what all the fuss is about, but be warned that it has borne the brunt of some graffiti over the years.

Bahrain International Circuit

On the other side of Jebel Dukhan, you'll find a completely different, thoroughly modern Bahrain attraction: the Bahrain International Circuit. This stunning track is a must-see for any motorsport fan, having played host to a number of high profile events. Not only was it the setting for the first ever Grand Prix to be held in the Middle East, it is also the home of the Formula BMW Race Professional Course, which aims to help Bahraini drivers pursue their dreams of becoming international Formula 1 drivers.

Tree of Life

Traditional dhow

Hawar Islands

You might not associate Bahrain with the fantasy of holidaying on a desert island, but that is exactly what you can do in just a 45-minute trip. That's how long it takes to reach the Hawar Islands, a group of islands situated just 20 kilometres from Bahrain's south-east coast.

On the nature trail

These undisturbed islands, with their pristine beaches and thriving ecosystems, are a far cry from the glittering skyscrapers, bustling malls and buzzing bars of Manama. Many refer to this group of 36 islands as the 'last frontier', an unspoilt natural habitat for flora and fauna, and a paradise for nature lovers. They are home to a number of endangered species, including the dugong, a type of sea cow. Birdwatchers flock to the area to spot falcons, kingfishers and the world's largest colony of Socotra cormorants.

Head for the Hawar Resort Hotel, which organises regular ferries between Al Dur Jetty on the Bahrain mainland and Hawar Island, the main island. There are plenty of leisure attractions and activities to keep you entertained, including watersports and organised excursions.

Sitra

You may not immediately consider adding Sitra to your Bahrain holiday itinerary, but there is more to this small island off the north-east coast than meets the eye. While it is predominantly an industrial area – it's home to a busy port and a number of factories – Sitra's treasures become apparent once you head down to its southern coast.

By the beach

At the renowned Bahrain Yacht Club you can try your hand at a variety of watersports such as sailing and windsurfing. Alternatively, you can also simply sit back, relax and enjoy the beautiful club house and beach. It's a great place to spend the day as a family, with a delicious beach barbecue in the afternoon and live music entertainment in the evening. Alternatively, splash out on a trip to the beautiful Al Bander Hotel & Resort, which boasts pristine swimming pools, golden beaches and plenty of bars. albander.com

Al Areen Palace & Spa

Manama

Novotel Al Dana Resort

Al Areen Palace & Spa

This superb Banyan Tree resort is just five minutes' drive from the Bahrain International Circuit. It boasts 78 luxurious pool villas, each with its own private butler. The centrepiece and highlight is a stunning courtyard containing a swimming pool and relaxing jet pool. alareenpalace.com

Mercure Grand Hotel

This popular accommodation option is well-suited to shopaholics, as it's situated within close proximity to the main malls in Seef. Unwind after a day of retail therapy with a pampering treatment in the Mercure Massage & Wellness Centre, or a spot of sunbathing by the rooftop swimming pool. mercurebahrain.com

Novotel Al Dana Resort

This newly-renovated four-star hotel has plenty to offer within the walls of its Arabic-inspired architecture, including extensive fitness and recreation facilities, as well as a private beach. A number of its bars and restaurants offer stunning ocean views while you dine and socialise. novotel.com

Regency InterContinental

This hotel is a great option for a city centre stay and has plenty of modern amenities. Active guests can take advantage of the swimming pool and 24-hour gym, and there are some excellent dining options including an Italian restaurant and authentic steakhouse. ihg.com/intercontinental

The Ritz-Carlton, Bahrain Hotel & Spa

This stunning seafront hotel has its own expansive private beach and marina. Plus, not only does it boast a host of fine dining options and the luxurious Ritz-Carlton Spa, the hotel also takes the stress out of planning by organising sightseeing trips. ritzcarlton.com

Luxury spas, swaying palms and sparkling pools await you in Manama

The Ritz-Carlton

The Gulf Hotel

Even if you don't stay at the Gulf Hotel, it is still well worth a visit as a dining destination in its own right. Boasting nine restaurants, nowhere else offers the same amount of quality and variety. Book a table at the Royal Thai restaurant, where masterchef Tawatchai Chuto serves up the freshest, tastiest seafood.

Bahrain
Places to stay

The Ritz-Carlton

Sofitel Bahrain Zallaq Thalassa Sea & Spa

Sheraton Bahrain Hotel
Located in the heart of Manama, this hotel has more than 250 guest rooms and suites, as well as a fitness centre and outdoor swimming pool. There are also several dining options to choose from, from Iranian cuisine to authentic Chinese fare, and the lounge boasts regular live entertainment nights. starwoodhotels.com/sheraton

Sakhir

Sofitel Bahrain Zallaq Thalassa Sea & Spa
This excellent hotel is the closest one to secluded Sakhir and makes a good base for exploring the surrounding attractions. It boasts stylish, spacious rooms, many of which have gorgeous views over the Gulf. sofitel.com/Bahrain

 The luxurious Sofitel is home to the first spa in a GCC nation to offer Thalassotherapy, which is the therapeutic use of seawater and marine by-products for healing and beautifying spa treatments. Try the seaweed wrap or a skin-toning massage using oxygen bubbles for the ultimate pampering experience.

Sitra

Al Bander Hotel & Resort
This family-friendly hotel located near Bahrain Yacht Club in Sitra is the perfect place for a summer holiday, thanks to its private beach, multiple swimming pools and watersports facilities. It has a range of international dining options, and enough activities to keep kids and adults entertained. albander.com

The Palace Boutique Hotel
A boutique hotel that's perfect for a bit of laidback luxury without the hustle and bustle of larger resorts. It's perfect for foodies, with the brilliant restaurant Masso's serving up delicious fare, and you're sure to spend plenty of time relaxing in the peaceful pool area and enjoying sundowners at the bar. thepalace.com.bh

Muharraq

Mövenpick Hotel Bahrain
This five-star hotel is located conveniently close to the airport, and has plenty of modern amenities to keep holidaymakers happy, including a pool, gymnasium, cafe and bar. There are three excellent restaurants to choose from, which frequently host exciting events such as live cooking demonstrations and themed nights. moevenpick-hotels.com

Mövenpick Hotel Bahrain

In the tracks of racing heroes

Experience F1 motorsports

Race to the finish
Plan your short break
for April if you want
to enjoy the buzzing
three-day weekend of
the Gulf Air Formula 1
Grand Prix.

When you're not cheering on your racing heroes during the Formula 1 Grand Prix, Bahrain's high-octane motorsports scene lets you get into the driver's seat and test your wits against a world class track.

Fans of motorsports can broadly be divided into two categories: those who are happiest cheering their heroes on from the sidelines, and those who dream of getting behind the wheel. Fortunately, Bahrain caters for both.

Since it became the first country in the Middle East to host a Formula 1 Grand Prix with the inaugural Gulf Air F1 Bahrain Grand Prix in 2004, thousands of fans have flocked to Bahrain to witness racing greats such as Lewis Hamilton, Jenson Button and Fernando Alonso tear around the Bahrain International Circuit (BIC). However, although the Formula 1 Grand Prix is undoubtedly one of the highlights of the motorsports calendar, the BIC has plenty of attractions and events on offer all year round for those with a need for speed.

Pole position

One of the most popular activities on offer at the circuit is the BIC Track Xperience, which allows you to power around the track in a world-class road car chosen from an impressive fleet that includes a Caterham G7, 210bhp Genesis and a Mitsubishi Evolution X. After being driven by a fully qualified instructor, you'll get behind the wheel for a few exhilarating laps of your own.

If you're nervous about hitting those thrilling speeds solo, the BIC Dragster Xperience is a great opportunity to enjoy some high-octane fun where you get to be a passenger in a Top Fuel Dragster – the fastest car in the sport of drag racing – reaching speeds of up to 260kmph, and experiencing G-Forces of up to 2Gs. For F1 junkies who aren't necessarily looking to get behind the wheel, a great option is to take part in the behind-the-scenes circuit tour of BIC, which takes in the landmark eight-storey Sakhir Tower, media centre, race control tower and even the Formula 1 circuit,

Need for speed

The Grand Prix sees some of the greatest F1 racers in the world put through their paces. However, no one has yet beaten the lap record of 1:30:252 set by Michael Schumacher during the inaugural Gulf Air Formula 1 Grand Prix.

depending on availability. It's advisable to book ahead to avoid disappointment.

Finally, for something a little bit different to the usual track day, consider the BIC's 4x4 Xperience, which involves getting behind the wheel of a Land Rover LR4 and pitting your wits and off-roading skills against a world-renowned 5.3km off-road course – great practice for the popular UAE activity of dune bashing.

Bahrain Grand Prix

The Gulf Air Formula 1 Grand Prix usually takes place over a three-day weekend in April. Tickets can be bought online through the BIC website at bahraingp.com. It's worth planning ahead as many hotels in Manama cater for this buzzing weekend by providing popular packages that combine tickets to the event with accommodation options.

Bahrain International Circuit

Middle East

Petra

Jordan

In just 72 hours, you can visit one of the New Seven Wonders of the World, the saltiest sea on the planet, and the Pompeii of the Middle East. Quite an adventure!

Flight time
3 hours 10 minutes

Door to door
30-40 minutes by car from the airport into central Amman

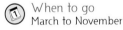

When to go
March to November

Packed with religious and historical sites, incredible archaeology, and friendly people, Jordan is a must-visit for any traveller. The capital Amman offers enough dining and cultural attractions to fill up a couple of days, but to truly experience the country, you'll need to venture out of the city centre.

The country's highlight is no doubt the magical ancient Nabataean city of Petra, one of the New Seven Wonders of the World, which is built into solid rock canyons. On your way, don't miss the opportunity to float atop the waters of the Dead Sea. History and religious experts will be fascinated by Jerash – Roman ruins that boast an unbroken chain of human occupation dating back more than 6,500 years – plus the many holy sites that dot the country: the brook where Jesus was baptised; the fortress where Herod beheaded John the Baptist; and the mountain top where Moses cast eyes on the Promised Land. Movie buffs shouldn't miss trips to the red desert Wadi Rum, where *Lawrence of Arabia* was filmed, while beach bunnies will enjoy Jordan's only coastal city, Aqaba.

Jordanians are incredibly welcoming, and despite being located between Iraq, Saudi Arabia, Syria and Palestine, it is one of the safest countries in the region. This is a place where you can live the life of desert nomads, scramble over the ruins of ancient monuments, float in the Dead Sea and walk in the steps of Moses – safely. You're advised not to travel within 3km of the Syrian border from the Sad Al-Wihdeh Dam up to, but not including, the Jabr crossing. But, with Ammam, Jerash and Petra to explore, there is still plenty to see and do.

A weekend to remember

Step back 5,000 years in just three days; there's plenty you can fit into a 48-hour trip. Aim to land on a Thursday, and stay in Amman, then start your Friday early by heading to the Dead Sea for a quick float – as well as some mud treatments – before continuing on your journey to explore Petra. On your return, stop by Wadi Rum and camp under the stars. Once back in the city on Saturday, spend your day exploring Jerash, known as the most preserved Roman site, before spending the evening watching the world go by at one of Amman's downtown restaurants. Be sure to sample the national dish, mansaf.

Jordan
Essentials

With its pleasant climate, it is possible to visit Jordan most months of the year. Avoid January if you're not looking for a snowy break!

SYRIA

LEBANON

Mediterranean Sea

PALESTINE

IRAQ

Ibrid

Queen Alia Intl Airport

AMMAN

Dead Sea

KINGDOM OF JORDAN

Petra

Wadi Rum

Aqaba

KINGDOM OF SAUDI ARABIA

Red Sea

This map is not an authority on international boundaries

Getting there
Fly from Abu Dhabi or Dubai to Queen Alia International Airport near Amman with Air Arabia, Emirates, Etihad, flydubai and Royal Jordanian, from Dhs.1,100 return.

Visas
Visitors from every country must obtain a visa to enter Jordan, but most nationalities can receive a tourist visa upon arrival at the airport, or arrange one beforehand at the Jordan Embassy or Consulate.

Time
One hour behind the UAE.

Climate
Summers are hot and dry, with cool evenings. From May to October, the weather is sunny with temperatures hovering around 23°C. Winters are cool to cold and wet, with temperatures dipping as low as 16°C. Most rain falls between October and March, and snow can occur between the months of December and February.

Language
Arabic; English is widely spoken and understood in urban areas.

Currency
Jordanian Dinar (JD).
1 JD = Dhs.5.

Vaccinations
Hepatitis A, Hepatitis B, Rabies and Typhoid.

Best for... outdoor exploration
Whether you want to snorkel in Aqaba, wander the ruins of Petra or explore the wilderness of Wadi Rum, you can enjoy the great outdoors when in Jordan. The Jordan Tourism Board is the go-to source for information on everything from cultural tours to outdoor adventures. Go to visitjordan.com when planning your itinerary.

Wadi Rum

Amman

The capital city of Jordan, Amman is a fascinating mix of historical and modern areas. Be sure to explore both.

Amman

Although not as widely publicised as neighbours Cairo and Beirut, Amman is a fascinating city of contrasts, featuring a unique mix of historical and modern. Relatively easy to get around (you can tour the whole city in less than half a day, for instance), the capital consists of old and new Amman. Old comprises various ancient sites as well as Downtown, while the new district is where you'll find grand villas for the rich, and international shops and cafes.

City views
Arguably the best spot to look over the whole city at sunset, the Citadel in Jabal Al Qalaa is the site of ancient Rabbath-Ammon, where Roman, Byzantine and early Islamic remains have been uncovered. The climb is steep, so it's better to take a taxi there.

Downtown Amman
Shopping for souvenirs? Then this should be your number one area to visit, as anything from ceramic mosaic dishes to handwoven rugs and evil eye house decorations to bath salts from the Dead Sea can be found in Downtown Amman. Plus, it is acceptable to haggle. English is less widely spoken in this old town, so it's best to visit with a local if you are hesitant about heading out on your own. The oldest souk here is Souk Al-Bukharieh, which is tucked away in a tiny alley with little shops lining it left and right.

The Roman Theatre
While in Downtown, don't forget to pass by the Roman Theatre, which was constructed during the time of Antonius Pius. This venue is still capable of seating 6,000.

Foul & falafel
Try Jordan's national dish, mansaf (saffron-dyed rice and lamb chops) at Al-Quds Restaurant (on King Hussein Street), known for its delicious homemade-style cooking. Meanwhile, Hashem (Prince Mohammad Street) is immensely popular for its foul, falafel and hummus. Finally, have a drink of fresh sugar cane juice at one of Downtown's many street vendors.

Amman Citadel

Local time

Like the UAE, Thursday marks the beginning of the weekend in Jordan. Amman's street life is best explored on a Thursday or Friday night; that's when the city comes alive.

Rainbow Street

Popular with Jordan's younger, hip crowd, Rainbow Street is a must-visit for anyone wanting to browse and buy products by local designers. Near the centre of Downtown Amman and currently in the midst of a cultural renaissance, this neighbourhood features wonderfully restored historic homes intermixed with boutique shops and art galleries. There are also a number of decent bars, shisha joints, ice-creameries and cafes. Travelling solo? Stop by Caffe Strada for a moment of reflection where everyone around you is working quietly. Fancy a cuppa? Turtle Green is Jordan's first tea bar in Jordan, offering everything from healthy green to the traditional black variety.

Nightlife

Although Amman's club and bar scene pales in comparison to nearby Beirut and, of course, Dubai, the Jordanian capital does have offerings for night owls, mostly in the trendy Abdoun and Sweifiyeh districts. Head for drinks at the guestlist-only Mimosa before joining the late-night crowd at its nightclub, Flow. Blue Fig and Seven Heaven are also worth visiting.

Cave of the Seven Sleepers

Just outside Amman, this is one of several locations claiming to be the cave where the 'seven sleepers' escaped persecution and slept for 309 years. Inside there are eight sealed tombs, while above and below the cave are the remains of two mosques.

Roman Theatre

The Dead Sea

Dramatic, beautiful and truly fascinating, Jordan's Dead Sea is the lowest point on the face of the earth. Located about an hour-and-a-half drive from Amman, it is surrounded by rugged crimson mountains – but the main attraction is, of course, the super salty water.

A swim in these waters, which are so salty that no living organism can survive in them, is an otherworldly experience as the salt causes you to bob about on the surface like a floating cork. Who can travel this far and not have a photo taken reading a book while floating on your back? A word of warning though – if you have any cuts or have recently shaved, the salt will sting!

Meanwhile, the Dead Sea's mud has healing powers – it is believed that the mud's rich minerals can soothe skin conditions such as acne and eczema.

Mud bath

No trip to the Dead Sea would be complete without slathering yourself in a thick layer of the gooey mud along its shoreline. Slap it all over, leave it to dry and then rinse off in the salty waters – your skin will thank you for it. Whether or not the healing properties truly exist, you will walk out of the water with softer, smoother skin than you walked in with.

The other benefit of being at the lowest point on the planet is the quality of the air, which contains 18 per cent more oxygen.

Day tripper

Any day trip from Amman to the Dead Sea should include a few stops along the way. Most notable are Madaba, home to the famous mosaic 6th-century map of Palestine in St. George's church; Mt. Nebo, the place where Prophet Moses gazed at the promised land before he died; and the River Jordan. visitjordan.com has a list of tour companies.

Aqaba

Combine a day trip to the Dead Sea with a visit to Aqaba (which is approximately 90 minutes away). This Red Sea resort offers some fantastic snorkelling and diving. Head to the Aqaba Marine Resort for glass-bottomed boat trips, beach volleyball, an aquarium and a shell museum.

Oval plaza

Glorious past

Day trippers to Jerash usually spend around two hours exploring the ruins, before visiting the religious sites in Anjura and the hilltop cultural centre of Umm Qais in the afternoon.

Jerash

Located about 50 minutes away from Amman, the ancient city of Jerash is one of the real highlights of any visit to Jordan. A short drive takes you more than 2,000 years back in time to one of the best-preserved Roman cities in the world. During the Roman Empire it was often called Pompeii of the East – and it is every bit as spectacular to visit today. Wander through paved and colonnaded streets to see the amazing ruins of temples, public squares, Roman baths and theatres.

Gladiator show

Immerse yourself in Roman life by heading to a performance of the Roman Army and Chariot Experience at the hippodrome in Jerash. The show – which runs twice daily – features 45 legionnaires in full armour in a display of Roman army drill and battle tactics; 10 gladiators fight 'to the death', and several Roman chariots compete in a classic seven lap race around the ancient hippodrome. It's recommended to book tickets in advance, as time slots do get filled up quite quickly. Visit jerashchariots.com for more information.

Wadi Rum

This UNESCO World Heritage Site is a timeless place, virtually untouched by man. It's a playground for hikers with its empty spaces, canyons and water holes, while campers will love sleeping under the stars in a real Bedouin atmosphere, complete with traditional camping equipment.

Off-road

It is possible to get a taste of the desert in just one day. Hire a 4WD from the tourist centre (wadirum.jo), together with a driver/guide to explore some of the best known sites. Hike across the 6km Burrah Canyon, climb the huge sand dunes (not for the faint-hearted), and visit the Anfashieh rock paintings. A traditional lunch and Bedouin tea are often included in organised tours.

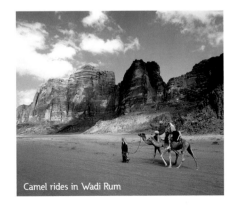
Camel rides in Wadi Rum

When exploring the ruins of Jerash, wear sensible clothes and comfortable footwear. Bring a hat, sunglasses and a bottle of water

Four Seasons Hotel Amman

Amman

The Boutique Hotel

Considering the price (around Dhs.100 per night), the cosy Boutique Hotel is a very nice little guesthouse in Downtown Amman. You're within walking distance of the Roman Amphitheatre and the Citadel. While the furnishings are simple, you can enjoy the wonderful ambience of staying in a traditional Egyptian house with friendly, helpful staff. the-boutique-hotel-amman.com

Four Seasons Hotel Amman

Set atop the highest of Amman's seven hills is this majestic luxury hotel with large rooms offering panoramic views of the city, and an indoor pool, gym and spa. Offering the perfect respite after a day of sightseeing, you can enjoy shisha Arabic, Asian and Italian a la carte, and poolside sundowners. fourseasons.com/amman

The Dead Sea

Crowne Plaza Jordan Dead Sea Resort & Spa

Stroll along the esplanade with panoramic views of the Dead Sea or cool off in the dazzling blue swimming pool. And with the spa's main ingredient – mud – in great supply right on its doorstep, there's a great choice of therapeutic treatments. crowneplaza.com/deadseajordan

Mövenpick Resort & Spa

A haven of tranquillity, right on the edge of the Dead Sea, this spa hotel is an oasis of lush gardens and olive trees in the desert wilderness. This Arabic village style resort transports you to another world; wake up to views of the sea or purple mountains; feast on a Mongolian BBQ; and if you want to avoid the sting of the saltwater sea, dive into one of the freshwater pools. moevenpick-hotels.com

Four Seasons Hotel Amman

Four Seasons Hotel Amman is a 40-minute drive from Queen Alia International Airport

Don't check out of your Dead Sea hotel without going for a spa treatment. The mud facials are probably one of the most natural you will ever experience in the region.

Wadi Rum

Kempinski Hotel Aqaba Red Sea

Wadi Rum

Classic Wadi Rum Camp

This camp offers traditional Bedouin-style accommodation, but is probably more suitable for groups of friends rather than families. All tents are equipped with mattresses, blankets and pillows, while showers and toilets are shared. Local dishes are served by the campfire. Rooms can be reserved via any hotel booking website.

Rahayeb Desert Camp

There are plenty of camps to choose from in Wadi Rum; one of the most popular is the Rahayeb Desert Camp. Offering a traditional Bedouin experience, the tents come with shared or private bathrooms, as well as a carpeted floor, linens and an extra blanket. Desert buggies, camel rides, and jeep safaris can be arranged, or simply unwind at a yoga class or with a body massage. rahayebcamp.com

Aqaba

Cedar Hotel

For something a little less pricey, head to the Cedar Hotel on Eshbeliah Street. Known for its excellent service, the three-star property is just a 10-minute walk from the beach, but guests also have the option of using its private Berenice Beach Club for an added fee. There's also a fantastic shop selling falafel near to the hotel – and really cheap too! facebook.com/cedaraqaba

Kempinski Hotel Aqaba Red Sea

Overlooking the Red Sea, this beautiful five-star resort has spacious rooms, each with its own private balcony. Take full advantage of the beachfront setting and enjoy the range of watersports, including jet-skiing, banana boat riding, parasailing, and scuba diving. It's only a five-minute walk to the shops and nightlife of Aqaba too. kempinski.com/aqaba

Mövenpick Resort Petra

The Mövenpick Resort Petra is one of the best places to stay in Wadi Musa, mainly because it is located a mere 50 metres away from Petra's entrance, plus the hotel's rooftop garden terrace offers stunning views of the hills at sunset. Each room has a private balcony, and all the mod cons you'd expect.

YOUR HOME AWAY FROM HOME.

FOUR SEASONS HOTEL

Amman

Handpicked hotel
Jewel in the Crowne

Crowne Plaza Amman
amman.crowneplaza.com

Distance from airport
30 minutes

Whether you're staying in Amman or heading out to Petra, this is the perfect base during your short break.

One of the beauties of Amman is that you are never too far from anything, no matter where you stay. The city is built on seven hills – each of which more or less defines a neighbourhood – and each of these hills has a traffic roundabout, or 'circle'.

Located near the 6th circle's trendy Suweyfeyeh shopping district is the Crowne Plaza Amman. One of the best known hotels in the capital, the property is a few minutes away from the city's landmarks, including the impressive Roman Theatre, and just 30 minutes from Queen Alia International Airport. A taxi service is available from and to the airport on request (approximately Dhs.160).

Choose your room

Although the property has a slight business feel to it, there's plenty for groups or families to do on site, so don't be put off by the number of businessmen meeting for coffee in the lobby and whatnot. Upon checking in, you have the choice between smoking and non-smoking rooms; however, a word of warning: most Jordanians seem to love to smoke, so do not be surprised if you find an ashtray in your non-smoking room as it is not considered breaking the law. Therefore, if you do have extreme allergies, make a point of letting reception know.

Food, glorious food

Crowne Plaza Amman is home to seven bars and restaurants, including Brasserie Oasis (international cuisine) and steakhouse V Lounge. Brasserie Oasis is best left for breakfast as its buffets are quite reminiscent of a typical Ramadan iftar available across hotels in the UAE – so perhaps spend time exploring something new.

The culinary highlight of this five-star hotel is, without a doubt, Al Halaby, which offers stunning views of the city from the rooftop, while providing delicious Aleppo specialties and desserts. This place serves traditional Syrian cuisine like no other, but also offers a few dishes with Jordanian influences. Try the mansaf or Palestinian-influenced mesakhan.

Football fan? You won't miss a game while on holiday (is that a good or bad thing?). Vienna Cafe shows matches from the English Premier League to the Spanish La Liga. Jordanians take the game very seriously, so don't be surprised if you see a group of locals fighting over whether FC Barcelona or Read Madrid is better!

Finally, if you have time during your short break to relax, make some time for a spot of sunbathing by the pool, or even get pampered with French body and facial treatments at the Thalgo Spa.

This five-star hotel offers two pools, a tennis court and a spa with massage facilities, plus seven different dining options

Suitable for all seasons

Crowne Plaza Amman caters to all seasons with its outdoor and indoor dining offerings, as well as a heated pool option when it's chilly outside. Room rates start from Dhs.500 (for two people), and the earlier you book, the better the rates will be. Bear in mind that rates will go up during peak holiday times, such as during Eid.

Monastery at Petra

Secrets of a lost city

Sightseeing in Petra

Best time to visit?
Go early morning or
late afternoon. The site
is open to visitors daily
6am to 6pm during
summer and 6am to
4pm during winter.

For many visitors, Jordan begins and ends with the magical city of Petra. It is without a doubt one of the Middle East's most spectacular, unmissable sights, battling it out with Machu Picchu or Angkor Wat for the title of the world's most dramatic 'lost city'.

Half-built, half-carved out of rock, this ancient city was originally cultivated by the Nabateans, the Arabs who dominated the region in pre-Roman times. It was, for several centuries, an important city on the silk and spice trade route.

In 1812, it was rediscovered by the Swiss traveller, Johann Ludwig Burckhardt, who tricked his way into the fiercely guarded site by pretending to be an Arab from India wishing to make a sacrifice at the tomb of the Prophet Aaron.

Today, Petra is considered one of the New Seven Wonders of the World, as well as being a UNESCO World Heritage Site. It spans a huge area, and takes several days to fully explore the whole site, which contains dozens of impressive remains of buildings and temples, as well a network of caves, mountains and gorges.

The main access into Petra is via a spectacular 1.2km natural passageway between two sheer rock faces. Known as the Siq, this concealed entranceway is dotted with interesting relics from the past: irrigation channels cut into the walls.

Obviously, expect to walk a lot in Petra, as cars or any type of motorised vehicle is not allowed within the archaeological space. You do have the option of being transported by donkey or horse, but after seeing the sorry state of the animals you won't be comfortable doing so. Additionally, the horse men are very difficult to deal with, and have a reputation for ripping off tourists – if anyone tells you a ride is free, don't believe it!

A valuable treasure

Also known as the Al Khazneh, the Treasury is Jordan's iconic poster image. Plus, it is the country's most famous blockbuster film location. Fans of the Indiana Jones series will recognise it as the home of the Holy Grail in the *Last Crusade*, although there is no interior behind the impressive facade – in reality though, the historical appeal of Petra doesn't really need much of a boost. This massive facade is 30 metres wide and 43 metres high, and carved out of sheer, dusky pink rock as the tomb of an important Nabataean king.

Make time to snap some photos of the urn atop the structure; it is rumoured to contain a pharaoh's hidden treasure, which explains the bullet marks that have been left by Bedouin travellers keen to find out.

The climb to Ad-Deir

If you've the stamina to do a bit of hiking, head to the Ad-Deir Monastery, the place of the 'high sacrifice'. Consisting of 800 steps, it is totally worth the climb as the site offers unrivalled views of Petra like no other.

Here, the crowds that fill the Siq and mill around the Treasury seem to thin out, as only a handful can persevere to the top. The hike generally takes 1.5 to 2.5 hours (up and down), and it is recommended to trek down the back side of the mountain to check out

the many fascinating tombs and carvings on the way. Be warned though; it's not for beginners and it is recommended you ask for advice on routes at the entrance before attempting it on your own.

Although there is plenty of information along the way, history buffs will enjoy a trip to Petra's two museums: Petra Archaeological Museum, and Petra Nabataean Museum, both of which house finds from excavations in the region and an insight into the city's colourful past.

Petra by night

Like the Great Pyramids of Giza, it is possible to visit this Jordanian marvel in the evening; however, if you've already seen the Treasury by day, this will seem less impressive. With a bunch of candles surrounding the area, visitors are entertained with Bedouin music and tea. It's a charming experience, but if you only have time to see Petra once, then go in the morning.

Petra by Night runs every Monday, Wednesday and Thursday from 8.30pm, and the best way to book is through your hotel. It shouldn't cost more than Dhs.65.

Road to Petra

A day trip to Petra from Amman doesn't come cheap. A private tour (which includes transfer, entrance fee, plus a two-hour private tour of Petra's sites) costs around Dhs.1,500 per person. A one-day entry ticket to Petra, meanwhile, costs Dhs.260. For more information, head to visitpetra.jo.

Middle East

Aerial view of Beirut

Lebanon

Ski in the morning, swim in the afternoon and party 'til dawn. However you plan to spend 48 hours in Lebanon, this is the ultimate city break with benefits.

Flight time
4 hours 5 minutes

Door to door
20 minutes by taxi from the airport to Beirut city centre; 90 minutes to ski resorts

When to go
January to December

With its unique combination of snow and sun, Lebanon manages to be all things to all people. The mountains are ripe for outdoor adventure, the ancient ruins are fun to explore, the food is sublime – and then there's the nightlife. Dubbed the 'Paris of the Middle East', Beirut is considered by many to have the best clubs and bars in the Middle East. And, like other cosmopolitan cities in the region, Beirut comes alive during Eid with street parties lasting through the night.

Despite suffering some knockbacks recently with conflicts both internally and externally, Lebanon has blossomed into a popular weekend getaway. In many ways it is an outdoor destination. Sunbathers pack the beaches along Beirut's Mediterranean coast from May to October, while skiers hit the slopes at Mzaar, just one hour out

of Beirut, from December to March. The capital's history is long and rich, with numerous ancient mosques, churches and synagogues, as well as a plethora of Roman ruins.

Outside of Beirut is just as interesting though, and worthy of a day trip or two; the massive Roman temples in Baalbek are not to be missed, and the many villages scattered throughout the country hold the key to Lebanon's incredible hospitality. If you're looking to swap city life for the mountain countryside, there's nothing better than a bike ride along the leisurely trails of Laklouk, a year-round resort at 2,000m.

The people of Lebanon make it a point to live life to the fullest, and even during times of unrest, you'll be sure to find the friendly locals carrying on as normal.

To travel or not to travel?

While travel warnings no doubt should be taken seriously, you'll find that a lot of western government websites advise against all travel to Lebanon. However, for the majority of the time, the country's capital is safe – as long as you avoid heading to the borders, you shouldn't encounter any issues. But do keep your eyes on the news before you book. Also note that, at the time of going to press, flights from the UAE to Beirut take longer than usual – four hours instead of three hours, 30 minutes – due to the fact that planes are currently not allowed to travel through Syrian airspace.

Lebanon
Essentials

Where else can you ski and swim, check out Roman ruins, visit vineyards and enjoy great nightlife – all in a long weekend?

SYRIA

Mediterranean Sea

Byblos
LEBANON
Jouneih
Mzaar
BEIRUT
Jeita Grotto
Beirut Intl Airport

Saida

Sour (Tyre)

SYRIA

PALESTINE

JORDAN

This map is not an authority on international boundaries

Getting there
Fly from Dubai to Beirut with Air Arabia, Emirates, Etihad, flydubai and Middle East Airlines, from Dhs.1,108 return.

Visas
Most nationalities can enter for free. Citizens from most North African countries can obtain a free tourist visa provided they have a two-way travel ticket, a hotel reservation/ place of residence and US$2,000.

Time
One hour behind the UAE.

Climate
Lebanon has a Mediterranean climate, with hot, dry summers (20°C- 32°C) and cold, wet winters (10°C- 20°C). There is virtually no rain between June and August. Autumn and spring have more rainfall, but without the tourist crowds and humidity of summer.

Language
Arabic; French and English are widely spoken.

Currency
Lebanese Pound (LBP). 1,000 LBP = Dhs.2. US dollars are commonly used.

Vaccinations
Hepatitis A, Hepatitis B, Rabies (for travellers interested in spending a lot of time outdoors, especially in rural areas) and Typhoid.

Best for... skiing and tanning
Beirut is probably the only destination close to the UAE that combines winter getaways with summer vacations. It is possible to stay at a ski chalet and hit the slopes in the mountains one day (p.276), then head to the sandy beaches in the city the next. The only problem you'll face is having to pack two wardrobes.

Roman ruins at Baalbeck

Four Seasons Hotel Beirut

A day in Beirut can take you anywhere from the beach to the mountains, or from the infamous Green Line to Gemmayze.

Beirut

It's true what they say: you haven't experienced the Middle East properly until you have been to Beirut. Although quite similar to Dubai in the sense that the city is modern and cosmopolitan, the Lebanese capital has much more soul — after all, its people have experienced mighty highs and lows, and there's no doubt that Beirut feels more 'local' so to speak. A day in the city can take you anywhere from the beach to the mountains; from the infamous Green Line and buildings peppered with bullet holes to the vibrant neighbourhoods of Gemmayze or Achrafieh. One thing is certain; Beirut residents are tremendously friendly and live for the moment. Get ready for fun times.

Beirut, old & new

You can savour the whole city with a leisurely two to three hour walk through the historical heart of Beirut. See where old and new Beirut collide as you stroll along Place D'Etoile, where Parisian-style boulevards stand alongside Roman ruins. Admire the beautifully restored 2nd century Roman Baths and the five spectacular Roman columns next to the Maronite Cathedral of Saint George; walk through the fragrant Gibran Khalil Gibran Garden (named after the Lebanese-American poet), stopping to admire the modern sculptures and a bust of Gibran himself; and then browse the art collections at the Robert Mouawad Private Museum. Martyr's Square is a focal point in the heart of Downtown Beirut which commemorates the Lebanese nationalists who died during World War I and is the final resting place of the late Prime Minister, Rafic Hariri. Beirut is also scattered with colourful gardens dotted with park benches, perfect for soaking up the atmosphere of the city.

Walking tour

A handy way of exploring the city's landmarks is through a walking tour mobile app (a popular one you can purchase is GPSmyCity.com). These apps come with detailed route maps and navigation features to guide you from one sight to the next. Plus, all the data is built in, so you can use it without internet access or a data plan. Perfect for a short break in Beirut.

Downtown Beirut

Al Hamra Street

One of Beirut's busiest neighbourhoods is Al Hamra Street. Lined with everything from one-off shops and restaurants to international franchises, this area is a must visit if you want to bag some unique souvenirs, fashion or accessories. Lose yourself in one of the many thrift stores that sell vintage t-shirts and other items; bookstores that sell English-language literature by some of Lebanon's finest writers; or venture into the popular Henry's Handmade shop, which lives up to its name so much that its banner outside is handwritten in marker pen. Here, you'll find plenty of jewellery – ranging from leather bracelets to silver rings – made by a man called, surprise surprise, Henry.

Eat like the locals

When your stomach starts growling, you won't be short of places to indulge. Cafe Hamra offers everything from Lebanese cuisine to burgers, while T-Marbouta is known for its hummus. Meanwhile, Cafe Younes – which opened in 1935 – continues to operate as a small family-run eatery. One place you shouldn't miss is Tawlet, for its kebbeh, freekeh and Armenian pastrami. Every day a different cook from a different area creates a traditional menu from a region of Lebanon. Tawlet also organises the Souk el Tayeb farmers market, held every Saturday at the Beirut Souk (or on the Waterfront during summer months). A mouthwatering event! tawlet.com

Snap (not) happy?

Many landmarks and historical buildings in Beirut are guarded by soldiers. While it may seem harmless to include them in your photos, it is advised not to point your camera at the guards; they will be less than happy and will ask you to delete the pictures..

Street art in Beirut

Near Al Hamra Street is the American University of Beirut. If you appreciate street art, take a walk outside the campus to check out the cool graffiti that adorns the wall. Many street vendors tend to loiter here; if you get the chance, buy some yummy cherry ice-cream.

Lebanon
Highlights

Beirut

After hours

Need somewhere to spend the early hours of the morning? Hypogeal nightclub BO18, located in Beirut's industrial Quarantaine neighbourhood, is popular with clubbers from 3am onwards. The club's site is believed to be the former Palestinian camp during the Lebanese Civil War.

Pubbing at Al Hamra

If you're in Al Hamra by day, stay into the evening and visit one of the pubs or shisha cafes that line the streets. However, if you only have time for one, make sure it's February 30. As the name suggests, it's out of the ordinary. The decor is topsy-turvy, where you feel as though your world has been turned upside down. No couch or bar stall, meanwhile, is like the other. From mopeds to barber's chairs, it has it all.

Discovering Uruguay Street

There's always going to be a place to see and be seen, and downtown's Uruguay is where Beirut's cool cats venture out to. Located directly behind Samir Kassir Square, this strip is home to bistro bars, such as Cassis, Tinto Tapas Bar and Patrick's.

Chilling in Gemmayze

For something a little more relaxed, Gemmayze would be your best bet. Beirut's artistic bohemian quarter is an old district full of narrow streets and beautiful historic buildings. Reminiscent of the ultra-trendy bar districts of London, Barcelona and Paris, this is the place to go 'bar-hopping' with a group of friends. Qahwet Laila is known for its coffee and great shisha hangouts, while pubs such as Spoons, Porto, Hemmingway's and Rocks are known for their chilled vibe, where barmen chat with punters and all sorts of music – from Latin to alternative – is heard blasting out onto the streets. For something a little 'out there' (and if you have the courage), head to a place called Drink & Sing, which does what it says on the box, so to speak.

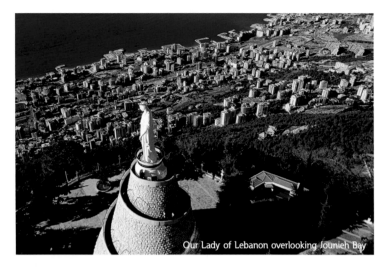
Our Lady of Lebanon overlooking Jounieh Bay

Jounieh and Harissa
Once a tranquil fishing village, Jounieh has now transformed into a mini Atlantic City. From 'super' clubs to the historic Casino du Liban, this area offers nightlife with a difference, but during the day is when it should be visited. Take a 'telpherique' cable car to the Our Lady (Harissa) of Lebanon for a sweeping view of what is considered to be one of the nicest bays in Lebanon.

Byblos
This ancient city is a UNESCO World Heritage Site as it is one of the oldest towns in the world, dating back at least 7,000 years. The rise and fall of nearly two dozen successive civilisations make this one of the richest archaeological areas in the country. For stunning views of the city, climb to the top of the Byblos Castle remains.

Ksara
Wine has been grown in Beqaa for thousands of years and a number of vineyards are in operation today. The magnificent village of Ksara was covered by sand for centuries, and its well-preserved caves were found by chance in 1898 by Jesuit priests. It is now the refuge of the well-known Ksara Chateau, where thousands of old wines are preserved – sample a number of exquisite local wines for yourself.

Day trips

It is well worth taking a day trip out of Beirut to check out what else the country has to offer. Popular trips include Jounieh and Harissa, the Jeita Grotto and Byblos. Most trips can be booked through your hotel's concierge, or through Nakhal & Cie.

Jeita Grotto
Located 20km north of Beirut, Jeita is home to one of the world's most beautiful caverns, the Jeita Grotto, which was a finalist in the New7Wonders of Nature competition. These natural caves comprise two sections – a dry upper gallery that you can visit on foot, and a lower cave that you have to travel through by boat. Unfortunately, photography isn't permitted inside the structures as it can damage the environment – so be respectful.

Baalbek
Towards the Syrian border (therefore check for any travel warnings before going) is Baalbek, home to the Heliopolis, a group of Roman temples, some of the most preserved in the country. Also, there is the Temple of Jupiter.

Byblos

Lebanon
Places to stay

Four Seasons Hotel Beirut

Beirut

Albergo Hotel

For trendy accommodation, the Albergo is a 10-minute walk from Mono Street in Achrafieh. All the furniture has an antique feel to it, with oriental rugs and crystal chandeliers. Meanwhile, each room features a hot tub bath. One of the stand-out features of the five-star property is the rooftop swimming pool, which provides stunning views of the Mediterranean. albergobeirut.com

Four Seasons Hotel Beirut

Rising high above the Beirut Marina, this stunning property features rooms, designed by Pierre-Yves Rochon, with floor-to-ceiling windows and balconies that offer panoramas of the courtyard, city or the Mediterranean. Meanwhile, the property's rooftop pool offers 360 degree views of sea, mountains and city. fourseasons.com/beirut

Jounieh

Old Souk Guest House

This is a nice hotel if you're looking to immerse yourself in history. Old Souk is in the middle of an almond plantation in the UNESCO town of Zouk Mikael. All rooms include air-conditioning, cable TV, private bathrooms and free wi-fi.

Portaluna Hotel & Resort

Looking for that Atlantic City vibe mentioned earlier on in the chapter? This resort is a five-minute drive away from all the clubs and Casino du Liban. Plus, some of the rooms feature a spa tub in front of floor-to-ceiling windows. portalunahotel.com

Regency Palace Hotel

Atop a hill in Adma, this Spanish-style hotel has rooms with balconies that offer panoramic views of the Bay of Jounieh. regencypalace.com

Four Seasons Hotel Beirut

Mzaar

Aux Cimes Du Mzaar

Located at the edge of the Jabal Dib slope and overlooking Mzaar Mountain is this five-star resort that features rooms with private balconies, a restaurant, sun terrace and cigar lounge. It takes less than an hour to get there from Rafic Hariri International Airport (which is 65km away). Meanwhile, most ski slopes are within a 1km radius; the hotel's reception can organise transportation for you. auxcimesdumzaar.com

InterContinental Mzaar Mountain Resort & Spa

Less than a hour's drive from Beirut, and nestled amid the peaks of Mount Lebanon, this luxury resort and spa offers year-round recreation. Ski direct from the resort with access to an 80km trail or enjoy a variety of activities including climbing, hiking, biking and rafting. ihg.com

The Four Seasons Beirut's pool bar offers stunning views of the marina

Handpicked hotel
A life less ordinary

Le Gray Beirut
legray.com

Distance from airport
20 minutes

With a dramatic rooftop swimming pool, Beirut's first designer hotel certainly knows how to work the 'wow' factor.

Ask anyone who has enjoyed a short break in Beirut recently, and they'll tell you that Le Gray is synonymous with holidaymakers from the UAE. Perhaps it's the city centre location that makes it perfect for those wanting to fully enjoy 48 hours in Lebanon; the high-octane – yet understated – glamour that attracts clientele that appreciate quality; or the beautifully personalised service for each and every guest staying in one of the property's 87 rooms... It's probably a mix of all three and then some.

Founded by Scottish hotelier Gordon Campbell Gray – he of the ultra-luxurious One Aldwych and Dukes in London, plus Antigua's Carlisle Bay – Le Gray Beirut opened its doors in November 2009, changing the face of hospitality in the Lebanese capital. Not only is it arguably unrivalled in terms of one-on-one service, it is also where you'll find Concierge Firas Musharafieh. What sets him apart from others is that he is a member of Les Clefs d'Or, a prestigious association that recognises concierges based on their quality of service.

Beirut 101

At check-in, try to meet the excellent concierge Firas – and within the first 15 minutes of being in town, you can have your break all mapped out. Firas and his team can advise you on anything from the best transport to take in the city centre and beyond, to day excursions, places to eat and more. Don't expect recommendations of the tourist hangouts and restaurants that are listed on every website. Instead, you'll get insider knowledge on the 'real' Beirut – from cheap restaurants that are always packed with local diners to the newest club that's open until 7am.

If you're not a fan of planned itineraries, the hotel's central location makes it easy to get around on foot or by taxi. Located in the smart downtown district, Le Gray faces the Mediterranean coastline and Mount Lebanon's peaks – so a spot of sunbathing or skiing is never far away – while there are plenty of things to see and do nearby. Next door is the Mohammad Al-Amin Mosque, while on the other side is the Rafic Hariri Memorial Shrine. Meanwhile, trendy Uruguay Street and the more relaxed Gemmayze are short walks away.

Live like a celeb

As for the hotel itself, the rooms are faultless. Book into a suite to enjoy the highlife: a spacious living room with balcony that overlooks the sea, comfortable beds, mini bar and coffee machine, plus double sinks and a wall TV in the bathroom. It's hard not to feel like a bit of a celebrity while staying here!

One top tip while at Le Gray; make sure you book a table at its Indigo on the Roof restaurant. While the hotel serves its daily breakfast there, you need to witness the sunset on the terrace, which offers 360-degree views of the city. And the cuisine is fantastic – order the seabass dish, one of the freshest in the region.

Check in

Le Gray Beirut is located in Martyrs' Square, Beirut Central District. Rates start from Dhs.1,000 per night, and you can email: reservations@legray.com for bookings.

The slopes of the Mzaar resort

Slope off for the weekend

Skiing in Mzaar

Be prepared...
Rental rates range from
Dhs.30-40 per day for
a ski or snowboard set.
Shops are located in
Faraya village leading
to the Mzaar ski resort,
or near the slopes.

Where else in the world can you ski and swim all in one short weekend? Visit Lebanon for a spring break with a difference.

Imagine a holiday where you have to divide your suitcase between shorts and flip-flops, and hats, scarves and gloves? While plenty of destinations can boast that they provide something for everyone, Lebanon fulfils this promise more than most: it's the only country in which you can ski in the morning and be swimming in the Mediterranean by the afternoon. And you can fly there in just over four hours.

Indeed, during the winter months, the temperatures in the mountains drop as low as -4°C while on the coast, the mercury rises to a balmy 17°C, so a sun, surf and ski weekend is technically feasible. However, if you're travelling from the UAE, chances are you've had your fill of beaches and are far more interested in seeing the snow.

Marvellous Mzaar

If that's the case, there's nowhere better than the Mzaar resort. Located at 1,850m, with 80km of runs, 18 lofts and heights reaching 2,465m, it's regarded as the best and most developed Lebanese ski resort.

The panoramic views from the chairlift really bring home the surreal contrast between the snow-capped slopes and the sundrenched coast, with the sparkling Mediterranean on the horizon. It's a timely reminder: hit the slopes early enough and you can hit the beach in the afternoon.

Unlike the tree-lined runs of European and North American mountain ranges, the Mount Lebanon range is rocky and bare. The level of skill on the pistes is very mixed and the resort is best suited to beginners and intermediates, although there are a couple of black runs. Fortunately, the pistes are wide and never crowded, so there is room to get out of the way of less experienced skiers.

Quiet times

Because the Lebanese weekend is Saturday-Sunday, it is almost guaranteed that the slopes are near-empty on a Friday. So, if you plan your weekend break from the UAE right, you should be able to jump back onto the lift without any of the queues you'd normally expect. Plus, the bars and restaurants are sure to be lively on Friday evening as revellers welcome the weekend.

Apres-ski

Not only is the landscape of the runs in Lebanon very different from its North American and European counterparts, so is the apres-ski ritual. If your idea of the perfect way to round off a day of skiing or snowboarding is to head to a bar in search of some vin chaud and while away your evening there, you'll have to hit the slopes early, as most of the (very few) piste-side bars only stay open for around half an hour after the lifts close. The best thing, therefore, is to do as the locals do and head back to your hotel to relax and refresh before going for a late dinner.

If your post-piste aches and pains aren't too severe, head to the buzzing area of Gemmayze (see p.270) after dinner to sample Beirut's famous nightlife.

When to go

The ski season runs from mid-December to early April, depending on the weather. The snow is not the most reliable, but has great potential if you catch good weather; March is considered the best month to go, as the snowfalls and weather are more consistent.

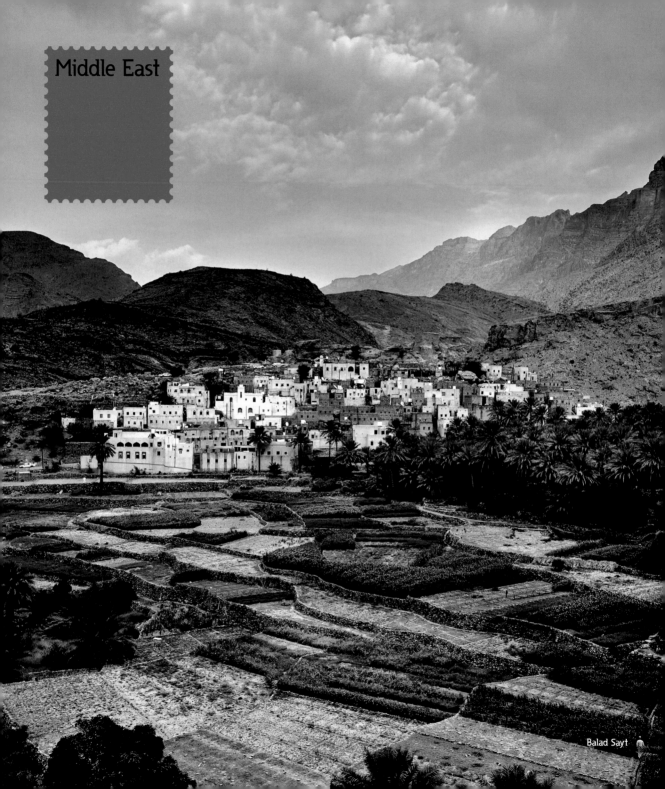

Middle East

Balad Sayt

Oman

Pack your walking shoes, bike and snorkel. It's time to hike along mountain pathways, drive through dramatic wadis, and explore the vivid colours of Oman's underwater world.

 Flight time
1 hour to Muscat;
2 hours to Salalah

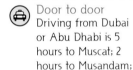 Door to door
Driving from Dubai or Abu Dhabi is 5 hours to Muscat; 2 hours to Musandam; 12 hours to Salalah

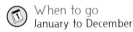 When to go
January to December

There aren't many places where you can lie on an isolated beach one day, enjoy the bustle of a city market the next, then escape to spend a night sleeping under desert stars. All of this and more is possible in Oman.

Nestled in the south-eastern quarter of the Arabian Peninsula, the Sultanate of Oman is phenomenally diverse. In the city centres, stout and pretty whitewashed buildings sit alongside ornate mosques, low-rise hotels and luxury villas. In Salalah, the land of coconut, banana and other tropical fruit trees, the lush greenery and cool weather combine to make this the ultimate short break from sticky desert climes elsewhere in the region. In contrast, there are the remote villages, natural lagoons and striking mountains of Musandam; known as the 'Norway of Arabia', this is home to

spectacular fjords that are best explored from the deck of a traditional dhow.

Oman's capital, Muscat, is a striking city sandwiched between rocky mountains and beautiful beaches. With strong connections to its history and culture, and some of the friendliest locals in the region, you'll want to visit again and again. Plus, there's the jaw-dropping views, fascinating wadis and lush oases and towering waterfalls of Western Hajar that combine for a simply other-worldly experience.

There's no end to the adventure in store here, and if you decide to drive the five-hour journey to Muscat, then the excitement begins the moment you enter the mountainous region. From beach holiday to exhilarating exploration, Oman is your ticket to a last-minute break from the city.

Whistle-stop weekend

Sometimes you just want to escape the blaring horns, back-to-back traffic and bright lights of Dubai or Abu Dhabi. Close to home, but worlds apart, Oman will get you at one with nature. In any country where you've got mountains, desert and beaches, there will be an abundance of 'natural' experiences — and Oman is no different. Camping on the beach, dune driving through the Wahiba Sands, and trekking along mountain paths — these are just a few of the outdoor pursuits that you can pack into a mini vacation in this magnificent country. To help plan your visit, go to omantourism.gov.om.

Oman
Essentials

The UAE's closest neighbour can feel like a whole other world, but is easily accessible from all seven emirates.

IRAN

Arabian Gulf

Khasab

Musandam

Dubai

Sea of Oman

ABU DHABI

UAE

Western Hajar

MUSCAT

Muscat Intl Airport

Sur

KINGDOM OF SAUDI ARABIA

SULTANATE OF OMAN

Salalah Intl Airport

YEMEN

Salalah

Arabian Sea

This map is not an authority on international boundaries

Getting there
Fly from Dubai or Abu Dhabi to Muscat with Emirates, Etihad, flydubai, or Oman Air, from Dhs.500 return. Fly direct from Dubai to Salalah with flydubai or Oman Air, from around Dhs.850.

Visas
Most travellers will be issued a single entry visa on arrival for Dhs.50. Dubai and Qatar residents do not require a visa if travelling direct, but single women may require a letter of no objection from their employer. Visitors to Dibba must pre-arrange their visa with their accommodation.

Time
Same time zone as the UAE.

Climate
Most of Oman has warm, sunny weather year-round. The climate is mild from October to April, but temperatures can reach the high 40s during the summer with humidity as high as 90%. Salalah has a tropical monsoon season from June to September, when it is cool, cloudy and rainy.

Language
Arabic; English is widely spoken.

Currency
Omani Rial (OR). 1 OR = Dhs.10.

Vaccinations
Diptheria, Hepatitis A and B and Typhoid.

Best for... off-road adventures
Venture off the beaten track in Oman and you'll be rewarded with astonishing scenery, secret picnic spots and a better insight into the heritage of the locals. Picking your way over desert dunes or rocky wadis in a 4WD is one of the most popular activities in Oman. Remember to take your passport with you, you'll need it at the Oman border.

Discover the nature of Oman

Majestic mountain ranges tower over teeming coral reefs. Red desert sands mysteriously shift as they whisper tales of a bygone era. Age-old traditions merge seamlessly with modern five-star service and Oman's world renowned Arabian hospitality. It's the perfect destination for your next holiday.

Beauty has an address - Oman

www.omantourism.gov.om | Visitor assist 800 77799

SULTANATE OF
oman

Ministry of Tourism

Mutrah Harbour

It's one of the most attractive and charismatic countries in the Middle East, which is why many count it as their favourite regional break.

Muscat

Oman's capital is visually striking, perhaps because it looks so little like a normal city; rather than a bustling CBD characterised by countless skyscrapers, gridlocked traffic and smog, Muscat has many separate areas nestling between the low craggy mountains and the Indian Ocean. The main areas worth exploring are around the Old Town and the fishing port of Mutrah, although walks along the beach in Qurm or exploring the lagoons in Qantab are recommended too.

Old Town

Located on the coast at the eastern end of greater Muscat, the Old Town is a charming cluster of pretty, whitewashed buildings sandwiched between rocky hills. It is home to the very interesting Muscat Gate Museum, which chronicles the history of Muscat and Oman from ancient times up to the present day. The view from the roof is worth the

Mutrah

visit alone. Other highlights include the striking Alam Palace, home of Sultan Qaboos, Bait Al Zubair, Jalali Fort and Mirani Fort overlooking the harbour.

Qurm Beach

Arguably the best beach in Muscat, this expanse of golden sand starts from the Crowne Plaza Muscat and stretches through Shati Al Qurum to Azaiba and beyond. It's well set up for visitors, with a number of picnic and shaded areas, as well as jet ski rentals. When the tide is low, nature lovers can take a scenic 4km walk towards the Embassies' area in Shati Al Qurum.

Qurm Park & Nature Reserve

This park and nature reserve is Muscat's main park and features sprawling lawns, a boating lake, beautiful gardens and a nature reserve made up of tidal wetlands and a mangrove nursery. It is home to the Sultan's Rose Garden and a large fountain, as well as the City Amphitheatre which seats up to 4,500 people.

Diving & snorkelling

For a nominal fee you can get a day pass to the Oman Dive Centre. Take a dive class or head out on an expedition, or just laze by the shaded pool and watch the boats come and go. There are 20 dive spots, all reached in between five minutes and 1.5 hours. Snorkelling gear and paddle skis are available to hire, and there is an excellent licensed restaurant. omandivecenter.com

Sailing trips

There's no better way to experience the beauty of Oman's magnificent coastline than with a sailing trip, and Ocean Blue Oman will help you do just that. It offers a range of experiences, from dolphin watching excursions to night charters. You can even splash out on a private charter for a special occasion, whether it's a party for friends or a romantic dinner for two in Mutrah Harbour. Ocean Blue Oman organises tours of the Damaniyat Islands, one of Oman's best snorkelling spots, aboard a 75-foot luxury catamaran. oceanblueoman.com

Ras Al Jinz Turtle Reserve

Watching nesting turtles lumber up the beach to lay their eggs, then make their way back into the sea, is to see nature at its most miraculous. You are virtually guaranteed a sighting at this reserve in Sur, south of Muscat, where you can camp overnight. After arriving, you'll be served a beach BBQ before night falls and the turtles come onto the beach. After a few hours' sleep, return to the beach to watch the mass of tiny hatchlings struggle out of their eggs and make their journey into the sea.

Haggling & bartering

One of the best markets in the region, the warren-like covered Mutrah Souk is a hotspot for souvenir-hunting tourists. Once inside, enjoy the mixed scent of frankincense, perfume oils, fresh jasmine and spices. The real excitement lies in exploring the side streets, where you'll discover a selection of tiny shops full of Omani silver paintings, pots, hookah pipes, and incense.

Eat like the locals

Sebalt Al Bustan offers a traditional Omani experience in Arabic tents set up in the hotel's gardens every Wednesday night during the cooler months. Even if your budget doesn't stretch to a night's stay, go for the legendary high tea in the Atrium Tea Lounge. al-bustan.dining.intercontinental.com

Into Mutrah

Mutrah Corniche is lined with pristine parks. Further east you'll find Riyam Park, where a huge incense burner sits on a rocky outcrop, while nearby is an ancient watchtower overlooking Mutrah – the view at the top is well worth the steep climb.

Muscat Gate Museum

Ras Al Jinz

Musandam

Beautiful fjords, rugged mountains and striking underwater coral beds combine to make this the region's outdoor epicentre.

Dibba Bayah Harbour
Dhow trips run from this attractive bay at the southern end of Musandam, taking you to unspoilt waters along the remote eastern coast. A boat trip is the best way to see the stunning scene, appreciate the scale of the fjords – and see dolphins!

Dibba Island
Take a trip from Dibba to this small rocky island, covered by a reef of corals. It's one of the best snorkelling sites around, especially for seeing turtles, and a real treat for divers who can expect to see the unusual jawfish (or hole goby). Once darkness falls, the island makes a lovely, easy night dive.

Jebel Harim
See the other side of Musandam on an off-roading experience through the mountains. Take a drive up to the plateau beneath Jebel Harim, the highest peak in the area at 2,087m. This is an excellent spot for camping, hiking and for views. Most of the year you can get to the top in a saloon car; in a 4WD you can carry on to explore tracks to more secluded places such as Sal Al A'la.

Western Hajar

This magnificent mountain range is home to some of Oman's biggest attractions, and a must for outdoorsy weekend breakers.

The High Country
Jebel Shams, the 'Mountain of the Sun' has a rugged terrain that is actually a fairly easy trek with several good camping locations. Below the summit, Wadi An Nakhur has some of the most stupendous views in the country as you drive through the 'Grand Canyon of Oman'. Sayq Plateau on top of Jebel Akdhar has beautiful mountain villages.

Al Hoota Cave
This long cave features a large subterranean chamber featuring some amazing rock formations and an 800m underground lake, which is home to a rare species of blind fish. There's a train that transports you into the cave, knowledgeable Omani guides, a restaurant and a natural history museum.

Nizwa Fort

Set in the oasis city of Nizwa is the 17th-century Nizwa Fort. Amid a verdant spread of date palms, this fine citadel features a maze of rooms, high-ceilinged halls, doorways, terraces, narrow staircases and corridors; its most striking feature is its colossal central tower, soaring 115ft above the fort. Nearby Jabrin Fort, notable for its ceiling decorations and secret passageways, is also worth a visit. Pick up some freshly made local halwa at Nizwa Souk.

Snake Canyon

This spectacular, challenging hike takes around three to four hours, and is something you'll remember forever. It's purely for the adventurous as it involves some daring jumps into rock pools and fair bit of swimming through ravines.

Wadi Al Abyad

Just over an hour west of Muscat, the pools of Wadi Al Abyad are a great place to visit throughout the year. From the end of the track, a short stroll will get you to increasingly larger pools where you can easily spend the whole day. Alternatively, you can take the easy two-hour hike through the wadi to the town of Al Abyad.

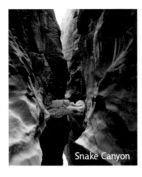

Snake Canyon

Make scents

The fragrant region surrounding Salalah has been exporting frankincense to kings and pharaohs for millennia. Visit the Museum of the Frankincense Land to learn more about this ancient commodity.

Salalah

Salalah

Escape the sizzling cities of the UAE from June to September and experience this southernmost region of Oman during the *khareef*, the monsoon season when temperatures are in the 20s and the rains turn the mountains green and lush. Along the rugged coast is a spectacular natural sight – the Al Mughsayl blowholes. Thundering waves have eroded caverns in the rock and explode through small openings underfoot. Visit Wadi Dawkah, a UNESCO World Heritage Site with over 1,000 frankincense trees. This reserve and the nearby caravan oasis at Shish are exquisite remnants of bygone times.

Jebel Shams

Oman
Places to stay

The Chedi Muscat

Muscat

The Chedi Muscat

This beautiful boutique hotel on the shore is famed for its clean lines, luxury and an impressive sense of calm. The stunning spa and outstanding restaurant don't hurt either. With an infinity pool, private beach and library, this is a destination for a break from hustle and bustle, and perhaps isn't an ideal choice for families. ghmhotels.com

Grand Hyatt Muscat

This established hotel is a hub of Muscat society, and the exuberantly decorated lobby indicates the plush furnishings found throughout. With several top-notch dining options, a beachfront location where local families promenade, and a buzzing pool area, it's a fun place to spend a few days relaxing, or a convenient base for exploring the city and its magnificently mountainous surroundings. muscat.grand.hyatt.com

Oman Dive Centre

Just south of Muscat, a stay here is an amazing and sociable experience; and one that is highly enjoyable whether you're a diver or not. You can book a barasti hut (they are actually made of stone, with barasti covering) for an average of OR.66 for two people (depending on season). The room price includes breakfast and dinner in the centre's licensed restaurant. For keen divers, the centre offers dive training and excursions, as well as boat tours in the surrounding area. omandivecenter.com

Shangri-La's Barr Al Jissah

With three hotels catering for families, business travellers and luxury-seekers, the Shangri-La is one of the most gorgeous resorts in the region. The hotels have several swimming pools and enough play areas to keep children occupied for days. The exclusive, six-star Al Husn is incredibly luxurious and perfect for a weekend of out-of-town pampering. shangri-la.com/muscat

Shangri-La's Barr Al Jissah Resort & Spa

There's a choice of five-star finery or cheap campsites to suit all budgets

The Chedi Muscat

The Absolute Adventure (adventure.ae) camp is an oasis of plantations and dorm-style rooms with bunk beds. It may not be luxurious, but a weekend here will provide more outdoor adventures than you can possibly imagine. From mountain biking and sea kayaking to canyoning, hang gliding and wadi bashing.

Juweira Boutique Hotel

Musandam

Golden Tulip Resort Dibba

Simple, clean and with a great beach and chilled pool, this is a good option for an affordable getaway. From the nearby Dibba port you can take a dhow cruise, and the hotel is also in a great location for some snorkelling. goldentulipdibba.com

Western Hajar

Sahab Hotel

After a scenic drive towards the summit of Jebel Akhdar, you'll arrive at this sleepy yet inviting hotel, 2,004m above sea level. It has everything a mountain explorer might need, including a clean and refreshing mountain breeze. Alternatively, ponder the dramatic backdrop poolside with a refreshing drink. sahab-hotel.com

 For a truly out-of-the-ordinary experience, head for Six Senses Zighy Bay, Musandam (sixsenses.com). This area of stunning natural beauty boasts rugged mountains and oceans teeming with marine life. It's a seriously luxurious hideaway with the opportunity for great hiking, mountain biking, snorkelling and diving.

Salalah

Hilton Salalah

The Hilton has a beautiful location among the lush palm groves on the shores of the Arabian Sea. From the grand entrance to the beachside restaurant, the poolside shisha to the beach spa pavilions, this is an excellent choice if you're looking for a romantic getaway or a weekend of sheer escapism. hilton.com

Juweira Boutique Hotel

This new hotel is on an inlet used by local fishermen. Each room has a terrace and overlooks the waterfront promenade, the fluffy cloud-capped mountains, the sea or the plentiful coconut trees that Salalah is famous for. Suites are spacious and light, a heavenly pool area has a bar and comfy sunloungers, and the seafood restaurant serves deliciously fresh Omani lobster. juweirahotel.com

Our Oman is Paradise...

Wadi Bani Khalid

An adventure playground

Explore wadis & mountains

Wadi Bani Awf

Ask the experts
For full itineraries, and extensive maps with GPS coordinates, get a copy of Explorer's *Oman Off-Road* (askexplorer.com/shop).

Beehive Tombs

Navigate rocky plateaus, wild wadis, drifting dunes and towering jebels by car, bike and foot.

Whether you're a committed off-roader in search of the path least travelled or an occasional weekend warrior with a taste for hiking or biking, there are plenty of routes that twist and turn their way through Oman.

Grand canyon

Some of the most dramatic yet accessible mountain scenery in Oman is along the route from Dibba to Wadi Bih, known as the Grand Canyon of the Middle East. This route passes through a twisting gorge called Wadi Khab Al Shamis, a green area that is refreshingly different to the stony sparseness of Wadi Bih. There's a steady climb up to the summit, with some of the most beautiful views in the country, before you head down on a graded track that drops 700m in just over seven kilometres – a real blast on a mountain bike. From the UAE you can also drive up to Khasab via Ras Al Khaimah, right to the tip of the Arabian Peninsula, passing mangroves, sabkha (salt flats) and desert to the famous fjords of Arabia.

Go west

The majestic Western Hajars are easily accessible from several different starting points in Oman. Driving from Muscat, head through the scenic Samail Gap; alternatively you can visit Wadi Damm, home to the ancient Beehive Tombs of Al Ayn and Bat. There's a back-breaking 70km road bike ride from Al Sheif up to Sayq Plateau, which lets you explore more than 30 villages. Travel north to the region's highest peak Jebel Shams, where there's an incredible choice of hikes. While here, head for Al Hoota Cave for an underground expedition and leave time for the hugely rewarding Abandoned Village Walk. Further north, the spectacular Wadi Bani Awf is a perennial favourite, from which you can head to Snake Canyon.

Wahiba Desert

For heart-thumping driving head for the Wahiba Desert, and take an exhilarating ride over the endless dunes of red and white sand, some of which are 200m high. Pull off just about anywhere for some serious dune-bashing fun, before spending the night camping on the dunes.

Dunes & dolphins

From the UAE, head to Nizwa first; on the way you can stop at Ibri, where daily auctions see residents haggle over dates, vegetables, honey and livestock; and then head to Bahla, an ancient walled city believed to be one of the oldest inhabited regions in Oman. A stop-over in Nizwa allows you to check out the souk, fort and Al Hoota Cave. Accommodation choice is a little limited in Nizwa itself, but try the Golden Tulip for a hospitable stay (goldentulipnizwa.com).

Next, head to Muscat for some luxury and culture – with attractions including Mutrah Souk on the Corniche, dolphin-watching trips from the coast and historical buildings. There are a number of five-star hotels to choose from in Muscat; a good option is the Shangri-La's Barr Al Jissah (shangri-la.com/muscat) which has great facilities for kids.

Just outside Muscat you'll find Bib Maryam's tomb and a dhow-building yard, Yiti and As Sifah beaches, as well as picturesque pools, waterfalls and date plantations.

Underwater kingdom

Diving Oman's coral reefs

Cooling off period
It is rarely too hot to be in the sea, where temperatures range from around 20°C in January to 35°C in July and August.

It may be on the doorstep of the UAE, but Oman's spectacular coral reefs, multi-coloured marine life and enticing shipwrecks make it a great diving destination.

From the calm waters in some of Muscat's natural lagoons to the more hairy conditions around Musandam's fjords, Oman is the ideal destination to experience the thrills of the deep. It's the sheer quality as well as the spectacular quantity of sea life that make it a great dive spot, for beginners and pros alike.

If you're new to diving, Oman has some wonderful places to learn. Fahal Island in Muscat has around 10 dive sites offering great diving in most weather conditions. In this area you can find isolated reefs, a swim-through cave and artificial reef balls. Not far from Muscat is Bander Khayran, an area characterised by a small fjord system, where you can dive down to 30m deep to see a diverse range of corals and marine life. The nine Damaniyat Islands, which span around 20km from Seeb to Barka, also have an extensive coral reef and abundant sea life.

What lies beneath

The Musandam peninsula waters are rich in plankton, and though not always clear, are abundant in healthy marine life. Turtle sightings are virtually guaranteed at Dibba Island, a small rocky island surrounded by soft and boulder coral reefs. If you're in a hurry, you can complete a circuit of the island in one dive, but only at high tide. Look out for the unusual jawfish, which build lovely drainpipe homes and line the walls with pretty shells to stop them from collapsing. Whale sharks also appear here seasonally.

Further along the coast, the Landing Craft is a sheltered dive site that is a wreck paradise. The Musandam has a well-preserved and undamaged wheelhouse, as well as a plane laid out on the deck; you can see propellers and the cockpit areas. After looking for shrimps, crabs and blennies in all the nooks and crannies, swim to the edge of the reef and you'll find a citron goby city.

Dive trips

You can book dive trips through Al Boom Diving (alboomdiving.com) and Al Marsa Travel & Tourism (almarsamusandam.com).

Shark spotting

Lying north of Dibba is Lima Rock, abundant with boulders, limestone caverns and reef life. Between 12m and 20m deep, the boulder field is covered with hard and soft corals, including orange and pink teddy bear coral. At 20m and deeper, numerous clumps of purple coral appear between the patches of sand. Look out for the yellow-mouthed rays that look as if they've just returned from the paint shop with their vivid markings. Moving deeper, whitetip sharks and leopard sharks are often seen resting on the bottom.

Oman's innumerable dive sites are well worth exploring. Get your flippers on, don your air tank and prepare yourself for a visual feast of turtles, stingrays and more.

Middle East

Qatar

Glitzy malls, hip hotels, stunning seascapes and unique cultural attractions – Qatar is one of the most fashionable destinations in the Middle East.

Flight time
1 hour

Door to door
40 minutes by car from Doha airport to the city centre

When to go
October to April

From the turquoise blue waters and sandy beaches along the Arabian Gulf to the rolling sand dunes of the desert and mangrove forests on the north coast, Qatar is an enchanting destination of natural beauty. Known as the 'Thumb of Arabia', the stunning country is also rapidly developing as a stylish getaway for a weekend of escape and discovery.

On the east coast of this small Arab nation is Doha – a dazzling capital city that fuses traditional culture and highly modern man-made treasures. It's a city of the moment, with futuristic skyscrapers, trendy shopping malls and designer restaurants all competing to transform the skyline. However, many of this ultramodern city's biggest attractions are rooted in tradition: to get the most out of Doha, you need to explore the plethora of art galleries, heritage villages, souks and traditional forts that celebrate the history and heritage of this former fishing and pearl-diving village. The famous Singing Sand Dunes and Al Wajbah Fort are popular cultural attractions that are well worth visiting.

Away from the city, the Inland Sea (Khor Al Udaid) in the south of the country makes a great day trip, while Mesaieed, Al Khor, Dukhan, Al Wakra and Al Shamal are perfect for outdoor adventures such as dune safaris, horse riding and camping. Tourism in these areas is still in its infancy, but the desert landscape is yours to explore.

Heart & soul of Qatar

Make the most of a weekend getaway with a jam-packed 48 hours in Doha. Stroll along the Pearl, widely known as the Italian Riviera of the Arabic world, peruse the world-renowned collections at the Museum of Islamic Art, and visit the striking Umm Salal Mohammed Fort – and all in just one day. That still leaves plenty of time to explore the Corniche, indulge at a luxury spa or simply laze on the beach. In the evening, there's no better place to be than Souk Waqif, a recently renovated bazaar that's perfect for eating, shopping and simply hanging out. Whether you choose to eat camel, drink mint tea and smoke shisha with the locals, it's all a matter of taste. After dinner, head to Sky View, an open air lounge bar that showcases amazing views of the capital at night.

Qatar
Essentials

Qatar makes a great short break for shopping, partying, fine dining and sporting activities.

Arabian Gulf

BAHRAIN

Madinat Al Shamal

Ras Laffan

Hawar Islands (BAHRAIN)

Al Khor

Bir Zekreet

Dukhan

QATAR

DOHA

Doha Intl Airport

Al Wakrah

Gulf of Bahrain

Mesaieed

KINGDOM OF SAUDI ARABIA

UAE

This map is not an authority on international boundaries

Getting there
Fly from Sharjah, Dubai or Abu Dhabi to Doha International Airport with Air Arabia, Emirates, Etihad and Qatar Airways, from Dhs.650 return.

Visas
Residents of GCC nations (Bahrain, Kuwait, Oman, Saudi Arabia and the UAE) with an 'approved profession', and citizens of a number of other countries can obtain a one-month visa on arrival, at a cost of 100 QAR (around Dhs.100), to be paid by credit card. Citizens of some countries will need to apply prior to travel. Check moi.gov.qa before you fly, and for a list of approved professions.

Time
One hour behind the UAE.

Climate
Mild winters and extremely hot summers. Temperatures can reach 50°C in July and August and feel even more uncomfortable than the UAE. The best time to visit is between October and April.

Language
Arabic; English is widely spoken.

Currency
Qatari Riyal (QAR).
1 QAR = Dhs.1

Vaccinations
Hepatitis A, Hepatitis B and Typhoid.

Best for... sporting events
Not only has Qatar been chosen to host the 2022 FIFA Football World Cup, it's also home to the annual Tour of Qatar cycle race. The best golfers in the world go head to head in the Commercial Bank Qatar Masters for a share of the $2.5 million prize, while the top tennis seeds compete in the Qatar ExxonMobil Open Tennis Tournament.

Souk Waqif, Doha

Doha Corniche

Away from the city, Qatar is a patchwork of tranquil fishing villages, dramatic desert landscapes and peaceful beaches.

Doha

Cultural Village of Katara

Katara is a unique development that combines traditional architecture with a diverse array of modern cultural attractions, including an outdoor amphitheatre, galleries and souks, and concert halls designed for opera, ballet and theatre. Since its opening, the Cultural Village has played host to a number of high profile events including the Qatar Philharmonic Orchestra and the Qatar Marine Festival. It is a hugely popular hub of activity and home to Doha's first public beach. By night, it comes alive as locals and visitors arrive to socialise, relax and dine at one of the many well-loved cafes and restaurants.

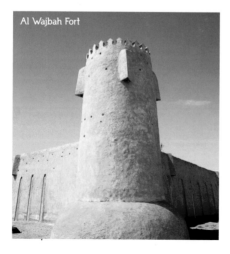

Al Wajbah Fort

Al Wajbah Fort

Al Wajbah Fort is considered by many to be one of the oldest forts in the country and, as such, it is a must-see for history buffs visiting the area. A source of great pride to the local community, the 19th century landmark was the site of a famous battle in 1893 when, under the leadership of Sheikh Qassim bin Mohammed Al Thani, the people of Qatar defeated the attacking Ottoman forces. Although it is currently unclear when or to what extent the fort's impressive two towers will be made accessible to the general public, Al Wajbah is nevertheless worth a visit.

Markets & malls

Visitors to Qatar in search of some retail therapy can rest assured that there is a host of shopping options, from traditional markets to modern malls and high-end boutiques. For a more authentic souk experience, the best of the bunch is undoubtedly Souk Waqif. This complex rabbit warren-like market boasts a wide variety of stalls selling exotic wares as well as plenty of dining options and cultural entertainment shows to keep weary shoppers happy. It's also one of the most traditional marketplaces in Doha. Keep in mind that purchases should be made in cash and that you'll need to try your hand at bargaining if you are to get the best deal. Afterwards, find a cafe, order a Turkish coffee or a mint tea and some apple-scented shisha, and simply watch the world go by.

Souk Waqif

Doha Corniche

Much of the action in Doha is centred on its popular Corniche, a hustling and bustling stretch of beach that simply begs to be explored. To make the most of the sunny weather, take a stroll along the promenade and grab a bite to eat at Al Mourjan, a Lebanese restaurant that's perfect for a leisurely lunch. If the weather is nice, choose a table on the terrace and admire the views. Afterwards, perhaps take a dhow trip from the jetty round the bay or to one of the near-lying islands. The Corniche is also the perfect place to view the ever-evolving skyline and the Arabian Gulf.

Museum of Islamic Art

Culture lovers should not miss a trip to this iconic attraction on its island of reclaimed land just off the Corniche. The masterful Islamic-influenced architecture is the work of IM Pei, the legendary architect responsible for the iconic pyramid of the Louvre in Paris. The museum houses a marvellous collection of temporary and permanent exhibitions, a cafe and a 200-seat auditorium.
mia.org.qa

Drinks in the sky

Round off a day of sightseeing with some delicious sundowners at Sky View. Located on the 15th floor of La Cigale Hotel, this chic lounge is quickly becoming one of the hottest spots in the city, attracting stylish revellers with its cocktails, nibbles and cool tunes.

Fort Tower, Umm Salal Mohammad

Sun, sea & lounging

If you're planning to hit the beach during your short break, the best option is to visit a hotel with a beach club. One of the finest is undoubtedly the Hotel InterContinental Doha, which is home to Doha's longest private beach, as well as a swim-up bar, and children's pool. During the week, you can get a day pass, although you'll need to be accompanied by a club member or hotel guest during holidays and weekends. The Grand Hyatt, with its white sand beach on West Bay Lagoon and indoor and outdoor pools, is another good choice.

 Don't forget to haggle during your souk visits; bartering for a bargain is part of the fun and is a traditional custom.

Qatar
Highlights

The Pearl

The Pearl Qatar

Doha's beloved Pearl is a stunning series of interconnected man-made islands that are perfect for a leisurely stroll, so much so that the area has been nicknamed the Arabian Riviera. One of the most popular areas is the island Porto Arabia, which boasts everything a visitor could possibly desire, from high-end shopping options to fine restaurants and cafes serving up international cuisine. Indeed, the Pearl Qatar is the perfect destination for foodies, who can indulge in everything from nouveau Mexican at Pampano to modern Japanese dishes at Megu. Perhaps best of all are the decadent treats on offer at Alison Nelson's Chocolate Bar. thepearlqatar.com

Fashion boulevard, The Pearl

A walk in the park

Doha has a number of excellent parks; one of the most popular is Rumeilah Park (also known as Al Bidda Park), whose convenient location opposite the Corniche means a lively, busy atmosphere, especially on Fridays. In spite of its sporadic opening times, it's worth the visit to see its open-air amphitheatre and heritage house. Sheraton Gardens has great views over Doha Bay.

Family fun

When the temperatures get painfully close to 50°C and the pool is too hot to swim in, the air-conditioned Villagio Mall is the perfect retreat. Go to a movie, ride a rollercoaster, race a go-kart and glide down the indoor canal in a gondola. There are shops too – plenty of them – but if you're holidaying with children you'll struggle to tear them away from the many novel rides in the Gondolania theme park.

Further afield

Just north of Doha is the village of Umm Salal with its traditional Emirati architecture. The Barzan Towers are an arresting sight as you enter the village, each providing stunning views of the surrounding desert. After passing the towers, head for the centre to see Umm Salal Mohammad Fort. Although not open to the public, its unique T-shaped architectural style is certainly worth a photograph or two. It was originally built as a residence for Sheikh Jasim Bin Mohammed in the late 19th century.

Museum of Islamic Art

Inside the fort at Umm Salal Mohammed

Outside Doha

Beyond Doha's city limits, the isolated farms, desert terrain, salt flats and small villages provide a complete contrast to city life and afford a glimpse of how life used to be.

Al Khor

If you're looking for a change of scenery from Doha, then a trip to Al Khor could be just the thing. This former pearl-fishing village is about 40 minutes' drive from the capital, and is a pleasant coastal town to visit, especially during the cooler months. There are plenty of picnic spots, including pristine beaches and lush green parks. Other attractions include a popular fish market in front of the harbour (fishing remains the area's chief industry), a museum on the waterfront that's free of charge and the charming old watchtowers.

Bir Zekreet

The beach destination of Bir Zekreet is one of Qatar's most popular spots for weekend warriors and camping enthusiasts alike. In addition to this, the desert landscape surrounding the city is a great place to spot the picturesque natural formations known as desert mushrooms. Also sometimes referred to as 'mushroom rocks', these top-heavy funghi-like structures make for great photographs, especially as the sun goes down. However, keep in mind that you will need a 4WD to get here.

Khor Al Adaid

A popular day trip destination also known as the Inland Sea, Khor Al Adaid is a wide inlet with narrows in the centre and widens out to a large, seawater lake. It's surrounded by crescent shaped dunes, and the border between Qatar and Saudi Arabia runs down the middle. Although strong currents make the narrows too dangerous for swimming, taking a dip around the shore is a popular and safe pastime. A number of tour companies organise trips to the area, so you don't need to hire a 4WD to enjoy this spectacular landscape, whether it's just for a few hours or a full overnight camping stay. Other popular activities in the area include dune bashing, camel riding and sand skiing.

Back to nature

Located in Al Shahaniya, the Oryx Farm and Equestrian Club is your best bet to view the Arabian oryx in natural surroundings. You need a special permit from the Ministry of Municipal Affairs and Agriculture to visit, so it's best to go with an organised tour.

Oryx in Al Shahaniyah

Singing Sand Dunes

A trip to Qatar's famous Singing Sand Dunes is a memorable experience. Just 40km south-west of Doha, the sand in this desert forms a natural amphitheatre and creates an audible, low-pitched humming sound. Centuries ago, Qataris attributed these noises to evil djinn or spirits, as did explorers such as Marco Polo. Today, it is known that this 'singing sand' is caused by a combination of factors, including how the sand grains shuffle down the slopes – which doesn't make it any less incredible to see (or hear).

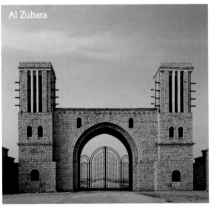

Al Zubara

Al Jassasiyeh

This collection of more than 900 ancient stone carvings, or petroglyphs, on the rocky hills that overlook Qatar's north-east coast is one of the most interesting archaeological sites in the country. Shapes vary from geometric patterns to representations of animals and boats.

 Visit Al Zubarah Fort – it's a long drive from Doha (roughly 100km), but is worth a photo if you're already in the area.

Qatar
Places to stay

Sharq Village & Spa

Doha

La Cigale Hotel

For the ultimate in five-star luxury and hospitality, opt for a stay at La Cigale Hotel. This gem boasts a range of high-end rooms and suites, fine dining options including Italian and Japanese cuisine, and exclusive amenities. After a day of sightseeing, relax in the excellent spa, which boasts traditional Arabian pampering treatments on its menu as well as a treatment room for couples. lacigalehotel.com

Courtyard Doha City Centre

If it's a shopping destination that you're after, the Courtyard Doha City Centre hotel has an adjoining mall that should fulfil all your retail therapy needs. This four-star gem boasts attractive rooms and plenty of modern amenities, including the luxurious Saray Spa. marriott.com

Grand Hyatt Doha

The Grand Hyatt is the perfect option for a summer break, as the majority of rooms enjoy stunning ocean views of the Arabian Gulf, and guests can relax on an expansive 400m private beach or at the outdoor swimming pool. Be sure to indulge in a pampering treatment at the luxurious Jaula Spa. doha.grand.hyatt.com

InterContinental Doha

This waterfront oasis is known for having the longest private beach and largest free-form pool in the city. It also boasts a wide range of dining options including Italian, Greek and Mexican fusion, and a poolside bar serving light refreshments. ihg.com

Mövenpick Hotel Doha

This slice of luxury close to the airport is perfectly situated for visitors hoping to explore the city's wealth of tourist attractions, including the ever-popular Museum of Islamic Art and the bustling Corniche. moevenpick-hotels.com

Grand Hyatt

The modern, spacious rooms at La Cigale really have the 'wow' factor

The Ritz-Carlton

La Cigale Hotel

You might not consider Doha to be a cycling destination, but this is a great way to see the sights, especially along the Corniche. There's even a cyclists' club called the Qatar Chain Reaction (qatarchainreaction.org) that organises rides and races during the cooler months for road and off-road biking trips.

Oryx Rotana

Mövenpick Hotel Doha

Oryx Rotana

The luxurious yet affordable Oryx Rotana boasts a fitness centre, outdoor pool and a spa. It also has an impressive array of entertainment options, including a pool-side restaurant, Mediterranean tapas bar and jazz club. rotana.com

The Ritz-Carlton Doha

Active holidaymakers will love staying in this sophisticated hotel, which offers a range of watersports. Refuel on the delicious French seafood served at La Mer before relaxing with an indulgent treatment in its popular spa, whose features include Roman baths and an indoor swimming pool. ritzcarlton.com

Sharq Village & Spa

This elegant hotel combines all the flair of traditional Qatari design with modern amenities and luxurious comfort. Sharq Village and Spa boasts a range of exquisite dining options, but the real highlight is the brilliant Six Senses Spa. The suites are a lavish treat worth every dirham. sharqvillage.com

Outside Doha

For the more intrepid travellers, one option may be to eschew all the official accommodation channels and try something off the beaten track instead. If you're feeling adventurous then, rather than staying in a hotel, why not pack up your camping gear and head out into the desert to sleep under the stars?

One of the most popular spots for doing so is Al Khor Island, which is 40km outside of Doha. Also known as Purple Island, the causeway that links this getaway to the mainland is surrounded by a mangrove forest, making it a must-see for nature lovers. If you're not very experienced when it comes to off-roading or desert camping, you can opt to do your trip through an organised tour instead. Plenty of travel companies offer desert safaris; while some involve day trips of just a few hours, many others include an overnight stay in Bedouin-style tents and traditional entertainment, such as Arabic music.

Doha's luxury hotels epitomise Middle Eastern opulence with a modern twist

Courtyard Doha City Centre

For a Doha stay that's slightly out of the ordinary, head to W Hotel and Residences (whoteldoha.com). This hip luxury hotel in West Bay is known for its impeccable service and is well suited to those who like a generous helping of nightlife. Enjoy the luxury beds and waiter service at the WET pool, before a spot of pampering in the Bliss Spa.

On your marks, get set, go!

Enjoy outdoor adventures

Adventure seekers
Get the most out of your short break with a travel company. Check out Qatar Adventure (qataradventure.com) for top trips.

Beyond its glitzy exterior, the Gulf nation has plenty to offer adrenaline junkies who are adventurous enough to go off the beaten track.

There's more to Qatar than chic restaurants and retail therapy. For those in search of bigger thrills than merely bagging a bargain, Qatar has a rich and diverse activity scene – whether you want to take on the immense desert sands with a spot of off-roading or get closer to nature by kayaking through the rich thickets of the mangrove ecosystem.

Dune bashing

Exactly as energetic, thrilling and adventurous as it sounds, dune bashing is a form of off-roading that's very popular in Qatar. There are plenty of tour companies that organise desert safari and dune bashing trips. As your driver approaches the desert, he'll reduce the tyre pressure to prevent the vehicle from sinking into the dunes. After that, it's just a case of buckling up and holding on tight for a rollercoaster ride across the sands.

Golfing

If you fancy getting out on the green and teeing off in the sunshine during your long weekend, then look no further than Doha Golf Club. While annual membership is fairly pricey and in high demand, it's possible to be a visitor on the 18-hole course during the quieter days of the week from Sunday to Wednesday. However, book in advance. There is also a nine-hole Academy floodlit course for less experienced golfers, shorter games or for teeing off after dark.

Kayaking

When it comes to watersports in Qatar, most people immediately think of beach attractions, such as surfing and sailing. However, if you're looking for something

Kick off

Qatar's profile is rising in the football world. It successfully staged the 2006 Asian Games and the 2011 AFC Asian Cup, and won its bid to host the 2022 FIFA Football World Cup. Key international matches are played at the sporting venues at Aspire Zone, also known as Doha Sports City.

out of the ordinary, head to the region's mangroves for some kayaking. Entalak Adventures (facebook.com/entalak) is well known for organising active tours to this unusual landscape.

Sailing

The warm temperatures and coastal landscape of Qatar make it the perfect destination for sailing enthusiasts. At the Regatta Sailing Academy, there's a range of courses for everyone from beginners to the more advanced, including lessons for children, ladies-only classes and private tuition. If you're already a proficient sailor, you can simply hire one of the boats. All staff are qualified instructors from the Royal Yachting Association.

Sandboarding

Snowboarders might think that their favourite hobby is going to be a distant memory during their stay in Qatar. However, this fun desert substitute provides just as much of an adrenaline rush. Sandboarding is very similar to snowboarding, in that both feet are strapped to a long, wide board, but instead of hitting the slopes, you hit the dunes. Find a tour company to organise your trip, and start with the smaller dunes if you've never tried either sport before.

Jumeirah Zabeel Saray

United Arab Emirates

When you're looking for a low-key, no-fuss break, remember that luxury hotels, beautiful beaches and outdoor attractions are all right on your doorstep.

Door to door
Journey times by car
from Dubai:
Abu Dhabi 1.5 hours
Ajman 30 minutes
Al Ain 1.5 hours
Fujairah 1.5 hours
Ras Al Khaimah
1.5 hours
Sharjah 30 minutes
Umm Al Quwain
45 minutes

When to go
January to December

From idyllic islands to sophisticated cities, many exotic holiday destinations are just a short flight from the UAE; so many, in fact, that it's easy to forget how many fantastic gems can be reached without even leaving the country.

The UAE comprises seven very different emirates – Abu Dhabi, Ajman, Dubai, Fujairah, Ras Al Khaimah, Sharjah and Umm Al Quwain – and each has a weekend break or overnight stay in them. They are all within easy driving distance of each other, and even a trip from Dubai to the northern-most emirate of Ras Al Khaimah takes less than two hours. In this sense, the UAE is the ultimate 'staycation' destination.

Living by the mantra that bigger is better, Dubai boasts architectural icons like Burj Khalifa and Burj Al Arab, and gargantuan resorts such as Atlantis, The Palm. Abu Dhabi, the capital of the UAE, is not far behind in the opulence stakes, from the $5 billion Emirates Palace to the thrill-seeking Ferrari World and Yas Waterworld. History buffs will find plenty to marvel at in the cultural capital of Sharjah, with its myriad of heritage attractions, and neighbouring Ajman has picture-perfect beaches.

When it comes to exploring the great outdoors, there's no beating the smaller emirates of the north like Ras Al Khaimah and Umm Al Quwain. Meanwhile, nearby Fujairah is an adrenaline junkie's paradise, with activities designed to make the best use of the rugged landscape, including wadi bashing, mountain biking and hiking.

Simply staycations

The close proximity of each emirate – most are just a couple of hours' drive or less from each other – means that it's easy to travel around the country. While going further afield requires forward thinking (as well as a bigger budget), it's entirely possible to plan a last-minute break in the UAE. This makes it the perfect place for the most relaxing holiday option of all: the staycation. Without the stress of visas and vaccinations, airport queues, jetlag and making sure you've got the right currency, you can enjoy a truly tranquil holiday. Plus, with so much to see right on your doorstep, why not take advantage of living in one of the most diverse and exciting countries in the world?

UAE
Essentials

One of the biggest advantages to taking a UAE staycation is the stress-free travel that it involves.

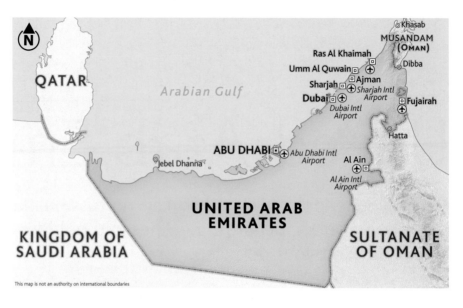

This map is not an authority on international boundaries

Getting there

If you're already familiar with the roads and own a car, it's easy to travel from one emirate to another, especially as fuel is so cheap. There are plenty of car rental companies to choose from, plus the option of hiring a 4WD. Of course, you might opt to take a domestic flight for some destinations – in the case of Sir Bani Yas Island, the flight from Abu Dhabi International Airport is a necessary (and fun!) part of the journey.

Driving is the best way to see more of the country. Just be sure to time your journey to avoid the rush hour traffic and weekend crowds if you can.

Climate

Between October and April, gorgeous sunny days give way to pleasantly cool evenings, with temperatures of 20-30°C – making it the perfect time for a UAE staycation. Even when the temperatures soar to the high 40s during the summer months (June to August), you can spend early mornings and late afternoons outdoors – or stay close to a pool to cool off. In Fujairah, the beaches overlook the Indian Ocean, so the water temperature stays a pleasant 32-33°C. Al Ain also enjoys slightly cooler temperatures year-round, as well as the more than occasional heavy downpour of rain.

Best for... residents' deals

When the mercury rises, prices drop. Many hotels and attractions offer brilliant promotional rates to UAE residents. You can stay at Atlantis, The Palm, for a discounted rate that includes access to Aquaventure waterpark. In Abu Dhabi, UAE residents can enjoy similar deals at Fairmont Bab Al Bahr and Yas Waterworld.

Sheikh Zayed Grand Mosque

Abu Dhabi

Once a quiet coastal village, today Abu Dhabi is a thriving metropolis populated by international luxury hotels, futuristic skyscrapers and modern malls, all surrounded by the pristine beaches and warm waters of the Arabian Gulf. The capital boasts some of the biggest attractions in the UAE, including Yas Waterworld, Yas Marina Circuit and Sir Bani Yas Island.

Ferrari World

Monte-Carlo Beach Club, Saadiyat

Thrills & spills

For outdoor entertainment, there's nowhere better than Yas Waterworld. The waterpark boasts several record-breaking rides that are sure to thrill adrenaline junkies. Slither down the world's first 'rattling' waterslide complete with special effects, or defy gravity on the Liwa Loop. Yas Island is also home to Ferrari World Abu Dhabi, the largest indoor theme park in the world, which boasts more than 20 rides and attractions. yaswaterworld.com

Sun, sand & sea

Located off the coast of Abu Dhabi, Saadiyat Island has a wide range of luxury accommodation, fine dining restaurants and leisure facilities – and its clean white sands and turquoise waters transport you to an island paradise. There's beachfront golf at the Saadiyat Beach Golf Club, watersports and sun loungers at the BAKE public beach, and VIP fun in the sun at the Monte-Carlo Beach Club, Saadiyat.

Walk on the wild side

The stunning Sir Bani Yas Island, located just off the coast of Abu Dhabi, is home to the Arabian Wildlife Park, a nature reserve with more than 10,000 species of animal including Arabian oryx, cheetahs, giraffes and hyenas. There are plenty of opportunities for enjoying the gorgeous landscape, from kayaking and mountain biking to hiking and horse riding. Stay over at the luxurious Desert Islands Resort & Spa by Anantara. desertislands.com

Abu Dhabi Corniche

Emirates Park Zoo

Both kids and adults are sure to enjoy a trip to the recently-renovated zoo which houses more than 2,000 species of animals, including white tigers, blue monkeys and brown bears. The emphasis is on allowing you to get close to your favourite animals through touch and interaction; for example, at the Giraffe Cafe, visitors can feed the giraffes and zebras. emiratesparkzoo.com

Abu Dhabi Corniche

No trip to Abu Dhabi would be complete without spending some time on the Corniche, where some of the city's best-loved attractions are found. Family Park is a definite highlight, with its leafy gardens, picnic areas and tree-lined walkways. At the Breakwater, you can stroll along wide pavements, watch fishermen casting into the Gulf and stop for lunch at Havana Cafe.

Hop on, hop off bus tour

When you have limited time for sightseeing, a great way to view as many tourist attractions as possible is through a city bus tour. The Abu Dhabi Big Bus Tour is a hop on, hop off service that takes in 11 stops, including the famous Sheikh Zayed Grand Mosque, Emirates Palace and Saadiyat Island. bigbustours.com

Dining out

Abu Dhabi's culinary scene is a highlight of any trip to the UAE capital. From afternoon tea at the Emirates Palace to the Marco Pierre-White-helmed Steakhouse & Grill at the Fairmont Bab Al Bahr, and Tiara, the revolving restaurant on the 55th floor of Marina Mall — many of the city's restaurants are destinations in their own right.

Coming soon

The Louvre Abu Dhabi and the Guggenheim Abu Dhabi are set to open in 2015 and 2017 respectively. Both will be located in the cultural district of Saadiyat Island. At 450,000 square feet, the Guggenheim will be the largest Guggenheim in the world, and the Louvre has been designed to be 'an island on an island'.

Emirates Park Zoo

 Abu Dhabi's iconic Sheikh Zayed Grand Mosque is open to visitors from 9am to 10pm daily (from 4.30pm on Fridays).

Abu Dhabi
Places to stay

Eastern Mangroves Hotel & Spa by Anantara

This is Anantara's first city-based hotel in the Middle East. The views are lush, green and skyscraper free, thanks to the resort's enviable location alongside the mangroves. Some of the leisure activities include kayaking and sailing. anantara.com

Emirates Palace

The $5 billion Emirates Palace is an Abu Dhabi icon. This 'seven-star' luxury hotel boasts nearly 400 rooms and suites, more than 1,000 chandeliers and almost 100 hectares of gardens. There's also a private marina, two huge swimming pools and a 1.5km private beach. kempinski.com

Fairmont Bab Al Bahr

With its luxurious rooms, outdoor pools overlooking the creek, and stunning views of Sheikh Zayed Grand Mosque, it's no wonder that the Fairmont Bab Al Bahr is a much sought after Abu Dhabi destination. It also has some of the best dining and drinking spots in the city. fairmont.com

Eastern Mangroves Hotel & Spa by Anantara

Emirates Palace

Liwa Hotel Abu Dhabi

This affordable holiday spot is perfect for a family holiday, with a dedicated children's pool and playground. However, there's plenty for adults to enjoy too, from the temperature-controlled outdoor pool (perfect for the summer months) to the luxury spa. almarfapearlhotels.com

Sofitel Abu Dhabi Corniche

For first-class comfort, exquisite service and top quality dining, look no further than the Sofitel. Its spacious rooms ooze comfort and luxury, and the stylish bathrooms with rain showers bring the spa experience right to your door. During the day, relax by the outdoor pool. sofitel.com

Yas Viceroy

As befits a hotel that first opened its doors for the debut Abu Dhabi F1 Grand Prix in 2009, the Yas Viceroy spans the track of the Yas Marina Circuit. It offers fantastic views over the track as well as Yas Island itself. Be sure to check out the rooftop pools and pool bars as well as the stunning Skylite lounge. viceroyhotelsandresorts.com

Yas Viceroy

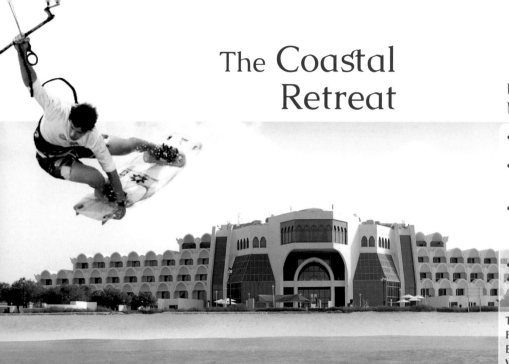

The Coastal Retreat

فـنـدق المـرفـا
MIRFA HOTEL

- 3 Meeting Room
  10-60pax
- 1 Conference /
  Banquet Hall
  200 pax
- Open Garden
  40 acre for
  Function &
  Team Building.
- 114 Rooms & Suites
- Water Sports
  Activities

T: +971 2 895 3000
F: +971 2 883 6400
E: rsvn@mirfahotel.com
W: www.mirfahotel.com

- 2 Meeting Room
  10-50pax
- 1 Conference /
  Banquet Hall
  120 pax
- Open Garden
  25 acre for
  Function &
  Team Building.
- 63 Rooms & Suites
  plus 3 Private Villas.
- Desert Activities

T: +971 2 882 2000
F: +971 2 882 2830
E: rsvn@liwahotel.net
W: www.liwahotel.net

LIWA
HOTEL

An Oasis of Tranquility

Ajman

Despite being the smallest of the emirates, Ajman still has lots to offer travellers, including fine dining, luxury hotels and pristine beaches, with a few heritage attractions thrown in for good measure. The relatively undeveloped coastline means that you can enjoy uninterrupted views of the Arabian Gulf as you soak up the sun on golden sandy beaches.

Ajman Museum

Ajman Corniche

A stroll along Ajman's bustling Corniche is a must-do during the milder months. It boasts plenty of amenities including cafes, shops and a tidal pool for safe swimming. There are some excellent traditional restaurants, too – try the seafood at Themar Al Bahar or the Middle Eastern cuisine at Attibrah – if you feel like lingering over a sit-down lunch in the sunshine.

Ajman Equestrian Centre

The Ajman Equestrian Centre is a great place to learn more about the emirate's traditional sport and get into the saddle yourself. It houses more than 100 well-trained Arabian horses, and offers a range of lessons and riding activities for visitors of all abilities.

Ajman Museum

This 18th century fort houses an astonishing collection of artefacts and archaeological findings. One of the highlights is an exhibition of an excavated cemetery discovered in the Al Muwaihat area; some of the pottery and jewellery found during the excavation dates back as far as 3,000 BC.

Souks & markets

For authenticity, skip the malls and head to the markets. Haggle for the catch of the day at the lively fish souk, where you can have your purchase seasoned and grilled onsite, and pick up handmade trinkets and pretty jewels in the city centre souk area.

Kempinski Hotel Ajman

The Ajman Palace

This gem is one of the newest hotels in the emirate, but is already establishing itself as a firm favourite. The spacious rooms combine modern luxury with traditional Arabian design influences, and the leisure facilities include an infinity pool, a private sandy beach with a lawn and sea terrace, and a fully equipped spa and fitness centre. There are also two speciality restaurants and a rooftop shisha lounge.

Kempinski Hotel Ajman

This beautiful five-star hotel offers the ultimate in luxury and hospitality. There's a stunning stretch of white sand beach overlooking the Arabian Gulf that's perfect for trying out watersports or simply soaking up the sun. You can even request to have a table set up in the surf for a romantic dinner for two. Be sure to sample the Indian cuisine at the excellent Bukhara or the Italian fare at Sabella's. kempinski.com

Ramada Hotel & Suites

This affordable hotel is conveniently located in the city centre. The rooms are comfortable and spacious, and there are a number of on-site amenities to choose from including a spa, fitness centre and an indoor swimming pool, which is perfect for the summer. Guests can use the private beach at its seafront sister hotel. ramadaajman.com

Spa delights

As well as boasting some of the best dining options in the emirate, the Kempinski Ajman is also home to arguably the best spa in the city. You can enjoy an indulgent massage at a spa pavillion on the beach or try a soothing and healing Ayurvedic treatment at the stunning Softouch Spa.

The Ajman Palace

Ramada Hotel & Suites

Al Ain Zoo

Hili Fun City

Al Ain

Also known as the 'green city' or 'garden city' due to the many parks, gardens and open spaces that it boasts, a visit to Al Ain is the perfect escape. Despite its modest size, there are plenty of attractions from the family-friendly Al Ain Zoo to the thrill-a-minute Wadi Adventure. Nearby Jebel Hafeet is a great place to hike.

Al Ain Zoo

This zoo is not characterised by small cages and meagre wildlife displays. Instead, it feels much more like a safari park, with spacious enclosures spread across its 900 acres interspersed with smaller exhibitions. Highlights include watching the hippos

Wadi Adventure

splash around in their 10m-long ravine, catching a glimpse of the rare white lions in their enclosure, and getting up close to the giraffes at their feeding station. awpr.ae

Hili Fun City

This green and spacious park boasts more than 30 rides and attractions for visitors of all ages, from white-knuckle thrills such as the terrifying Sky Flyer and Thunderbolt, to gentler rides such as the Hili Express Train. Even if you're not a fan of theme park rides, Hili Fun City is still a lovely spot to spend a sunny afternoon. Simply bring a picnic basket and enjoy the open green spaces, outdoor BBQs and colourful play areas. hilifuncity.ae

Jebel Hafeet

The highest peak in the UAE, Jebel Hafeet towers over the border between Al Ain and Oman at an imposing 1,240 metres. It forms an impressive backdrop to the scenery; drive to the top to be rewarded with fantastic views over Al Ain.

Wadi Adventure

A must-visit for adrenaline junkies, here you can pit your wits against three world class white water rafting and kayaking runs, totalling more than 1km in length. If that's not enough, there's also a challenging airpark of tree-top obstacles, canyon swings and a climbing wall to take on. Surfers can ride the perfect wave time and time again at the surf pool. wadiadventure.ae

ENJOY YOUR STAY FOR LESS
AT DANAT AL AIN RESORT

Unwind at Danat Al Ain Resort & experience our newly refurbished rooms and lobby. The earlier you book, the more you can save!

• Book your room 3 days prior to your arrival and get up to 15% discount on best available rate
• Book your room 7 days prior to your arrival and get up to 25% discount on best available rate
• Book your room 14 days prior to your arrival and get up to 30% discount on best available rate

Call +971 3 704 6000 or email reservations.alain@danathotels.com for more information.

Danat
Al Ain Resort

*Subject to availability. Terms & conditions apply.

Managed by Danat Hotels & Resorts, a Division of National Corporation for Tourism & Hotels
PO Box 16031, Al Ain, United Arab Emirates T. +971 3 704 6000 | F. +971 3 704 6009 | E. info.alain@danathotels.com | www.danathotels.com

Al Ain
Places to stay

Hilton Al Ain

Al Ain Rotana

This popular city centre spot is a hit with residents as well as visitors. In fact, it's a nightlife hub, thanks to six popular dining spots which include the lively Trader Vic's and the excellent Lebanese restaurant Min Zamaan. The rooms, suites and chalets are attractive and spacious, and the swimming pool and gardens are great spaces for soaking up the rays. Plus, there are great fitness facilities for keeping active during your short break. rotana.com

Danat Al Ain

Well-known for being one of the UAE's most enjoyable inland resorts, with its luxurious guestrooms and deluxe villas; the landscaped gardens and swimming pools are the perfect places for enjoying the sun. There are plenty of family-friendly facilities on offer too, including a family pool. Adults are sure to enjoy the luxury spa and the swim-up pool bar, as well as the Horse and Jockey Pub. danathotels.com

Hilton Al Ain

The Hilton's location right in the heart of Al Ain makes it the perfect base for a spot of sightseeing, especially if you're planning to venture to Jebel Hafeet or visit Al Ain Zoo. When you're not out and about, there are landscaped gardens, tennis courts and swimming pools to enjoy, as well as a nine-hole golf course. Unwind in the evenings at the Hiltonia Sports Bar and Paco's Bar. hilton.com

Mercure Grand Jebel Hafeet Al Ain

This hotel's spectacular location near the summit of Jebel Hafeet means that visitors can enjoy spectacular views of Al Ain. The rooms here are simple and comfortable, although you may not be spending much of your time indoors with three swimming pools to choose from, a waterslide and a mini-golf course. When you get peckish, there are two restaurants, as well as a coffee shop and bar. mercure.com

Danat Al Ain

Al Ain's hotels are social hubs for the city's best dining and nightlife

Al Ain Rotana

Mercure Grand Jebel Hafeet Al Ain

A dramatic landscape and moderate temperatures make Al Ain an ideal destination for outdoor activities. On the Omani side of the city, you're 30 minute's drive from amazing hiking and off-roading routes including the Hanging Gardens and Jebel Rawdah. There are some great camping spots too.

The Dubai Mall

Dubai

As one of the most sought after holiday hotspots in the world, Dubai may be the ultimate staycation destination: why would you go anywhere else with so many riches right on your doorstep? With its luxury hotels, gourmet restaurants, pristine beaches and gargantuan malls, this larger-than-life emirate has everything you need for a non-stop short break to really brag about to your work colleagues on a Sunday morning.

Burj Khalifa

New Dubai

Downtown Dubai is home to some of the city's biggest attractions. Burj Khalifa (burjkhalifa.ae), the tallest building in the world, is a must-see; the observation deck on the 124th floor offers spectacular 360° views. Head downtown in the evening and you'll be treated to a show from the Dubai Fountain, the largest dancing fountain in the world. Performances take place daily at 1pm and then 6pm to 11pm at 30-minute intervals. The bars and restaurants of Souk Al Bahar provide some of the best views. Nearby, The Dubai Mall (thedubaimall.com) offers plenty of indoor entertainment including an ice rink, the theme park Sega World and the Dubai Aquarium and Underwater Zoo.

Old Dubai

Away from the gleaming skyscraper valleys lies a very different Dubai. Head for Bastakiya in Bur Dubai, close to Dubai Creek, and you'll find an atmospheric heritage area of traditional windtowers, courtyards and winding alleyways. A myriad of cultural attractions such as Dubai Museum and the historic Sheikh Saeed Al Maktoum's House are located nearby. Stroll along the creek to the abra station and cross the water to explore the bustling souks on the Deira Side, or take a dhow cruise with traditional food and drink as the sun sets over the city. Beyond the city limits, Dubai's desert landscape provides plenty of opportunities for outdoor adventures, from dune bashing to Bedouin-style camping and desert safaris.

Ski Dubai

Aquaventure

Aquaventure

This popular waterpark at Atlantis, The Palm has something for everybody, whether you're a thrill-seeking adrenaline junkie or a family looking for some relaxing fun in the sunshine. One of the highlights has to be the legendary Leap of Faith, a 27-metre near vertical drop that shoots you through a tunnel surrounded by shark-infested waters. There are plenty of gentler rides too, for young children. atlantisthepalm.com

Dubai Dolphinarium

A fantastic indoor attraction where bottlenose dolphins and fur seals are the stars of the show. These fascinating creatures dance, juggle, play ball, jump through hoops and even paint. The evening shows feature illusions and aquatic acrobatics, and there's the opportunity to swim with dolphins on selected afternoons. Before or after the show, leave time to explore the UAE's only mirror maze – a dizzying labyrinth. dubaidolphinarium.ae

Ski Dubai

Located in the Mall of the Emirates, Ski Dubai is the first indoor ski resort in the Middle East and boasts more than 22,500sqm of real snow, as well as a snow park for the kids. With temperatures at around -3°C, this is a great place to cool off. It's also home to a colony of snow penguins that visitors can see through specially organised 'Peng Friend' encounters or during the March of the Penguins show. skidxb.com

Wild Wadi Water Park

This 12-acre attraction next to Jumeirah Beach Hotel boasts more than 30 rides and attractions. While it can be a bit of a wait for some of the popular rides on busy days, Wild Wadi is nevertheless well worth a visit, especially for rollicking rides like Wipeout, a permanent rolling wave. Be sure to check out Breaker's Bay, the largest wave pool in the Middle East. For fun with friends, head to the four-seater Burj Surge, and if you really want to test your bravery, opt for the Jumeirah Sceirah and its near-vertical drop. jumeirah.com

Wild Wadi Water Park

DUBAI DOLPHINARIUM

Wet, Wild & Totally Wonderful!

Dolphin & Seal Show
Mon to Thu - 11am & 6pm
Fri & Sat - 11am, 3pm & 6 pm
Swimming with Dolphins: Mon to Thu - 1pm to 4pm

Swim with our dolphins
Book Today!

Lose yourself in the UAE's only mirror maze at Dubai Dolphinarium!

MIRROR MAZE

Magical, Mystical & Totally Mind-bending!

Open everyday 9.00am - 7.30pm; Sunday 9.00am - 5.00pm

Location: Creek Park, Gate 1, Dubai, Call: +971 4 336 9773, Toll Free: 800-DOLPHIN (800-3657446)
Book your tickets online at www.dubaidolphinarium.ae

Our Vision: To create an excellent city that provides the essence of success and comfort of living.

Bab Al Shams Desert Resort & Spa

Al Maha Desert Resort & Spa

Combining the wild beauty of the desert with the luxury of a top-class resort, the Al Maha Desert Resort and Spa is designed to resemble a traditional Bedouin camp. Each suite is utterly luxurious and comes with its own butler and private pool. al-maha.com

Atlantis, The Palm

This hotel opened with a bang (literally) in 2008, with a launch that included a $15 million firework display. Today, it continues to attract discerning guests from all over the world, drawn by its luxurious rooms, stunning Nasimi Beach Club and world-class restaurants including Nobu, Ossiano and Ronda Locatelli. atlantisthepalm.com

Al Maha Desert Resort & Spa

Burj Al Arab

An icon of the city's skyline, the Burj Al Arab symbolises Dubai luxury at its finest. Each suite spans two floors and is serviced by a team of butlers, and guests can make use of a completely private beach. If you can't stay the night, check out the restaurants; try the afternoon tea at the Skyview Bar. jumeirah.com

Bab Al Shams Desert Resort & Spa

Set against the stunning backdrop of the serene desert dunes, this beautiful resort was built in the style of a traditional Arabic fort. Facilities include a kids' club, pool with swim-up bar, and the luxurious Satori spa. You can also organise a range of activities through the hotel including morning yoga classes and desert safaris. meydanhotels.com

Desert Palm

Traditional Arabian charm meets modern luxury in this chic five-star hotel located south-west of central Dubai. Despite its proximity to the city, Desert Palm enjoys lush green surroundings thanks to its setting in the midst of a 150-acre polo estate, which includes four championship polo fields. desertpalm.peraquum.com

Atrium, Burj Al Arab

Jumeirah Zabeel Saray

For an unforgettable pampering experience, there's nowhere better than Jumeirah Zabeel Saray, a structural wonder that can lay claim to being the home of Talise Ottoman Spa, the biggest spa in the Middle East. It also boasts beautiful interiors combining Arabian and Turkish design influences, its own private stretch of beach and several top quality restaurants.
jumeirah.com

Sofitel Dubai Jumeirah Beach

This chic seafront hotel, which stands tall on JBR's The Walk, is the perfect weekend retreat. Enjoy all the luxuries of a suite that's bigger than some apartments (and even has a butler!), gather with friends in the infinity pool bar, and dine by candlelight in the innovative Italian, Rococo. Pay the extra for a suite and enjoy bubbly and canapes with ocean views; head to the main restaurant for a breakfast of kings. sofitel.com

XVA Art Hotel

The XVA Art Hotel is housed in what was once a traditional windtower house located in the heart of Bastikiya, one of the city's oldest districts. It's one of the few truly boutique hotels in Dubai, as well as being one of the city's hippest hidden gems; within the hotel, you'll find an art gallery, a popular vegetarian cafe and a number of cool stores. xvahotel.com

A personal butler, Club Millesime access, and a Nespresso machine beckon you to a suite at the Sofitel

 Dubai's luxury hospitality scene shows no signs of slowing down. Anantara is set to bring its Asian-inspired brand of five-star luxury to the new Anantara Dubai Palm Jumeirah Resort & Spa, and construction has already begun on the first Four Seasons Dubai hotel, set to open in 2014.

Atlantis, The Palm

Bab Al Shams Desert Resort & Spa

Snoopy Island

Fujairah

Fujairah may be just a one-hour drive from Dubai (or two hours if you're travelling from Abu Dhabi) but the dramatic landscape of this east coast gem makes it feel like a different world. The journey itself takes you through the spectacular Hajar Mountains before arriving at this picturesque location along the Gulf of Oman.

Outdoor pursuits

Fujairah is the perfect place to visit if you're looking for an active holiday that makes the most of the great outdoors. The areas that lie on the border between Fujairah and Ras Al Khaimah, such as Wadi Sidr, Wadi Tayyibah and Wadi Asimaf, are particularly well-suited for hiking and mountain biking weekends away.

Let's camp!

Of course, if you're feeling adventurous, you could skip the hotel completely in favour of a night under the stars. Fujairah is a very popular spot for camping, with many intrepid travellers opting to pitch their tents on the pristine beaches of Dibba or Al Aqah.

Fujairah Fort

Dhow cruise

One of the quintessential travel experiences when you're visiting Fujairah is to go to Dibba for a dhow cruise. Plenty of companies organise journeys in these traditional boats, with trips designed to take in the dramatic coastline on the way to Musandam, an enclave of nearby Oman. Your itinerary could include anything from scuba diving and snorkelling to simply sunbathing on the deck.

Snoopy Island

Snoopy Island, so named because of its resemblance to the beloved comic book dog, is a popular snorkelling spot in Fujairah located about 100m off the shore of Sandy Beach Hotel in Al Aqah. The hotel's beach is a pleasant place to sunbathe, and the island is just a short swim away, although you can rent a kayak to get there, as well as snorkelling equipment. For the best visibility, aim for an early morning snorkel; expect to be rewarded by an abundance of sea life including turtles and rays.

Culture & heritage

Located just outside Fujairah city, the Fujairah Heritage Village is home to a collection of fishing boats, traditional dhows and tools depicting what life was like in the UAE before the discovery of oil. There are two springfed swimming pools for men and women. It's also worth paying a visit to the nearby Fujairah Museum (although it is closed on Saturdays).

Fujairah Rotana Resort & Spa – Al Aqah Beach

This resort puts its beachside location to good use, with each of the 250 guest rooms and suites boasting its own balcony with views over the sea. Some of the highlights of the hotel include its private beach, the swimming pool with pool bar and the indulgent spa offering plenty of pampering treatments. You can even opt to have a massage in a hut on the beach with an ocean view. rotana.com

Le Meridien Al Aqah Beach Resort

This family-friendly hotel has an enviable location on a 230-metre stretch of beach overlooking the Indian Ocean with the stunning Hajar Mountains providing the background. Set within lush, green grounds, it boasts excellent outdoor and indoor play areas, as well as dedicated kids' and teens' clubs. For adults to enjoy, there's an extensive spa, a dive centre, a cinema and a range of restaurants and bars. lemeridien-alaqah.com

Fujairah Rotana Resort & Spa

Le Meridien Al Aqah Beach Resort

Beside the seaside

Ras Al Khaimah's Al Qawasim Corniche is a social hub that's perfect for a family day out. Enjoy the natural beauty of the mangroves or stop at one of the cafes for a refreshing drink. You can even hire bikes for exploring the area. Round off your evening by sampling the Italian fare at the delightful restaurant Pesto.

Ras Al Khaimah

Nature lovers, take note: Ras Al Khaimah boasts the best natural scenery in the UAE. With the stunning Hajar Mountains as its backdrop and the sparkling waters of the Arabian Gulf on its shore, the northernmost emirate is the perfect destination for an outdoor break with plenty of opportunities for camping, hiking and soaking up the sun.

Bassata Desert Camp

The classic desert experience. Indulge in traditional Arabian cuisine with an extensive BBQ dinner buffet, enjoy a spot of dune bashing and witness traditional Bedouin entertainment, belly dancing and Tanoura (folk dancing).

Ice Land Water Park

This polar-themed waterpark is one of the most popular attractions in Ras Al Khaimah and the newest addition to the giant WOW RAK tourist destination. It boasts more than 50 rides including Penguin Falls, Snow River and Mountain Cyclone. icelandwaterpark.com

Prince of Sea

Hop aboard this fabulous yacht for a daytime, sunset or dinner cruise. Depending on which excursion you choose, you could enjoy swimming in the Arabian Sea, snorkelling off the coast of Al Marjan Island (look out for the rare green turtles) or simply dining on delicious barbecued seafood as you watch the sun go down. The evening trips usually include a welcome drink, DJ music and a buffet dinner, as well as traditional Arabian entertainment such as belly dancing. rasalkhaimahtourism.com

Ras Al Khaimah Country Club

This newly opened equestrian club is already proving popular with local horse riding enthusiasts and visitors from the UAE and abroad. As well as boasting superb equestrian facilities and expertly trained staff, there's also a restaurant and bar for lingering over a delicious meal or relaxing drink, and a large, scenic swimming pool for cooling off while you soak up some sun. Riding lessons and excursions are available to visitors of all ages and experiences. Contact info@rasalkhaimahtourism.com for more information.

Prince of Sea

Ras Al Khaimah beachfront

Banyan Tree Ras Al Khaimah Beach

Set within the impressive desert landscape of Wadi Khadeja, this stunning resort combines the wild beauty of its surroundings with the luxury and quality that Banyan Tree is known for. There are two excellent restaurants and bars, including the signature venue Saffron, which serves up top quality Thai and South Asian fare, and each of the 101 villas boasts its own private pool and sun deck. The perfect getaway for a special celebration – or just because... banyantree.com

The Cove Rotana Resort

This sprawling resort comprising more than 200 rooms and 72 villas has the feel of an old Mediterranean hill town, thanks to its location built into the hillsides overlooking the Arabian Gulf. The centrepiece is undoubtedly the lagoon that it is built around, which is protected from the sea by 600 metres of pristine beach. rotana.com

Hilton Ras Al Khaimah Resort

With 1.5km of private, white sandy beach, six swimming pools, five-star service, loads of watersports on offer and some super fine dining options, you won't really need to leave. As well as rooms in the main building, there are 151 quaint villas with direct beach access, and for all that's on offer, it's actually rather good value. hilton.com

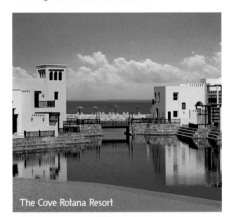
The Cove Rotana Resort

Banyan Tree Ras Al Khaimah Beach

Find paradise in Ras Al Khaimah

Located just 45 minutes from Dubai International Airport, Ras Al Khaimah offers a variety of entertainment and relaxation facilities including exclusive hotels & resorts, international cuisines and world-class spas, all at great value for money. With a wide range of adventure and sports activities covering desert camps, golf courses, light aviation and watersports, the emirate of Ras Al Khaimah offers the ultimate outdoor experience.

Ras Al Khaimah

A RISING EMIRATE

www.rasalkhaimahtourism.com
www.Facebook.com/VisitRasAlKhaimah

Al Qasba

Sharjah

Dubai's neighbouring emirate is the cultural capital of the UAE, with a well-preserved heritage area, an ever-evolving arts scene, some wonderful museums and a thriving cafe culture. Regular events such as the Sharjah Light Festival and Sharjah Biennial draw visitors from all over the UAE and beyond; in the city centre, it seems like there's always something new to see and do.

Heritage Area

Al Qasba

Sharjah gets the European alfresco vibe spot on, and is home to some great hangouts where people gather to eat, socialise and promenade. Canalside hub Al Qasba is packed with popular cafes and restaurants, and has some attractions worth a look, such as Maraya Art Centre and the Eye of the Emirates observation wheel. Al Majaz Park is good for little ones; there are plenty of kids' play areas including a lovely splash park. Restaurants along the waterfront overlook Khalid Lagoon, where Sharjah's nightly answer to the Dubai Fountain is a colourful affair.

Sightseeing by bus

If you're short on time but want to see as much of Sharjah as you can, check out the City Sightseeing Sharjah bus tour. This hop on, hop off journey takes in a range of highlights including Central Souk, Al Qasba, the fish market, Al Majaz Park and the Maritime Museum. Tickets are valid for 24 hours. city-sightseeing.com

Heritage Area

In 1998, Sharjah was named the Cultural Capital of the Arab World by UNESCO — and the Heritage Area makes it easy to see why. Sitting alongside Sharjah Creek, you'll find traditional architecture dating back as far as the 19th century as well as recently-renovated buildings and courtyards designed in the authentic Arabian style. There are souks and exhibitions to explore, too.

Al Tamimi Stables

Museums, old and new

As an emirate that is renowned for its dedication to preserving the treasures of the past, it's little wonder that Sharjah is home to some truly outstanding museums. One must-see is the Museum of Islamic Civilisation. Once a traditional souk, today this stunning building houses more than 5,000 artefacts from the Islamic world including ceramics and manuscripts. The exhibits are packed with information, and include a beautiful gold-embroidered curtain for the door of the Holy Ka'ba. Sharjah Maritime Museum, adjacent to Sharjah Aquarium, is another destination for history buffs and showcases Sharjah's illustrious pearling traditions. For a more modern attraction, head for the Sharjah Classic Car Museum, a must-see for petrolheads. This impressive museum is home to more than 100 classic cars. Some of the models were manufactured as early as 1917, while others date back to the 1960s. Having newly re-opened after a recent renovation, the museum now has more kid-friendly facilities including interactive areas.

sharjahmuseums.ae

Al Tamimi Stables

This recently-opened facility sounds like it should be a home for horses only, but in fact boasts gazelles, reindeer, oryx, ostriches and more. It's the perfect place for a family day out; kids are sure to love spending time with the cute creatures at the petting zoo. Al Tamimi is a professional stable too, housing over 30 horses. There are plenty of activities to keep kids and adults entertained including horse riding, falconry and art classes.

tamimistables.com

Go east

Beyond the city boundaries, Sharjah emirate spans deep into the desert where you'll find one of the UAE's most popular dune playgrounds, Big Red, as well as the impressive Fossil Rock. East coast enclaves Khorfakkan, Dibba Al Hisn and Kalba all have stunning coastlines.

See the light

The Sharjah Light Festival, which takes place in February, is widely regarded as the highlight of Sharjah's cultural calendar. Visitors and locals attend the event to see the emirate transformed by a spell-binding symphony of colours, music, lights and animation, and even vivid 3D imagery.

Sharjah Light Festival

Al Majaz Waterfront

Sharjah Grand

Coral Beach Resort

The highlight of this popular hotel is undoubtedly its close proximity to a pristine sandy beach, and kids are sure to love the swimming pool with waterslide. There's a host of activities and sports facilities on offer to keep guests entertained, as well as a spa and hammam where you can wind down after a long day exploring the city. Be sure to try the excellent seafood at the restaurant Casa Samak during your stay.
coral-international.com

Marbella Resort

Sharjah's hotels are extremely family-friendly; the emirate's zero-tolerance drinking laws mean that it's a very wholesome, safe place to spend time. Marbella is another resort with good kids' facilities, and it has a lovely location overlooking Khalid Lagoon and close to Central Souk. The resort has two temperature-controlled swimming pools, tennis courts, squash courts, a fitness studio and gym, as well as a few dining options.
marbellaresort.com

Radisson Blu Resort

This reliably smart hotel chain has a five-star offering in a great location close to the city's historic centre and with its own beach. Facilities are plentiful and include temperature-controlled swimming pools, watersports, tennis courts, a spa and a fitness centre, as well as several cafes and restaurants. For a five-star hotel on the beach, prices are incredibly reasonable.
radissonblu.com

Sharjah Grand

If there's one hotel that's sure to keep guests more than entertained throughout their stay, it's the Sharjah Grand. This beachside resort boasts an extraordinary array of activities and leisure facilities from watersports and fitness classes to volleyball and table tennis. There's also a large temperature-controlled swimming pool overlooking the ocean for a dip or a spot of sunbathing.
sharjahgrand.com

Radisson Blu Resort

Laze by the sea Coral Beach Resort is just a 20-minute drive from Dubai

Coral Beach Resort

Sharjah's east coast enclaves currently lack in accommodation options, but there is the recently refurbished Oceanic Khorfakkan Resort & Spa, and Kalba's Breeze Motel. The future is bright, however, with the Chedi Khorfakkan, from the same people behind the popular and uber-luxurious Chedi Muscat, expected in 2015.

Dreamland Aqua Park

Umm Al Quwain

A visit to Umm Al Quwain is a great way to see traditional Emirati life; fishing and date farming are still the main industries, as they have been for centuries. It has plenty of modern attractions too; its beach resorts are popular hangout spots among UAE expats, and you can even go skydiving (see emiratesdropzone.webs.com for details).

Dreamland Aqua Park

Barracuda Beach Resort

This comfortable, laidback resort is perfect for a short break or even a quick weekend getaway. There's a variety of rooms, but you might prefer one of the lagoon-side one-bedroom chalets, each of which accommodates up to five people. These are fitted out with kitchenettes and barbecues, which make them ideal for private overnight parties, and the hotel boasts a large pool and Jacuzzi too. barracuda.ae

Dreamland Aqua Park

This impressive waterpark is both huge and hugely popular. Perfect for a family day out, there are more than 30 rides, including four 'twisting dragons' that promise white-knuckle thrills. There's also a lazy river, a wave pool and a play area if you're looking for something a little more relaxing, as well as a high-salinity floating pool. Dreamland is a great attraction for a weekend trip as you can camp overnight, even staying in one of the tents or huts provided. However, note that Fridays and public holidays are for families only. dreamlanduae.com

Flamingo Beach Resort

This cheap and cheerful hotel is perfect for nature lovers, as it's surrounded by a shallow lagoon and green islands that attract a variety of fauna, including visiting flamingos. The hotel organises a variety of excursions to keep guests entertained, including flamingo tours, crab-catching and deep sea fishing trips. flamingoresort.ae

Index

Photography

Serbia
p.228 (Paragliding in Serbia) D. Bosnic, Archive NTOS
p.229 (Farm in Serbia) D. Bosnic, Archive NTOS

Jordan
p.250 (left - right) Jordan Tourism Board
p.252 (Amman) Jordan Tourism Board
p.252 (Amman Citadel) Jordan Tourism Board
p.253 (Roman Theatre) Jordan Tourism Board
p.254 (top) Jordan Tourism Board
p.255 (Oval plaza) Jordan Tourism Board
p.255 (Camel rides in Wadi Rum) Jordan Tourism Board
p.257 (middle left - right) Jordan Tourism Board
p.258 (Wadi Rum) Jordan Tourism Board
p.258 Kempinski Hotel Aqaba
p.262 (Monastery at Petra) Jordan Tourism Board

UAE
p.337 (Sharjah Light Festival) Sharjah Commerce and Tourism Development Authority
p.337 (Al Majaz Waterfront) Sharjah Commerce and Tourism Development Authority

And special thanks to...

Goa: Amarya Shamiyana; Dwarka; Goa; Incredible India (India Tourism Dubai) Marriott Resort & Spa; Grand Hyatt Goa; Taj Exotica; The Leela Goa

North India: Incredible India (India Tourism Dubai); Lebua Lodge At Amer; Taj Lake Palace; Taj Mahal New Delhi; The Manvar Resort & Camp

Kerala: Incredible India (India Tourism Dubai); Kerala Tourism; Soul & Surf, Varkala; The Leela Kovalam; Vivanta by Taj Malabar Kochi

Maldives: Kuramathi Island Resort; Maldives Marketing & Public Relations Corporation; Niyama; One&Only Reethi Rah, Maldives; Taj Hotels Resorts and Palaces

Nepal: Kantipur Temple House; Nepal Tourism Board; River Bank Inn; The Dwarika's Resort Dhulikhel; The Dwarika's Hotel; The Last Resort; Waterfront Resort, Pokhara

Sri Lanka: Amaya Hills; Heritance Ahungalla; Barry Allan; Heritance Kandalama; Heritance Tea Factory; Jetwing Lighthouse; Mount Lavinia Hotel; Sri Lanka Tourism Promotion Bureau

Egypt: Egypt Tourism Authority; Fairmont Nile City, Cairo; Four Seasons Alexandria; Four Seasons Resort Sharm El Sheikh; Mena House Hotel; Rixos Sharm El Sheikh

Ethiopia: Arequ Guesthouse; Ethiopian Embassy, UK; Radisson Blu Hotel, Addis Ababa; Sheraton Addis

Kenya: &Beyond; Chris Goldstraw; Giraffe Manor; Kenya Tourist Board; Sankara Nairobi; Sarova Whitesands Beach Resort & Spa, Mombasa; Segera Retreat; WaterLovers Beach Resort

Seychelles: Air Seychelles, Four Seasons Seychelles Resort & Spa; Kempinski Seychelles Resort; Le Meridien Fisherman's Cove; New Emerald Cove Hotel; Seychelles Tourism Board; Sunset Beach Hotel

Azerbaijan: Atlantis Holidays, Dubai; Excelsior Hotel Baku; JW Marriott Hotel Absheron Baku; Ministry of Culture and Tourism of the Republic of Azerbaijan; Qafqaz Riverside Resort Hotel

Cyprus: Almyra, Paphos; Amathus Beach Hotel, Limassol; Aphrodite Hills, Paphos; Cyprus Tourism Organisation

Georgia: Aurora Chan, Boombully Rooms & Hostel; Courtyard by Marriott Tbilisi; Georgian National Tourism Administration; Radisson Blu Iveria Hotel; Tbilisi Marriott Hotel

Turkey: Ecce Navigo; Empress Zoe Hotel; Hotel Ibrahim Pasha; Kempinski Hote l Barbaros; Medium Rare Advertising & Marketing on behalf of the Turkish Cultural & Tourism Office in Dubai

Serbia: National Tourism Organisation of Serbia

Bahrain: The Gulf Hotel Bahrain; The Ritz-Carlton, Bahrain Hotel & Spa

Jordan: Crowne Plaza Amman; Four Seasons Hotel Amman; Mövenpick Resort Petra

Lebanon: Four Seasons Hotel Beirut; Le Gray; Lebanese Ministry of Tourism Representation Office, Dubai

Oman: Grand Hyatt Muscat; Juweira Boutique Hotel; Ocean Blue International

Qatar: La Cigale Hotel; Sharq Village & Spa

UAE: Danat Al Ain Resort; Mercure Grand Jebel Hafeet Al Ain; The Ajman Palace; Ras Al Khaimah Development Authority; Al Tamimi Stables; Coral Beach Hotel; Sharjah Grand Hotel

Explorer Products

Residents' Guides
All you need to know about living in and loving some of the world's greatest cities

 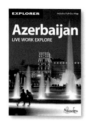   

Visitors' Guides
The perfect pocket-sized Visitors' Guides

Calendars
A whole year's worth of stunning images

Activity and Lifestyle Guides
Drive, trek, dive, sail and swim... life will never be boring again

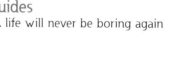  

Maps
Never get lost, no matter where you are

Photography Books
Beautiful cities caught through the lens

Retail Sales
Our products are available in most good bookshops as well as online at askexplorer.com/shop or Amazon. Please contact retail@askexplorer.com

Bulk Sales & Customisation
All products are available for bulk purchase with customisation options. For discount rates and further information, please contact leads@askexplorer.com

Licensing & Digital Sales
All our content, maps and photography are available for print or digital use. For licensing enquiries please contact licensing@askexplorer.com

Check Out
Search for information and inspiration, as well as connect with other expats and share your experiences on askexplorer.com

Directory

Tourism boards

Abu Dhabi	tcaabudhabi.ae
Ajman	acm.gov.ae
Al Ain	tcaabudhabi.ae
Azerbaijan	azerbaijan.tourism.az
Bahrain	moc.gov.bh
Cyprus	visitcyprus.com
Delhi	delhitourism.gov.in
Dubai	dubaitourism.ae
Egypt	egypt.travel
Ethiopia	tourismethiopia.gov.et
Fujairah	fujairahtourism.ae
Georgia	gnta.ge
Goa	goatourism.gov.in
Jordan	visitjordan.com
Kerala	keralatourism.org
Kenya	magicalkenya.com
Lebanon	lebanon-tourism.gov.lb
Maldives	visitmaldives.com
Nepal	welcomenepal.com
Oman	omantourism.gov.om
Qatar	qatartourism.gov.qa
Rajasthan	rajasthantourism.gov.in
Ras Al Khaimah	rasalkhaimahtourism.com
Seychelles	seychelles.travel
Sharjah	sharjahtourism.ae
Sri Lanka	srilanka.travel
Turkey	tourismturkey.ae

Embassies & consulates

Armenia	uae.mfa.am
Azerbaijan	azconsulatedubai.ae
Bahrain	mofa.gov.bh
Cyprus	cyprusme.com
Egypt	egyptianembassyinuae.com
Ethiopia	ethcodu.com
Georgia	mfa.gov.ge
India	indembassyuae.org
Jordan	jordanembassy.ae
Kenya	kenyaembassy.ae
Lebanon	lebembassyuae.com
Maldives	foreign.gov.mv
Nepal	nepalembassyuae.org
Oman	ocodubai.com
Qatar	mofa.gov.qa
Romania	mae.ro
Serbia	mfa.gov.rs
Seychelles	mfa.gov.sc
Sri Lanka	srilankaembassyuae.com
Turkey	dubai.bk.mfa.gov.tr

Airlines

Air Arabia	airarabia.com
Air Seychelles	airseychelles.com
Azerbaijan Airlines	azal.az
EgyptAir	egyptair.com
Emirates	emirates.com
Ethiopian Airlines	ethiopianairlines.com
Etihad Airways	etihadairways.com
flydubai	flydubai.com
Indian Airways	airindia.com
Jet Airways	jetairways.com
Kenya Airways	kenya-airways.com
Middle East Airlines	mea.com.lb
Mihin Lanka	mihinlanka.com
Qatar Airways	qatarairways.com
Royal Jordanian	rj.com
RwandAir	rwandair.com
SriLankan Airlines	srilankan.com
Turkish Airlines	turkishairlines.com

Travel vaccinations

Cedars Jebel Ali International Hospital	cedars-jaih.com
Disease Prevention & Screening Centre	ahs.ae
Dubai Health Authority (DHA) Travelers Clinic	dha.gov.ae
Dubai London Clinic	dubailondonclinic.com
Health Bay Polyclinic	healthbayclinic.com
Manchester Clinic	manchester-clinic.com
Mediclinic	mediclinic.ae
Panacea Medical & Wellness Centre	panacea.ae
The Clinic	theclinic.ae
Top Medical Centre	topmedicalcentre.com
Unicare Medical Centre	unicaredubai.com
Up & Running Integrated Sports Medical Center	upandrunningdubai.com